MAKING GOD LAUGH

*A Memoir of Psychiatry,
Dublin, and the Electric Chair*

Other Titles by

R.C. GOODWIN

Short Stories

The Stephen Hawking Death Row Fan Club

Novel

Model Child

MAKING GOD LAUGH

---

*A Memoir of Psychiatry,
Dublin, and the Electric Chair*

R.C. GOODWIN, MD

Copyright © 2024 R.C. Goodwin, MD

All rights reserved. No part of this publication may be reproduced, distributed, or transmitted in any form or by any means, including photocopying, recording, or other electronic or mechanical methods, without the prior written permission of the publisher, except as permitted by U.S. copyright law.

For privacy reasons, and for maintaining patient confidentiality, some names and identifying data have been changed.

For permission requests, contact the author at juderob@cox.net.

For information about this title or to order other books and/or electronic media, contact the publisher:

Secret Harbor Press, LLC
www.SecretHarborPress.com
secretharborpress@gmail.com

Cover and interior design by The Book Cover Whisperer:
OpenBookDesign.biz

Publisher's Cataloging-In-Publication Data
(Provided by Cassidy Cataloguing Services, Inc.)

Names: Goodwin, R. C. (Robert Clare), author. Title: Making God laugh : a memoir of psychia-try, Dublin, and the electric chair / R.C. Goodwin, MD. Description: First edition. | [Charleston, South Carolina] : Secret Harbor Press, [2024] Identifiers: ISBN: 978-1-7331439-7-4 (paperback) | 978-1-7331439-8-1 (ebook) | LCCN: 2024916312 Subjects: LCSH: Goodwin, R. C. (Robert Clare) | Psychiatrists--United States--Biography. | Psychiatry. | Authorship. | Dublin (Ireland) | LCGFT: Autobiographies. | BISAC: BIOGRAPHY & AUTOBIOGRAPHY / Medical. | BIOGRAPHY & AUTOBIOGRAPHY / Memoirs. Classification: LCC: RC438.6.G66 A3 2024 | DDC: 616.890092--dc23

Library of Congress Control Number: 2024916312

978-1-7331439-7-4 Paperback
978-1-7331439-8-1 eBook

Printed in the United States of America

FIRST EDITION

To The Washington Diner Breakfast Club

*In Memory of Erik Linnolt, Charlie Boren,
and Father John Kiely*

The past beats inside me like a second heart.
— John Banville, THE SEA

CONTENTS

Chapter I: GROUND RULES
1

Chapter II: BACKGROUND
7

Chapter III: CULVER AND YALE
30

Chapter IV: SOMEDAY YOU'LL BE A WONDERFUL DOCTOR
56

Chapter V: CÉAD MÍLE FÁILTE
66

Chapter VI: THE DEFAULT PSYCHIATRIST
85

Chapter VII: THE COURT OF LAST RESORT
100

Chapter VIII: SURVIVING DIVORCE AND REMARRIAGE, MORE OR LESS
121

Chapter IX: PSYCHIATRY IN THE ROUGH
135

Chapter X: A DAY IN THE LIFE
151

Chapter XI: THE LONG SHADOW OF TODD KILMER
171

Chapter XII: NIRVANA UNIVERSITY
189

Chapter XIII: EXPIRED PASSPORTS
199

Chapter XIV: THE WRITTEN WORD
223

Chapter XV: A TERRIBLE THING TO HAPPEN TO A LITTLE BOY
240

Chapter XVI: INTERVIEW
256

ACKNOWLEDGMENTS
267

AUTHOR BIO
269

CHAPTER 1

GROUND RULES

On a bright June day in the late 1980s, I found myself strapped into an electric chair.

At the time I was working as a psychiatric consultant at a maximum-security prison in Connecticut, and I was researching an article on the death penalty. My friend Ron, another psychiatrist, asked me if I'd like to see the state's electric chair. "It's in the basement, under F-Block. I'll get a correctional officer to take us there."

I nodded with a certain morbid curiosity. Ron summoned a correctional officer (CO), and the three of us went down a creaking stairwell. From there we made our way through a dank and ill-lit corridor, a forgotten walkway in the bowels of the prison. We turned a corner and entered a small enclosure, about fifteen by twenty feet, easily overlooked. And there it was, the electric chair, a yard or two away from us.

A first impression: It was surprisingly attractive, made of varnished oak with graceful curves and fancy lathe work. Almost elegant—too elegant to have been the apparatus in which eighteen people died. The chair had eight leather straps, all of them about two inches wide and a quarter of an inch thick: two for each arm, one for each ankle, one apiece for the chest and lap. They had to be strong, these straps. Not just to restrain the prisoner but strong enough to withstand the violent contractions that would occur when the switch was thrown, contractions as powerful as those you'd see in a grand mal seizure. Built into the base of the chair were what looked like miniature pillories to encircle each ankle.

The CO told us prisoners had built the chair in the woodworking shop of a former state prison in Wethersfield, a town just south of Hartford. You have to wonder how they felt about the task at hand, making something for the express purpose of killing other inmates. In any case they did a commendable job. Apart from the thick leather straps and ankle restraints, it wouldn't have looked too bad in someone's den.

Walls of cinderblock lined the room. Directly behind the chair was the death cell, where the condemned inmates spent their final hours. Other doors led to a utility closet and the executioner's station. In front of the chair, behind long rectangular windows, was an area for witnesses. Two dozen people, maybe a few more, might have crammed into it. In the absence of recent executions, it now served as a catch-all storage space containing folding chairs, a plastic trash bag, and a Monopoly game.

We stood in front of the chair, quiet and respectful. Then I walked around it slowly, touching it, examining it from different angles, admiring its craftsmanship. Ron broke the silence. "We can strap you in, if you want. Give you more of a taste of the real experience." I nodded again, not without a measure of apprehension.

They fastened straps across my chest and abdomen and straps that held my arms and legs in place. I tried to imagine what it must have been like to sit there as an inmate with only moments left to live—hooded and barely able to move, listening to the hum of the generator as two thousand volts were about to be administered to my shaven scalp. Wondering if I'd be knocked out right away or remain conscious as I was burned alive from the inside out, waiting alone with my fear and maybe my regrets, waiting even then for a reprieve, a miracle.

They unstrapped me and I stood up, slightly shaky. No reason for shakiness. The electric chair, unplugged for decades, was as innocuous as a Barcalounger. Despite that, though, it was an unsettling experience. It took a while for my heart rate to go back to normal. This field trip had made the chair more than a symbol or a point of law. It was quite real.

SEVERAL DECADES LATER, AS I began to think of writing a memoir, the idea first struck me as kind of preposterous. I haven't amassed great wealth or power. I'm not a Nobel laureate or an inventor of something that changed the world. I haven't won an Oscar or Emmy or performed Tom Brady-style heroics in a Super Bowl. I'm not an exonerated death row inmate or a survivor of ethnic cleansing. Which is to say, I've done none of the things that often lead to the writing of such a book. Except for a scattering of relatives, friends, and patients, I'm mainly unknown beyond the small town in the small New England state where I reside. If I look at my life with a cold hard eye, I see it as unremarkable at its core. Writing a memoir smacks of chutzpah.

Then I remembered my time in the electric chair.

It occurred to me that perhaps my life hasn't been as humdrum as I'd supposed. I've done psychiatric work in private practice, jails and prisons, homeless shelters, nursing homes and substance abuse facilities, and at a university with twenty-three thousand students. My clientele has included teenagers and centenarians, captains of industry and serial killers, priests and pimps. They've come from St. Lucia and South Africa and South Korea, and hundreds of points in between. I've appeared as an expert witness in cases involving child abuse, crimes committed during blackouts, and murder; one of the trials was a death penalty case. I've also learned something about therapy—individual, group, and couples—from the other side of the desk. (Gratuitous advice: never trust a therapist who doesn't have significant familiarity with pain.) These experiences have ranged from life-altering to marriage-saving to kind of *meh*.

Apart from my work, I've managed to see a fair bit of the world, from Barbados to Bruges, from Prague to Panama City, from Florence to Fairbanks. I'm old enough to have gone to Cuba before Castro and Haiti before Duvalier, old enough to have flown in DC-3s as well as 777s. I've seen the Sistine Chapel and Auschwitz, reasonable candidates for the bookends of the human experience, the best and worst humanity can offer. I've heli-hiked in the Canadian Rockies and zip-lined over Costa Rican rainforests. I've seen the phenomenal Boston Celtics of the Larry Bird era and Hall of Fame baseball players—Carl Yastrzemski and Jim Rice, Goose Gossage, and Carlton Fisk. In New Orleans, I've dined on crayfish étouffée, and in Quebec City on caribou (okay, but a bit gamey), and in Anchorage on reindeer sausage (pretty good, once you get past the idea of eating Rudolph). Also haggis in Edinburgh (interesting, only do not ask what's in it).

I've paid my respects to the Louvre and Prado as well as lesser institutions like the sadly defunct Liberace Museum in Las Vegas, which has to be among the hokiest tourist attractions that ever existed. I've heard Yo-Yo Ma, Joni Mitchell, Dave Brubeck, Nadja Salerno-Sonnenberg, Miles Davis, and Jim Morrison in the flesh. I've heard the Boston Symphony Orchestra and the Dukes of Dixieland.

World events within my lifetime? God, where to start? The use of two atomic bombs, the end of World War II, and the inception of too many other wars to count. The establishment of the U.N. and NATO, the building and tearing down of the Berlin Wall. Men on the moon and a rover on Mars. Antibiotics, AIDS, oral contraceptives, Ebola, and near-routine organ transplants. Fifteen presidents to date, one of them assassinated and attempts on four others.

As I write, we've just experienced the COVID-19 pandemic, apropos of momentous events. I'm old enough to remember the scourge of polio in the 1950s, before the Salk vaccine, when hitherto healthy children ended up in iron lungs. I missed a month of school, quarantined at home because I played with Suzy Glosecki one weekend; the next week she was diagnosed with it. A red tape stretched around the house, covered with the word *QUARANTINE!* in bold black letters. It was like the yellow *CRIME SCENE* tape you see on cop shows.

Also, as I write, America is experiencing marked angst and agitation over racial matters. I'm old enough to remember Martin Luther King's "I Have a Dream" speech at the Washington Mall and to have been a Freedom Rider as an undergraduate, in the course of which I experienced a degree of fear previously unknown to me. Never, before or after, have people glared at me with that degree of unvarnished hatred.

IN THE BOOK AT hand I've changed the names and identifying details of patients, including the incarcerated ones, as well as some of my colleagues, classmates, friends, and intimate partners. In fact, I've changed the name of anyone when I thought that using a real one might cause consternation or embarrassment.

A few words on the title. There's a classic quote about making God laugh by telling Him your plans. It's often attributed to Woody Allen, although there's an earlier version, a Yiddish proverb: *Man plans and God laughs*. Whatever the source, I feel it's singularly appropriate to my own life. I believe it's quite possible that I've given the Old Boy a few chortles along the way. I'd like to think so. A serious business, running a universe or a multiverse as the case may be, and He could probably use some comic relief. Perhaps that's why He allowed the human race to evolve in the first place.

CHAPTER II

BACKGROUND

One saturday morning in late september, in the second decade of the new millennium, I sit in the living room drinking coffee. My wife, Judy, is on the sofa opposite. Penelope, our cat, parks herself on an adjacent chair, close enough to be fussed over but far enough to maintain her vaunted feline independence. Penelope is a splotched calico with a lot of Maine Coon in the mix, with a tail that looks as if it makes up half her body weight. I feed her before I have coffee in the morning, I find it near-impossible to walk by her without petting her, and I give her treats on demand throughout the day. Face it, I am whipped.

Autumn has just begun, the season that makes Connecticut worth the trouble. Worth the blizzards and heatwaves, not Floridian but hot enough. Worth the heavy taxes and clogged interstates. Glancing outside, I discern early hints of the coming panorama, the spectacle of red and gold and purple of which I never tire.

I reflect on what has been so far my considerable good luck in life. It both awes and humbles me.

Consider my birth. Six weeks premature, I weighed in at under five pounds. This occurred long before medical advances enabled babies who weighed half that much to survive. My low birth weight meant I might well have died or experienced serious cognitive or physical disabilities. Moreover, I breathed easily and cried lustily. Preemies often had critical respiratory problems, treated at the time with high concentrations of oxygen. But oxygen administered this way can be toxic to the infantile retina, and babies exposed to it can be permanently blinded.

My luck also held in the matter of geography. I was born in 1942, in New York City to Jewish parents. Had I been born on the other side of the Atlantic, there's a fair chance I wouldn't have made it to 1943.

More luck concerned my family. My parents, Robert and Eileen, were intelligent, caring, and more or less patient. Robert, a young doctor completing a residency in dermatology at the time of my birth, eventually built a busy practice. During my early childhood, my parents had to keep track of every dollar, but they never lacked for basics.

Eileen Marjorie Mandl was born in 1918. She died of a cerebral hemorrhage four months before her one-hundred-and-first birthday. Her life encompassed eighteen presidents, from Woodrow Wilson to Donald Trump, and the rise and fall of the Third Reich and the Soviet Union. It included the coming of TV and computers, of astronauts, and wide-bodied jets (she was born less than fifteen years after the Wright brothers' first flight). Women couldn't vote when she was born, and she lived long enough to see one come within inches of the Oval Office.

∽

My paternal grandmother, Clara, had already had three miscarriages before my father's birth. In the course of the last one, she almost died herself. Clara told me about regaining consciousness after a massive postpartum hemorrhage and finding a nurse on her knees praying for her, in tears. "I didn't think you'd make it," said the nurse.

The couple gave up on having children, but Clara became pregnant for a fourth time. By now her husband, also named Robert, was in his forties, and Clara in her late thirties. Clara was terrified, and Robert, who adored his wife, was distraught. "Clara," he told her, "I'd give my right arm for you not to be in this predicament."

"It wasn't your right arm that got me into this predicament," she retorted.

Despite her past obstetrical mishaps, their son was born in 1911 without complications. The sun rose and set on him, this only child born to parents on the verge of middle age. Named after his father, he would be known as Robert. His father went by Bob. When I joined the family thirty-one years later, I became Rob (in childhood, Robbie).

Both of my parents grew up in comfortable circumstances. My paternal grandfather bought and sold commercial real estate in Chicago. Eileen's father, a biology teacher in the Bronx, had also started a school for medical assistants in New York City. It trained young people to become lab workers, X-ray technicians, and medical secretaries. The Mandl School—it still bears his name almost four decades after his death—has since expanded to include courses in respiratory therapy, ultrasound procedures, and healthcare administration.

Their parents' success gave them educational opportunities barely imaginable to their forbears, and they made the most of them. My mother graduated from Cornell at nineteen, Phi Beta Kappa. She ultimately focused on music, an abiding passion of her life, having studied piano from the age of eight. After majoring in English, she went to Juilliard. It's an interesting reflection of the times that her overprotective parents had no qualms about letting her go to Grand Central unaccompanied at age *ten*. Then she walked half an hour to her piano lesson. When it ended, she walked back to Grand Central and returned—again, unaccompanied—to their home in the suburbs. Parents who allowed their children to do this now would deservedly wind up arrested.

When they met, my father felt more for my mother, much sooner, than she for him. In his case, it sounded suspiciously like love at first sight. She considered him charming and attentive, smart and funny. She thought him handsome. None of that meant she was ready to marry him. Years after my father's passing, she told me about the particulars of his proposal. "But, Robert," she told him. "I don't love you."

"You'll learn to," he replied. In any case, despite her uncertainty, she acquiesced. Quite possibly, he wore her down. He had a way of doing that.

Did she learn to love him as he predicted? I've learned in both my personal and professional life that any marriage is ultimately a closed book to everyone except the two principals. As far as the question of whether or not my parents loved each other, I can cite evidence either way. In the balance I think they probably did. If they didn't, they gave a good approximation of it, at least at times.

WHEN MY GRANDFATHER WAS driving my father to college in the late 1920s, the young man had yet to choose a career or profession.

He asked his father for advice. "Well, Robert," his father replied, "business doesn't look so good right now. Maybe you should go into medicine."

"All right," said his son, and the discussion ended. It impressed me that his trust and respect for his father was such that this simple exchange had settled everything so easily.

My father's grades were high enough to get him into medical school without much difficulty. There was, however, one bump along the way that had lasting consequences for the family. He applied to Harvard, as well as less exalted institutions. At Harvard, he was interviewed by a condescending old WASP, a dean with the Dickensian name of Pennypacker. "So, Mr. Goldstein (the family name at the time)," the dean asked him, "who will take care of your uncle's delicatessen if you come to Boston for medical school?"

My father never did forget the slight. The University of Illinois College of Medicine accepted him—he never told me if Harvard accepted him as well. But the Pennypacker interview had deepened his awareness, already considerable, of antisemitism. This awareness wasn't softened by European events of the 1930s and 1940s. He had a deep knowledge of Jewish trials and tribulations through the millennia, from biblical times to the Holocaust. "Every time you see a Jew," he said repeatedly, "you're looking at a living miracle."

Fast-forward: When my father completed his training and went into private practice, he changed the family name to the ethnically neutral *Goodwin*. He wanted colleagues and potential patients to judge him by his merits and not his ethnicity. Years later, he told me he came to regret this decision, which he deemed unnecessary and a bit cowardly.

He did well in medical school, but his circumstances were far from easy. His parents had to sell their spacious home as a result of the Depression, and the three of them moved to a small apartment. He did much of his studying in the noisy, crowded confines of the L during the train ride between his home and classes. Here he was, a formerly coddled youth with newly impoverished parents. The family never lived in congregations of the homeless known as Hoovervilles or stood in breadlines, but the security they took for granted had vanished. My father's later prosperity enabled him to travel the world from Greece to the Galapagos Islands, to drive a Mercedes and wear a Patek Philippe. But he never fully trusted it, saying "All of us whose families lost everything in the Depression were never quite sane on the subject of money."

MY FATHER'S LIFE INCLUDED a stint in the military. His tour of duty resulted in a turn of events that affected the family everlastingly, although *luck* might not be quite the right word for it. Without it, in fact, there might not have been a family. The particulars: A few years after medical school, he enlisted in the army shortly before America entered World War II, and he wound up serving in the First Cavalry. In the course of its recent history, the First Cavalry has focused on non-equine methods of warfare such as artillery and helicopters. Back then, however, you could still find a number of horses in it.

He could be a consummate smartass when he chose to be. On one such occasion, his regiment had a full dress inspection with the equine contingent groomed and gussied up. A visiting general approached him, beaming. "Well, Lieutenant," the general asked, "how do you like our horses?"

My father was supposed to say how wonderful they were, how

noble and beautiful. What he said instead was, "Sir, I can't stand the goddamn stinking beasts. They're stupid fuckers, and they make my asthma worse."

They couldn't court-martial him for his irreverence, although they might have liked to. Instead, they transferred him to Fort Bliss, in El Paso, Texas, during the worst of the summer doldrums. The posting was as close to Devil's Island, the horrific French penal colony off the South American coast, as you could get in the U.S. Armed Forces. But his irreverence quite possibly saved his life. Most of his unit wound up in Bataan, on the Death March. Some of the captured Americans had their teeth knocked out so the Japanese could get at their gold fillings, others were summarily shot when they asked for water, and others were randomly killed by bayonet. The Japanese were also known to have buried some of them alive. In total, as many as six hundred Americans died, along with eighteen thousand Filipinos. But my father wound up his tour in Northern Ireland, of all places, which the British and Americans used as one of their staging areas for Operation Torch—the North African landings—and subsequently for Normandy.

MY OWN LUCK HELD up in the when and where of my formative years. I grew up in Springfield, Illinois—middle-sized, middle-class, a place where life flowed in mainly navigable currents, especially if you were the white offspring of a professional man. World War II was over, and the *Sturm und Drang* of the 1960s lay safely in the future. An unlikely event led to the family's moving there. Around that time, the city's sole dermatologist committed suicide, and local doctors were desperate to find a replacement for him. Dr.

Goodwin—he'd changed the family name by then—made a quick decision to relocate there. My grandmother Clara, newly widowed, joined us shortly thereafter. My three younger siblings were yet to come along.

Before the opportunity arose, it's unlikely my father gave Springfield more than a passing thought, and he probably hadn't been there. Eileen most likely hadn't thought of it at all. They subsequently found themselves living in a city of not quite 100,000 in the middle of the prairies, far from most of the people they cared about.

The Springfield of my childhood had right-angled streets, most of them due north-south and east-west. It had a number of parks with broad, inviting landscapes. It had a plethora of small businesses in the days before the malls and most of the chains. You bought groceries at Gruenwald's or The Avenue Food Shop, and fish at Robert's, and pastries at the B & Z Bakery. When the broiling summers were at their worst, you could avail yourself of the tepid but cooling waters of Lake Springfield. The city's most striking structure was the state capitol, its silver dome visible for miles in all directions.

Small things tell a lot, as always. Parents allowed children to trick-or-treat alone, even quite young ones. Often treats consisted of homemade cookies and hand-dipped caramel apples, not hard to take. Anyone who suggested Halloween offerings should be X-rayed for hidden razor blades would have struck people as a paranoid twit. Harry Truman received boos and Dwight Eisenhower cheers when they appeared in newsreels, an add-on to every feature film. Truman's popularity plummeted when the Korean War began.

Springfield took pride in being the epicenter of the Land of Lincoln, and still does. It's where he practiced law, and it's where he lived in the only house he ever owned. It's the town from which he left when he headed to Washington for his first inauguration, and it's where he lays entombed now. Lincoln sites remain major tourist attractions. His legacy notwithstanding, though, Springfield was never a paradigm of racial harmony. I had all-Caucasian classes throughout grade school, and I recall precisely one Black classmate in my years in Springfield High. The city may have been Lincoln's home, but it was also the site of a horrific race riot. In 1908, after the alleged rape of a white woman by a Black man, three days of murder and mayhem ensued. The result, sixteen dead including two men lynched, and the destruction of whole blocks of Black-owned homes and businesses. A mob went through the town, chanting, "Curse the day that Lincoln freed the niggers!"

TV was still a novelty for much of my childhood. Howdy Doody hung around with Clarabelle, Chief Thunderthud, and an Indian princess named Summerfall Winterspring—no one used the term *Native American* yet. They advertised cigarettes shamelessly. *MORE DOCTORS SMOKE CAMELS THAN ANY OTHER BRAND!* Married couples on TV shows slept in twin beds until the Flintstones came along a decade later. Playing with your friends was unsupervised and unscripted from around the time you turned six. If you needed adults and your parents were unavailable, the neighbors most likely would fill in. You knew them and they knew you, and they kept an eye on you.

THE GOODWINS HAD DINNER together, like most families. Conversation could take you anywhere, from contemporary medicine to the Civil War, always of interest in Lincoln's hometown. Apropos, my lifetime has included the death of the last surviving

Civil War veteran, Albert Woolston (1850-1956). Despite the growing popularity of television, we often listened to the radio, sometimes during dinner. There was Groucho Marx on *You Bet Your Life* ("Say the secret word and divide a hundred dollars between ya!") and *The Shadow* ("Who Knows . . . What Evil Lurks . . . in the Heart of Man?") and *Amos 'n' Andy* (dated, politically incorrect to the nth, with the leads played by two white guys).

If my parents weren't carping at each other, one could learn a great deal at the dinner table. Books read and movies seen, the Army-McCarthy hearings, the execution of the Rosenbergs, the prospects of an up-and-coming young senator named John F. Kennedy might all be on the agenda. Both parents had done well in their respective Shakespeare courses, and they liked to quiz each other on Shakespearean trivia. An enjoyable pastime: The Webster's Dictionary of a thousand or fifteen hundred pages sat on a wooden stand near the table. My father would challenge those present to find a word he or my mother didn't know. It didn't happen often. I only remember two of them—*callythump* (a noisy or boisterous parade) and *wallydrag* (the runt or last-born of a brood or litter; also a dwarfed and feeble creature).

Family life could be likened to the opening of *A Tale of Two Cities*: . . . the best of times, . . . the worst of times. The best of times meant an appreciation of my parents' wit and breadth of knowledge, their conversations going anywhere and touching on anything, and their wide and varied circle of friends. The best of times also meant an impassioned shared commitment to their children's well-being, although Eileen enjoyed them more than Robert did.

The worst of times could be ugly. A pleasant meal could turn into a full-blown skirmish in a flash. They could argue or bicker over anything, however trivial—they actually had a major fight one night over the crucial question of whether Burl Ives, the actor, had a beard. The word divorce came up often. I sometimes wished they would divorce. It might have been an improvement on the status quo.

My father was nothing if not mercurial. He could be affectionate, cold, quick to praise, impossible to please, friendly, enraged, charming, mean-spirited, a pleasure to be with, or someone to be avoided altogether. A talented mimic, he could be as amusing as any of the Marx Brothers, his favorite comedians, or as humorless as a hanging judge. He was maddeningly unpredictable, and his moods could turn on a dime.

In fairness, his wit could be quite amusing as long as you weren't the target of it. Once, talking about an acquaintance known for his indolence, he said that Stan Sherman was being treated for testicular gangrene. "Yes," Dr. Goodwin explained, straight-faced, "he sat on his balls, and he was too lazy to get up." On another occasion, he found himself next to a boring, talkative man on a long flight. "Excuse me," he said politely. "I have narcolepsy, and I feel an attack coming on." With that, he dropped his head to his chest and feigned sleep, complete with snoring. The rest of the flight passed uneventfully. We should note that his mordant wit could be directed on occasion toward himself. One morning, toward the end of his life, he came to breakfast with a sardonic smile. "Big day for me," he told the rest of the family, "I woke up with a medium-on."

Despite the vagaries of his moods and temper, he wasn't violent. Precisely once in my life did he lay a hand on me, and I deserved it. At the age of three or four, I woke him up as he tried to sleep late on a Sunday morning by repeatedly thumping him on the head with a wooden toy hammer. The sleeping giant didn't take it well. Lying on his stomach with one arm hanging over the edge of the bed, he sent me flying across the room with an underhanded slap on the butt. Was I remorseful? Not a chance. I turned to my father and reproached him— "You hit me." I don't recall his response to this.

As my father's practice prospered, my advantages and opportunities multiplied. I enjoyed summer camps in Minnesota and Wisconsin and family vacations from Montreal to Miami. On frequent trips to Chicago, I swam in Lake Michigan. I visited the Brookfield Zoo, and the Shedd Aquarium, and the Museum of Science and Industry, where I particularly liked their sprawling model train exhibit. Beyond those well-known attractions, I loved the skyscrapers of Lakeshore Drive, and the Buckingham Fountain, and endless blue-green stretches of the lake. Put simply, I regarded the city as the most exciting place in the world.

My parents believed their children should have every educational and cultural opportunity. Music, a case in point. When I was in the third grade, my father made this offer: "Robbie, your mother and I will arrange for music lessons in any instrument you choose. What do you think you'd like to play?"

"The double bassoon," I answered.

For once Dr. Goodwin was taken aback. "Do you know what a double bassoon is?" he asked after a brief silence.

"No, Pop, but I like the way the words sound."

They settled on the clarinet instead.

We should note that my father, unlike my mother, had no musical aptitude to speak of, but this didn't stop him from impromptu performances. A self-taught pianist of meager talent, he did a great imitation of Liberace, then at the height of his fame and popularity. Draping my mother's fur stole around his shoulders, flashing Liberace's trademark smarmy smile, using the Hanukah menorah as a candelabra, he fudged his way across the keyboard to the great amusement of my three younger siblings and me. Sometimes he sang along as he played. A favorite oeuvre was Dvorak's Humoresque Number Seven, with changed lyrics. His version:

> *Passengers will please refrain*
> *From flushing toilets in the train*
> *While the train is standing in the station*
> *I love YOUUUU, Dear*
> *Going out in Central Park*
> *And goosing statues in the dark*
> *If Sherman's horse can take it*
> *So can YOUUUU, Dear*

I don't know if he wrote this himself or filched it from another sentimentalist.

SOME OF THE BEST parts of my formative years involved Clara, my paternal grandmother. She lived with us from 1947, when her husband died, until 1970 when she died herself. She dearly loved my siblings and me, and we still routinely reminisce about her. If something went wrong, from a scraped knee to a romantic crisis to a set-to with our parents, she was unconditionally there for us. She kept contraband for us in her underwear drawer: my cigarettes—I smoked in my teens—and my brother's *Playboys*. She was always willing to offer advice, but only when we asked for it. And she never failed to offer us a sympathetic ear.

Clear of mind, with an excellent memory until the end, she was quick to share details of her life with us. I credit her for contributing to my love for history, my undergraduate major—she made it personal and real. She talked about the great flu epidemic of 1918 when people literally fell off trolley cars and dropped dead. She talked about life on the home front during World War I, a fear-ridden era when German-Americans were afraid to speak their native language and sauerkraut became known as liberty cabbage. When JFK was assassinated, she described how she and my grandfather were at the Pan-American Exposition in Buffalo in 1901. They'd stood about a hundred yards away when President McKinley was shot.

IN SCHOOL, OUR HIGHLY structured education emphasized rote learning and memorization. I can still rattle off the state capitals, and if pressed I could probably name the presidents in order. A very different education compared to that of our children and grandchildren. My stepdaughter came home from a junior high biology class and began to talk about the hypothalamus, a part of the brain I first heard about in college. My youngest grandson already knew about Van Gogh and Picasso at age nine.

I remember the teachers, almost all female, as benign and encouraging. A disproportionate number of them were single—spinsters, to bring back an outdated word. Benign, yes, but they also ran tight ships. Misdeeds resulted in visits to the principal, Mr. Head, a middle-aged bald man who wore bowties, about as threatening as Father Christmas. The greater threat, by far, was a note to one's parents. Children behaved in class, mainly because bad behavior was not an option.

Despite the growing unreliability of my memory, I recall the names of most of my classmates in grade school and my two years in Springfield High School. More than that, I remember much about their personalities, goals, and families. I remember Connie's determination to go to medical school, no ordinary goal for a girl back then, and I wonder if she made it. Ted's father was a reporter who covered state politics and would later win a Pulitzer for exposing governmental corruption at the statewide level. Marlene's father was a Major League umpire inducted into the Baseball Hall of Fame.

To be a child in Springfield during the late 1940s and 1950s meant, in my case, to live a life anchored in routine. Except in the foulest weather, I rode my bike to school. In the eighth grade, boys went to another school for shop class each week, and girls had home economics there. No cafeteria, so most students went home for lunch, and dual-income families had yet to become the norm. Recess, featuring innumerable games of kickball, broke up the school day. More games took place after school, or maybe you watched TV with friends, or maybe you went biking in a park.

Weekends had their own routine. Saturday afternoon usually meant movies or roller-skating. The Esquire, a theater within walking distance, had double features, a cartoon and a newsreel. A dollar covered a ticket and popcorn, and you still came home with change. Roller-skating took place at Moonlight Garden, where you made your way around a large wooden oval for three hours, give or take. I loved it, for reasons that escape me now.

On Saturday nights the entire family (including Clara, now in her late seventies and the least violent person I've ever known) sat enraptured by televised wrestling, exciting and wonderfully camp.

It was theater, pure and simple. Combatants had names like Yukon Eric and Farmer Don Marlin, Argentina Rocca, and Killer Kowalski. Gorgeous George, the most outrageous of them all against stiff competition, assumed the persona of an English dandy. He came to the ring accompanied by a butler who sprayed his corner with perfume before the match.

～

Some of my best youthful memories involve the lake. Quite a few of them occurred in 1960, the summer before I started college. I had a job on the riprap crew. The crew consisted of a group of young men, mainly high school and college students, who boarded a diesel barge in early morning. The barge, already loaded with a high pile of rocks and concrete rubble, set out for a leisurely circuit of the lake. The crew literally threw the rocks and rubble against the shoreline at points where the water eroded it. Many of them required two or more to lift and hurl it as the barge puttered around all day. Hard, sweaty work, but the crew took periodic swimming breaks. Never, before or since, did I have more upper body strength or a better tan. No one gave thought to a risk of melanomas.

I had a job that was fun, a job that put money in my pocket—not much, but I didn't need much. I had a girlfriend. I had a car, a Karmann Ghia predictably named Carmen, a stylish version of a Volkswagen, no longer made. Yale had accepted me, and I looked forward to going there with excitement and self-confidence. A bit too much self-confidence as it turned out. The brand new decade of the 1960s began with the best of omens. Who could have foretold how it would end?

In reconstructing a childhood, there's always the danger of an unrealistic idealization, although my own formative years were better than all right. It was hardy paradise, of course. The Korean War had turned into a grinding stalemate. The Cold War, with its Russophobia had hardened into an ongoing reality. Schoolchildren practiced crouching beneath their desks, unlikely to provide much safety if atomic bombs began to fall. Jim Crow reigned throughout much of the country, Senator McCarthy accused and bullied, and women lived lives of curbed and limited opportunities.

Hardly paradise, and yet the world—my world, in any case—was pretty much the way it should be, as long as you didn't look too closely at it.

FROM AS FAR BACK as I could remember, I wanted siblings. I thought of them as a source of close and easily available companionship. I envied schoolmates who had them.

There was something else I didn't grasp fully at the time. As an only child, I felt the undivided weight of parental demands and expectations, my father's in particular. His attention to my performance, to almost every word or deed (scrutiny would be the better word) could be extreme and oppressive. Anything could ignite a firestorm: a *B* on a book report, a chore ignored, a belatedly written thank you note for a birthday present. He was a helicopter parent long before the term came into use.

There's an old Jewish joke, not side-splitting, about a little boy who brings home a report card. He'd gotten five A's and a B+. His father looks at it and scowls. "So, Irving, since when does the alphabet begin with B?" A summary of Robert's expectations.

If I had siblings, or so I imagined, his attention and expectations might be diluted. Not to mention the vagaries of his temper and the scorch of his tongue.

⁓

My mother, like my grandmother Clara, had her share of obstetric problems. When I was two or three, she gave birth to a premature baby boy who only lived for a few hours. After that, my parents tried unsuccessfully for years to have more children. It was rarely discussed, but at some point midway through my grade school years, my parents and I became resigned to the near certainty I'd remain an only child. An OBG said the likelihood of another pregnancy was slim to nil. We don't know if God actually laughed about this, but He might have smirked a bit.

In 1952, my parents had a second son, whom they named Thomas. The fall of 1954 saw the arrival of my sister, Lisa. The spring of 1956 saw the arrival a second daughter, Laura—or Lolly, as she's known within the family. Eileen, in fact, was pregnant with her at my Bar Mitzvah. My maternal grandmother, still unaware of the pregnancy and rather vain about appearances, chided her daughter for having gained so much weight.

I took pleasure in the arrival of the much younger siblings. I gave them shoulder rides, teased them, read to them, and swam with them in Lake Springfield. The age difference spared me from sibling rivalry, so I could simply enjoy them. Which I did, for the most part.

It's a psychiatric maxim that no two people have the same family. This is true in ways obvious and not so obvious. It's obvious, for instance, that I have three younger siblings while Lolly has three older ones. Less obvious is the fact that I was born in the early 1940s while my siblings were born in the quite different epoch of the mid-1950s. My parents, moreover, were twenty-four and thirty-one at the time of my birth. In Lolly's case, they were thirty-seven and forty-four.

The trajectories of our lives make for striking contrasts. I married twice. The first one lasted ten years; so far the second one has lasted close to fifty. Tom married once, and it lasted about two years. Neither sister married, although both have had long relationships. I sidled into medicine with a strong side interest in writing. I always loved art but had no talent at all for it. Tom, on the other hand, won his first art prize at age four before he eventually gave up the visual arts and turned to the jazz saxophone; he has also engaged in the buying and selling of musical instruments.

Lisa gravitated toward the culinary arts, gourmet baking in particular. At different points, she has worked in restaurants, private clubs, and a culinary institute in California. She lived with my mother for the last decade of her life, assuming the role of her main caregiver. She shopped, cooked, paid bills, kept track of doctors' appointments and a host of medications, as well as providing companionship. I firmly believe her presence added five years or more to Eileen's lifespan. Lolly, artistically the most talented one, became a glassblower, but she has experience in virtually all the visual arts. Two of us live in New England, one in New Mexico, and one in California.

Still, there are similarities. Among the things we have in common: an irreverent and often raunchy sense of humor—Lolly, more than the others, has my father's talent for mimicry. All share staunchly Democratic leanings with a visceral loathing of the former and current president, a man who believes Hitler had some good ideas. A Robert-like penchant for creative insults ("hung like a cocktail sausage" was how Lisa described one of her less impressive male consorts. When I'm upset, she describes me as looking like a perturbed owl.) An abiding love of cats. A juvenile tendency to laugh about flatulence. A more than passing acquaintance with depression. A fondness for oysters on the half shell—any one of us could eat a dozen or two at any given time. A high tolerance for flawed people, more so with humanity at large than with each other. An affinity for underdogs. A tendency toward stubbornness and sarcasm. A problem with forgiveness, although Lolly does better with it than the rest of us.

Relations among the four of us have run the gamut and fluctuated wildly, from extreme closeness to long periods of estrangement. We know things about each other no one else does, including our parents, significant others, and various therapists. Above all else we share this bond, if at times we appear to share few others: of the eight billion people in the world, we're the only ones who know what it's like to have had Robert and Eileen Goodwin as our parents.

WHEN I WAS IN college, my time in Springfield became haphazard. After starting medical school, I didn't spend an entire summer there until 1968 when I worked with a brilliant if curmudgeonly chief of pathology, Dr. Grant Johnson, at one of the area's main hospitals. I assisted at autopsies and preparing slides of specimens; I also listened to Dr. Johnson's often fascinating digressions. The most memorable once concerned the death of a colleague, a veterinary pathologist, who died while conducting an autopsy on a whale. He allegedly drowned in the whale's aorta.

One summer, as I tried to navigate the shoals of late middle age, I found myself seized by a peculiar yearning to go to the Illinois State Fair. Throughout my childhood and early adolescence, I'd gone there devotedly, year in and year out.

The fair has been in Springfield permanently since 1894. Its expanse includes a racetrack and grandstand, a midway ("Happy Hollow"), a campground, a garden pavilion, and a swine barn. It has hosted farmers, governors, artisans, presidents, sellers of funnel cakes and candy apples, con artists, and children and octogenarians for eleven days each August. Lisa, the only family member still living there at the time, put me up, and we made the state fair pilgrimage together.

We gazed upon a cow carved of butter, a fair hallmark for generations. Lisa humored me as we inspected sows and piglets, ewes and lambs, prizewinning pies and cakes, and booths on the midway where you could play unwinnable games of chance. We rode the Ferris wheel. We ate junk food galore, although Lisa, a vegetarian, did not participate in my quest for the perfect corn dog, the epitome of Midwestern soul food. We should note that Springfield, while posing no threat to Paris or Lyon, has made its own contributions to haute cuisine. In addition to the corn dog, reputedly invented there, they also invented the horseshoe sandwich in the town. This is a Welsh rarebit-type creation with cheese smothering ham and turkey or any other combination of meats that inspired the chef and topped with french fries. The kind of food that could shorten your life by ten years if you ate it regularly.

Stands now sold crepes and sushi as well as deep-fried s'mores, and there were newer gravity-defying rides, and now there were

Filipino and Lithuanian booths in a recently designated Ethnic Village. Still, in most essential respects the fair had remained the same.

I can't speak for Lisa, but I thoroughly enjoyed myself. It also deepened my awareness that, for all the years I spent far away from it, Springfield had become an absolutely integral part of who I am. Furthermore, it would remain so, for the duration.

WHILE I MAINTAIN A steadfast fondness for it, I don't fancy Springfield as an earthly paradise. For one thing, there's the matter of the weather. The summers can scorch like a blast furnace, the winters can render you numb with cold, and an occasional tornado may enliven things. Apart from that, however, I had often been restless there. I'd always loved to travel, and I did a fair bit of it growing up. The family made trips to the upper Midwest with its sprawling forests and sizeable lakes, lakes that made Springfield's seem like little more than a wading pool. We went to Montreal and Quebec, where people actually spoke a language other than English. We went to Florida: my first exposure to the ocean. I especially liked the verve and excitement of cities. Springfield had its virtues, but verve and excitement would not rank high among them.

It would be inaccurate to say that Springfield never changed. Many of its small shops and other businesses have been replaced by CVS and Walmart and their ilk. Movie theaters have given way to a Cineplex. The two main hospitals, the main teaching hospitals for the city's medical school, appeared to have doubled in size. Even so, much about the Springfield of my youth has persisted. The starkly geometric layout of its streets. The silver-domed grandeur of the state capitol, the sprawling state fairground. The isolation—fifteen minutes from town and you're in the middle of farms and prairies, and you felt a million miles from anywhere.

At some point in my youth, long before I had a semblance of a plan—before I could have found the words to fit the thought, I knew I'd leave someday. The wider world, about which I knew so very little, beckoned. I knew I'd leave and so I did, for better or worse, or more likely both.

CHAPTER III

CULVER AND YALE

There's a swathe of north central Indiana with an abundance of lakes and rivers that break up a rolling countryside of hillocks and verdant valleys. Maxinkuckee, the largest lake in the area, lies roughly halfway between Chicago and Indianapolis. No less a personage than Kurt Vonnegut Jr., an Indiana native who went there frequently, has written fondly of it. On its shore sit two private secondary schools, the Culver Military Academy for boys and a sister academy for girls. It's possible that there are more pleasantly situated schools in the United States, but I've never seen one.

Starting at the Military Academy in September of 1958, and attending for my last two years of high school, I graduated in June of 1960. I consider the chance to go there as having been one of the singular pieces of good fortune in my life.

∼

I WANTED TO GO to Culver. Some people I've known find this unfathomable. They regard military schools (or at least the idea of them since they've rarely had firsthand exposure to one) in a negative light. They regard them as semi-correctional facilities for incorrigible sons of wealthy parents who can afford them (think of Trump). Or else as dumping grounds for offspring deemed inconvenient or frankly disliked. Neither group included me.

I knew about Culver before becoming a cadet. In the early 1950s, I attended their summer Woodcraft Camp, which I loved. I swam and canoed on Maxinkuckee, hiked through adjacent woodlands, and played volleyball and softball. I tried badminton and pitched horseshoes. Campers wore vaguely military outfits—blue flight caps, short sleeve chambray shirts, Bermudas and knee socks—and our tents underwent cursory inspections. But the quasi-military ambience was mild and benign, and you could never confuse the place with Camp Lejeune.

The main reason I wanted to go involved my father. Our relations continued to deteriorate as I reeled through adolescence, and I yearned to get the hell out of Dodge. While I doubt he and I would have killed each other if I'd stayed in Springfield, I can't rule it out completely. For the record, I don't believe he was a terrible parent. During the worst of times, I never lost sight of his wit and intelligence and his no-holds-barred devotion to his family. But adolescents are notoriously hard to control, and my father was as controlling a man as I've ever known. Moreover, he ignored one of the cardinal rules of dealing with your teenager: *Everything, potentially, is a battle, so pick your battles carefully.* With him, there was no such thing as a trivial battle with his children. Every clash was Gettysburg or Guadalcanal.

WHEN I LOOK BACK on my time at Culver, I think first and foremost about the teaching. Put simply, it was the best I've encountered, from my first day in kindergarten until my last day as a psychiatric resident. No matter the subject, from English to history to chemistry, I never had a teacher there who wasn't excellent. My two favorites, against stiff competition, both taught English.

I had John Edgell my first year. Like many Culver teachers, he was a veteran of World War II, a naval officer who served in the South Pacific. Not a martinet, but he never lost a certain military bearing. From time to time he told stories of life on the jungled islands, and the fighting there, with a vividness that let you see and hear and smell it. In his classes, he found the proper balance between presentation and discussion, as did most of the Culver teachers. His assigned readings ranged from the Bible as literature to *Macbeth* to short stories of John Steinbeck and William Faulkner, both still alive and productive. He favored writing rich and evocative in detail but with no words wasted. When he returned your papers, he might have written almost as much on them as you did.

The following year my English class was taught by Arthur Hughes. A bit warmer and less formal than John Edgell, Mr. Hughes had more of a flair for the dramatic. He paced as he read out loud, his deep voice rising and falling, his face smiling or frowning as appropriate for the material. He favored more plays than Mr. Edgell, teaching those of Henrik Ibsen, Clifford Odets, and Arthur Miller. But his classes could take you anywhere. He even devoted time to fables, from Aesop's to *Animal Farm*. The latter provided my introduction to George Orwell.

I still think about Mr. Edgell and Mr. Hughes when I'm writing. I imagine them peering down over my shoulder, approving or disapproving of what I've done, goading me to find a better word or turn of phrase, scowling at clichés. Or simply telling me to forget a page or paragraph and start over.

Teachers' involvement with their charges went beyond the classroom. They advised the student-editors of the yearbook and literary magazine. They met with students after class, they lent them books. From time to time cadets were allowed to invite them to join them for dinner in the mess hall, and they usually accepted. Cadets, in turn, might be invited to their homes. Another of my favorite teachers, Peter DeTroy, was the advisor for my Honors English paper. His home bordered on Maxinkuckee and the dining room faced west, affording views of spectacular lakeside sunsets during dinner.

A telling detail—during my two years at Culver, the faculty included two PhDs, one in history and another in chemistry. For PhDs to teach in secondary schools was uncommon if not rare in the 1950s. Their presence said a lot about Culver's efforts to put together the best possible faculty.

THE MILITARY ASPECTS OF life at Culver were nonthreatening but omnipresent. Cadets woke up at reveille and went to bed at taps. They wore uniforms throughout their waking hours, underwent room inspections, and had to keep their ties straightened and shoes shined. Twice a day, they sought to turn their shoes into mirrors. One consequence of this: six decades after I graduated, I still hate shining shoes.

Cadets marched in weekly dress parades accompanied by a marching band. Some cadets were on horseback. The best of the cavalrymen were members of the Black Horse Troop, an elite outfit that usually participates in presidential inaugurations. A first year cadet, or plebe, opened doors for an upperclassman and addressed the latter as *sir*.

Culver's military character could be mildly onerous. At times I got sick of it when I wanted to sleep or stay up late and when marching became tedious (too hot, too cold, too rainy). I didn't care for close-order drill, which involved an M-1 rifle. Like all cadets, I was taught how to take it apart, clean it, and reassemble it, but I was never any good with it. Once, at a drill, my unit was given an order to *PRESENT ARMS!* Which means: holding the M-1 diagonally in front of me, disengaging the safety catch, and opening the bolt. The inspector, either a cadet officer or a member of the Academy's ROTC staff, could then peer into the rifle's guts to make sure it was properly cleaned and assembled. On this occasion I had reassembled the rifle particularly ineptly, and a piece of it flew out and hit the inspecting officer in his chest. So much for my career in weapons engineering.

On the other hand, if I'm honest about it, I kind of enjoyed the parades and marching. I enjoyed the sense of being part of something larger than myself, a common enough phenomenon, as benign as being part of a crowd at Fenway Park or as malignant as attending a Nuremberg rally.

I also did well with the structure, and I had enough self-awareness to know I needed a great deal of it. Years later, when I began to treat adolescent patients, I was struck by how they hated structure and rebelled against it at virtually every opportunity but also how they craved it and commonly thrived in it. One of my private patients, a girl of sixteen, was talking about her family when she interrupted herself in mid-sentence. "Your desk is too neat!" she declared. "I have an urge to go over there and mess it up!" But she later told me she thought her parents weren't strict enough with her brother and her, and she thought they'd both suffered for it.

A FEW YEARS AFTER I graduated, I came back to the Academy for a summer visit. I met with a history teacher I'd always liked, and conversation turned to the military aspects of life at Culver. "It was interesting," my former teacher said. "You weren't a leader, and you weren't a follower. For the most part, you were oblivious to the whole thing."

I believe he had a point.

MOST CADETS CAME FROM families that lived comfortably but weren't unduly wealthy. One of my roommates was the son of a founder and CEO of a small intercity bus line, another the son of a jeweler. Other classmates' fathers included a neurosurgeon, a law professor who became a federal judge, a three-star general, and a liquor distributor. The father of at least one cadet had died in World War II.

They came from both coasts, but more commonly from the Midwest and South. The Academy had yet to admit African Americans or American-born Latinos, but a handful of cadets came from the Caribbean and Central America. One classmate grew up in Cuba, where his family had known prominence and an affluent lifestyle. During the winter break of 1959, when Fidel Castro assumed power, he and his family suddenly found themselves without a home or a homeland. Such events have a way of underscoring the point that major news stories are more than abstract happenings in far-off places. They're events involving real people, and they have consequences that can be matters of life and death.

I mainly got on well with fellow cadets despite my nonmilitary take on things, and a few became lifelong friends. Culver did provide my introduction to anti-Semitism though. No physical attacks or swastikas were drawn on my door, and anyone engaged in such acts would have been expelled. But I saw and heard enough evidence of prejudice to gain my attention. Culver was where I first learned about the concept of Jews as Jesus-killers, for instance. How do you counter the illogic of that, of holding a group of people responsible for someone's death that occurred two thousand years ago? Culver was also where the word *kike* became part of my vocabulary. Springfield had its faults, but I recalled no instances of anti-Semitism throughout my childhood there.

***

Two hundred nine cadets graduated in the Class of 1960, along with a small number of faculty daughters in the days before Culver became formally coed. Five of the graduates went to Yale, three to Harvard, one each to Princeton and Dartmouth. Among the graduates' other schools: Duke, West Point, the Virginia Theological Seminary, and the *Escuela Superior de Comercio* in Madrid. Not bad for a small military school in the middle of North Central Indiana. I was among the five who went to Yale. I doubt I'd have made it to the Ivy League if I hadn't gone to Culver.

Glancing through the yearbook, I was struck by the innocence and naïveté on our faces. A survey included in the book contains telling results. Eisenhower was the most admired international figure, edging out Churchill, with Nixon coming in third. The most popular movie stars included Rock Hudson and Doris Day. *Playboy*, on the cutting edge of risqué, was voted the most popular magazine. Ninety percent of the graduating class described Culver as *excellent* or *good*.

I've gone to a number of Culver Reunions. At one of them, they invited alumni to sit in on classes. I attended one in history, focusing on American history in the second half of the twentieth century. The teacher asked me if I'd answer questions about the 1960s and 1970s, and I agreed to do so.

The questions were thoughtful, the discussion lively. *How did you feel when JFK was elected? What was it like when the president, Bobby Kennedy, and MLK were assassinated? Were you frightened during the Cuban Missile Crisis?* (Yes). *Did you think civilization as we knew it might be destroyed?* (Possibly but unlikely). *Did LBJ push through the Civil Rights Act out of principle or political expediency? We studied how Vietnam divided the country—how did it affect your own family?*

The teacher threw in his own questions and comments, and the hour-long discussion went by in a heartbeat. I was gratified to note that the quality of teaching, as evidenced by the classes I attended, had remained as high as when I'd been a cadet myself.

IN THE EARLY SUMMER of 1959, my parents and I spent two weeks traveling to points east. The trip combined my father's medical meeting in Washington, seeing my maternal grandparents in New York State, and my visits to prospective colleges. My grades at Culver, combined with high SATs, had made me a candidate for some of the best schools in the country. Even Yale.

I remember the interviews there, conducted by genteel academic types, but mainly I recall the campus. There were ten residential colleges, now numbering fourteen. There was a hodgepodge of architectural styles, from neo-Gothic to Georgian to Federalist, which somehow jibed. Greenery adorned the walls of many buildings; there really was a lot of ivy in the Ivy League. I recall few interiors of the buildings except for the Sterling Library, a repository of four million books (now with more than three times that), with its inviting, deep leather chairs. As congenial a place for reading as you could imagine.

The geography of Yale is deceptive. About four thousand undergrads attended in 1960, with perhaps a thousand more in graduate and professional schools. Its buildings occupied roughly four square miles. It would take you an hour, give or take, to get from the School of Divinity at the northeast end to the medical complex in the southwest, assuming you walked briskly. The buildings are spread throughout the central city, so the university does not seem cramped or claustrophobic.

Impressive. Hard not to be impressed, what with the stately architecture, the grounds and meandering paths and wealth of trees. Statues and paintings of famous alumni abounded within and outside the buildings, from Nathan Hale (Class of 1773) to John Calhoun (Class of 1804, since removed because of his embrace of slavery). Put simply, Yale was like no place I'd ever seen.

I applied, and Yale accepted me. In September 1960, when my parents dropped me off, I felt ready for it. I'd graduated with honors in English, French, and history, and I'd contributed to the school's literary journal, and they'd done a cover story on me in their alumni magazine. I'd even won a gold watch for the student who made the greatest cultural contribution to the corps of cadets. You might compare me to a Triple A minor league baseball player with marked potential. This did not mean, however, that I was ready for the big leagues. Especially for a team like the 1927 Yankees. What I hadn't known—or if I did, I suppressed it—was a simple fact, *that everyone there, with few exceptions, had excelled.* While I met classmates who were merely pretty smart, classmates admitted because they came from illustrious families and their great grandfathers had been Yalies, such classmates made up a distinct minority.

⁓

Rummaging through some old papers a few years ago, I found a calendar for the opening week of Yale College for incoming freshman in September 1960. It was four pages long, filled with small print. Events began as early as 8:00AM and often went on until late evening.

They offered campus tours and films about Yale and the city of New Haven. They offered meetings for students interested in ROTC, and in trying out for football, and in doing volunteer work at mental institutions. There was a welcoming address from the university president and a reception at his home, a recital by the university organist, and an outing at Hammonasset Beach on Long Island Sound. A presentation on "Religious Opportunities at Yale" (mandatory attendance) by William Sloane Coffin, the university chaplain, later to become a nationally-known opponent of American involvement in Vietnam. Discussion group meetings with counselors and faculty members. A formal welcoming dinner with entertainment provided by the Yale Glee Club.

I have long been intrigued by the vagaries of memory. I remember most of the major events of my life in detail: weddings, births of my son and grandchildren, the JFK assassination, and the 9/11 attacks. But I can remember a lot of the minor stuff as well. Passages from a novel read in the 1960s or parts of a movie seen in the 1970s.

Of my first week at Yale, however, I remember nothing. Not a fragment of conversation, nor moving into my dorm, nor a recollection of a meal or a speech or a concert. Why not? I have a general sense of the week as pleasant enough, and in any case it wasn't traumatizing. I wasn't drunk or stoned, and I don't think I was homesick. Perhaps I suffered from an overload of stimuli. So much happened, so much came at me from all directions, that none of it stuck.

THE YALE COURSES WERE incalculably harder than what I was used to. Case in point, I'd signed up for an introductory biology course but missed the first class because I had a cold or something. Biology class at Springfield High had not proved taxing. We looked at amoeba and paramecia through microscopes. We learned the differences between mammals, reptiles, and amphibians. The most demanding task had been dissecting a fetal pig.

When I showed up for the second Yale biology class, the professor had filled a blackboard with a diagrammatic representation of the tricarboxylic acid cycle. It's also known as the Krebs cycle, the common terminal metabolic pathway for aerobic organisms. I looked at the diagram, dumbstruck. An epiphany: I was no longer at Culver, much less Springfield High School. I had no further exposure to the Krebs cycle until I was in medical school, taking biochemistry.

Another case in point, I'd done well in French at Culver. But I'd studied it primarily in written texts instead of through the spoken word. This wasn't Culver's fault. That's how they did it then, and language labs were still uncommon. Babies don't learn languages by reading about them. As a result, I could read French without too much difficulty. While you'd never confuse me with Victor Hugo, I could write it. I could even speak it, sort of; I could think fast enough to translate something in my head. But that was not a two-way street.

I drew a blank if people addressed me in fluent idiomatic French, and they might as well have been talking to me in Farsi.

When I walked into my first Yale French class, the professor introduced himself. "I'm Joseph McMahon," he said in English. And that was it: his last English words for the rest of the year, with almost no exceptions.

Apart from my classes, there was also the matter of my classmates. I'd known bright types at Culver. One of them had graduated with honors in all his subjects, and he'd also achieved perfect SATs. But nothing prepared me for the supernova brilliance of several fellow Yalies. You may get a sense of this from their postgrad accomplishments. Their CVs include: senior astrophysicist at the Center for Astrophysics, operated jointly by Harvard and the Smithsonian . . . chief of the biological psychiatry branch of the National Institute of Mental Health . . . president of the University of Michigan . . .

While those mentioned achieved prominence in STEM, the humanities and social sciences had their own superstars. Bill became an author and filmmaker, a political activist, and a founding father of the disability rights movement. My freshman counselor, another Bill, was a graduate student in Comparative Literature, among Yale's most demanding fields. He knew Latin, Greek, Old English, French, Italian, and German; he also had a strong background in history, philosophy, and comparative religions.

In other words, these were men—no co-eds yet—who made you feel as if you'd been a three-toed sloth throughout your life.

MY CAREER AT YALE ran the gamut. At times I did all right, particularly in history and the social sciences. The quality of teaching varied since scholarly achievement doesn't always translate into classroom brilliance. But much of it was good to excellent, and some of it was genuinely inspiring. John Morton Blum not only taught twentieth century American history with verve and eloquence, he also wrote books about two of its leading lights, Theodore Roosevelt and Woodrow Wilson. Edward Zigler provided my first introduction to abnormal psychology, peppering his lectures with clinical vignettes and case histories. While not teaching, or writing or editing one of his forty or so books, he kept busy developing Head Start. Vincent Scully, perhaps Yale's most popular professor, gave SRO lectures on the history of architecture. A dramatic figure who paced and danced around the podium as he thrust his pointer at his slides—no PowerPoints yet—he expounded on the Parthenon and the Guggenheim and everything in between. I cannot attest to the accuracy of this, but he reputedly fell off a podium while lecturing, broke his collarbone, and went on lecturing without missing a beat.

If such teachers did not inspire you, no one could.

I surprised myself by receiving high marks in another biology course, in Comparative Anatomy, which included fascinating references to biodiversity and evolution. However, the other science course I took, in physics, proved disastrous. I did all right in introductory economics and in my one philosophy course. But I foundered in courses that should have played to my strengths. Creative writing, for instance.

Why was my Yale performance so inconsistent? Why was it so often mediocre, if not worse? Lack of discipline played a role, no doubt. Discipline at Culver was a given, but at Yale you had to provide your own. I cut classes, and I frequently read what I wanted but neglected assigned readings. That was only a part of the story though. I could still be quite disciplined if it suited me. *If.*

For another thing, I was preoccupied. Among the sources of my preoccupation, a knack for unhealthy relationships. I was prone to falling in or out of love or recovering from a breakup. Relations with my family preoccupied me too. A geographic separation didn't mean all the problems between my father and me had vanished. And there were times when I missed the rest of the family acutely: my mother, my siblings, and Clara.

Also, not to make excuses for myself, but I was often depressed as hell. The *Diagnostic and Statistical Manual of Mental Disorders* (DSM5) of the American Psychiatric Association lists nine specific symptoms for a major depressive disorder. They include such things as serious sleep impairment—insomnia, hypersomnia, or both; diminished interest or pleasure in almost all activities; feelings of worthlessness or inappropriate guilt. If five or more of these symptoms occur, the diagnosis of a major depressive disorder is deemed warranted. Looking back on much of my time at Yale, I note I had six or seven of them.

A relevant digression: In 2007, I took a half-time job as psychiatric consultant at the main campus of the University of Connecticut (UConn). At that point I was medical director at a community mental health facility, a job for which I had little interest and less aptitude. I liked treating patients and supervising psychology interns, but administrative nonsense stultified me. According to the prevalent mindset, all problems could be addressed by more paperwork or more meetings. The meetings, especially, made me crazy. I fantasized about bringing in an Uzi, just to add a bit of zest to them.

I took a five-digit pay cut when I went to UConn. The best money

I ever lost. I supervised graduate students in clinical psychology and social work, I gave presentations on subjects ranging from psychiatric drugs to sociopathy. I sat in on case conferences and staff meetings. But most of what I did was *treat*. And (I make no bones about this) I strive to be the kind of shrink I badly needed in my own undergraduate years. We all have our own agendas in life.

YEARS AFTER I LEFT New Haven, I heard a Yale professor give a lecture on the value of intellectual wandering, a crucial part of the undergraduate experience. By which she meant the taking of courses simply because they interest and challenge you, apart from having any bearing on your plans for a profession or career. A wonderful idea, in my opinion. I did so at least twice at Yale.

The first involved Greek classics in translation, also known as Classy Civ. The professor, Laurence Richardson, a quietly passionate man who favored velvet smoking jackets, including a rather fetching purple one, focused on the plays of Sophocles, Euripides, and Aeschylus.

You could ask what relevance Greek tragedies might have in the contemporary world. The answer, none at all, until you watch any evening newscast or pick up any newspaper. Until you consider religious, racial, and clan hatreds passed from generation to generation, sometimes through the millennia—until you consider things like ethnic cleansing, hardly a modern phenomenon. Until you witness an array of world leaders often motivated largely by hubris, possessing nukes. Until you learn the cataclysmic results of crimes of passion. The Greeks may not have invented them, but they did turn them into an art form.

Another case of my wandering involved my sole anthropology course, a field about which I knew nothing. The subject of the course intrigued me though: the high native cultures of the New World, focusing on the Aztecs, Mayans, and Incas. The course was taught by Michael Coe, a man still in his thirties. Only a few years out of graduate school, he'd already done field work in the Yucatan Peninsula, the Peruvian highlands, and the broad mesas encompassing Mexico City. He'd also done a stint in the early days of the CIA, which I only learned fifty years later when I read his memoir.

With contagious enthusiasm Professor Coe talked about the brilliance and brutality of the Aztecs, given to precise astronomical predictions and human sacrifice. About the Incas and their practice of a primitive socialism. Their achievements included magnificent architecture and textiles, although they hadn't invented a wheel or developed an alphabet. Coe lectured about the inferences that could be made about diet, health, and lifestyle from examining coproliths—the stony remains of age-old feces—and the difficulties of bringing them through U.S. customs. He paraphrased the dialog, which went something like this: "Sir, do you have anything to declare?" "Yes Officer, a hundred pounds of human excrement, several thousand years old."

Michael Coe, among the half dozen best teachers I had anywhere, in any subject.

REGARDING THE DIVERSITY OF its undergraduates, Yale from 1960 to 1964 might be termed a work in progress. In my class, Black and Hispanic students comprised one percent apiece. Fifty years later, the figures were six and nine percent respectively. During that same time, the percentage of international students rose from 3.5 to 13.7. I met those whose forbears came to the colonies before American independence and those born abroad. At least two classmates were sons of famous men, Joe DiMaggio and Mike Wallace. I didn't know Joe Junior, but I did know Peter Wallace, outgoing and warm, with an engaging sense of humor. Pete died the summer between his freshman and sophomore years in a hiking accident in Greece.

The classmate to whom I felt the closest was Samuel Edgar Wilhite, aka Hite, my roommate for three years. We were something of an odd couple. Hite, the quieter and by far the steadier one, had a keen analytic mind and Lincolnesque physique (tall, thin, dark-haired but no beard). As noted, I could be undisciplined and flighty, and my grades were all over the place. Hite's were consistently high, good enough to get him into Stanford Law School. After Stanford he moved back east, to Washington, where he became a federal public defender.

He and I remained connected through the years, meeting in places as varied as Dublin, New York City, and Isle Royale National Park in the middle of Lake Superior. We shared good and less than good times, including the vagaries of married life and one divorce apiece. We also forged a professional connection. Occasionally I flew to Washington and did a psychiatric evaluation on one of his clients. It gave us a chance to catch up and take in a museum and a few excellent meals. Hite, on his part, provided invaluable information on criminal law when I began to try my hand at writing crime fiction.

I was struck by his efforts on behalf of his clients, some of whom had committed heinous acts. He harbored no illusions about their innocence, but he never lost sight of their essential humanity, believing the differences between the best and worst of us are smaller than generally imagined. A belief I came to share when I began to work in correctional settings.

We remained close until Hite succumbed to a massive stroke, much too early, in the first decade of the new millennium.

YALE IS KNOWN FOR its secret societies. The most famous of these is Skull and Bones, housed in a windowless, imposing if bleak edifice known as the Tomb. Through the years its members have disproportionally included the very wealthy and very powerful. Consider 2004, when George W. Bush ran against John Kerry, ensuring that the president would be a Bonesman. New members of the societies were chosen ("tapped") toward the end of their junior year by members of the preceding class.

The university has a number of other societies, less prestigious. In the spring of 1963 one of them, Ring and Candle, tapped me.

Its format and purpose involved a great deal of self-disclosure with feedback from the other members. The society chose fifteen members each year, and my group was definitely a mixed bag. It included jocks and intellectuals, introverts and extroverts, the son of a captain of industry and the son of a steamfitter. We came from New England and the West Coast, from Atlanta and Springfield, Illinois. Some of us had a clear sense of what we wanted to do when we graduated, and some had none. Politically we ran the gamut from Goldwater Republicans to those far left of center. Some were devout—one became an Episcopal clergyman—and some were godless. We supported, encouraged, and sometimes confronted each other unsparingly. The twice-weekly meetings had elements of leaderless group therapy with overtones of self-actualization programs popular in the 1970s and early 1980s.

Looking back, I view the Ring and Candle experience as one of the most important and enlightening parts of my Yale experience. Among other things it gave me a chance to know (for the first time, beyond superficialities) an African American, a man with severe physical disabilities, and a man with roots in Central Europe whose father had fought on the other side of World War II.

The members of our group included a classmate named Terry Holcombe. He became, along with Hite, one of the two classmates with whom I established a lasting intimacy. My relationship with Terry survived long periods of geographic separation and no contact. Terry spent years in Brazil and Venezuela, working for a global nonprofit called *Accion* while I spent years in Dublin.

Terry originally came from the New Haven area. When I returned to New Haven for an internship, I found Terry had come back to Connecticut as well. Notwithstanding the passage of six years since we'd seen each other, and intervening events like marriage and parenthood, we reestablished an easy and immediate rapport.

Terry and I remained close for over half a century. We and our families have shared New Year's Eves and Fourth of July picnics and football games at the Yale Bowl. We've shared meals in restaurants where we've embarrassed ourselves with raucous laughter. We've shared trips to New York City and to tiny hamlets in Vermont and New Hampshire and theatrical productions from *Macbeth* to *Cabaret* to *Chicago*. We've also shared deaths of parents, relatives, and friends, and all manners of family dramas and dilemmas and health crises. Along the way, and I still find it hard to wrap my head around this, we've morphed from undergraduates into grandfathers.

DESPITE ANGST AND SELF-ABSORPTION, I did strive to be a useful member of the campus community, at times. Dwight Hall is a Yale institution dedicated to community service and social justice. Founded in 1886, its activities have ranged from helping New Haven's homeless to providing meals to the Depression's unemployed to organizing blood drives.

I was involved in two of their programs. The first involved visits of students to meet with long-term patients at Connecticut's largest state mental hospital. I only remember one of them, an unassuming middle-aged man named Lou. There was nothing about him that suggested psychosis or any other serious mental difficulties. After our meetings ended, I learned Lou had killed a woman in the course of a paranoid episode. While acquitted (not guilty by reason of insanity), he was remanded indefinitely to the hospital, which meant a de facto life sentence.

In the 1960s Dwight Hall was drawn into the emergent crisis over civil rights. It chartered buses and organized Freedom Rides, and I signed up for one. This particular trip would take us to Maryland's Eastern Shore. The group, mostly Yalies, included students from other New England colleges. Most of us hadn't been on a previous trip, so we had no clear notion of what to expect when we arrived there.

A group of twenty-five or thirty met us, or maybe twice that many. They were almost exclusively white males in their thirties and forties. My most vivid recollection is of their faces, beyond angry, contorted with hate. If looks could kill, everyone on the bus would have died ten times over. Some of them had baseball bats. It occurred to me, *I might not get out of this alive.*

No one, in fact, was hurt, and the bus wasn't damaged (on several trips a bus had been torched and demolished). The ride back to New Haven was uneventful, the mood notably more somber than it had been when we headed down.

THE ROMANTIC RELATIONSHIPS I had at Yale ran the gamut. They included long and short ones, those lastingly remembered and those mainly forgotten, the good and the bad and the ugly. Two were particularly noteworthy. The first of them was with Alexis.

Alexis Iphigenia Bartoli was from my hometown, Springfield. Her parents were born in Trieste, in Italy's extreme northeast, near the Balkans. This made for an exotic background by the standards of Central Illinois in the 1950s. In the early grades I remember her as a good student, affable and pleasant but on the shy side with an appealing giggle. As we made our way through the seventh and eighth grades, the acquaintanceship grew into a friendship. We talked together between classes and spent hours on the telephone. The conversations touched on everything. Our families—skirmishes between my father and me, her mother and her. We talked about classmates and teachers. About books; she listened patiently when I raved on about how wonderful *Catcher in the Rye* was. About our plans and hopes and fantasies.

In high school we saw less of each other. We had different classes and activities. We made new friends, and we both had the requisite infatuations with other people. Still, I cherished our shorter and less frequent phone calls, despite our not seeing each other for a week or so at a time. Then I went to Culver, and our contacts decreased to close to nil.

By the following March, we were no longer seeing other people. She was at the University of Wisconsin, in Madison, and we'd kept in touch by occasional letters and phone calls. On a whim I invited her to New Haven for spring weekend, and she accepted.

Through the years I've learned to pay attention to patients' first sexual encounters. That they're important is almost too obvious to state. Imagine a boy and girl, scarcely removed from childhood, who don't know each other well or care about each other much. Imagine them having sex in a nervous hurry, in one of their homes, fearing parents might come home from the movie earlier than expected. Now imagine another couple who've known each other for most of their lives and were friends and confidantes since well before their teens. They have no sexual expertise, but they're not completely ignorant about sex either. They're in a motel six states away from either set of parents. They have time enough to touch and explore, time enough to culminate a relationship that has waxed and waned but then waxed again for years. So it was for Alexis and me.

A line of William Wordsworth is relevant here. *To be young is very heaven.*

So, what happened? Maybe Madison and New Haven were simply too far apart. Or maybe the lure of other relationships were too strong, and we weren't ready for commitment. Even so, on more than a few occasions, before and after spring weekend, I was certain Alexis and I would wind up together. No doubt this made God laugh, possibly with a touch of melancholy.

THE OTHER QUITE NOTABLE relationship began in Evanston, just north of Chicago, during the summer between my junior and senior years at Yale. It occurred at Northwestern University. I was taking a year-long course in inorganic chemistry condensed into ten weeks. At that point I'd decided I wanted to become a doctor after all, but I wondered if I had the calling; I really did liken it to the priesthood. Among the reasons I felt ready to commit to it (not the healthiest one): I thought I'd regret it for the rest of my life if I didn't.

Living in a dorm no more than a ten-minute walk from Lake Michigan, I arrived at Northwestern knowing no one on campus. I became friendly with an undergrad named Roy, also taking a summer course. Roy lusted after a tallish redhead who didn't much reciprocate his interest. But the redhead had a friend, a sorority sister named Alice Hughes, and one evening the four of us went out for a pizza. Alice, slender and petite, had well-filled curves, and she moved with a dancer's grace. High cheekbones, shoulder-length jet black hair, and dark arresting eyes. I've always been a connoisseur of eyes.

Clearly, Alice and I made a favorable impression on each other. "I'm thinking I might marry her," I told Roy when we got back to our dorm. When they went back to their sorority house, Alice told the redhead something similar.

When not in classes, Alice and I spent almost all our waking time together. We made full use of the lakefront, practically living on our beach blankets. We went to open air concerts, frequented Old Town's bars and bistros and traversed Grant and Lincoln Parks. Another favored site was Buckingham Fountain, its multicolored heights of water arching up into the twilight against the city's skyline. We may have gone elsewhere, to museums and the aquarium, but I can't remember. Mostly I remember spending time with Alice, doing commonplace things, wishing the summer would go on and on.

Throughout the next year, the most salient feature of our

relationship was separation. In the face of our limited one-to-one contact, we mainly wrote letters: soulful, long, and passionate. Also riddled with plenty of angst. They referenced a shared future together, although the specifics of that future remained vague. They tended to have a somber tinge—neither of us was a stranger to pitch-black moods. Above all else, they were intimate. Intimacy can be easier when distance between intimate partners is considerable and time together minimal.

Every several months we managed to see each other. The occasion I remember best was the weekend before Thanksgiving in November 1963. Alice came to New Haven for the Harvard Game, always a big deal, full of Ivy League pageantry. Also a time Americans of a certain age remember in unforgettable detail, the weekend of JFK's assassination. Alice and I, as shocked and disbelieving as the rest of the country, spent the weekend quietly talking with a few close friends, trying to process what had happened. Taking comfort in the physicality of each other's presence. Trying to come to grips with the widespread belief that American life would never be the same, that it had changed in some basic and ominous way. The novelist, Don DeLillo, described what happened in Dallas as accurately and concisely as anyone, "the ten seconds that broke the back of the American century."

An intriguing *What If* with profound historical consequences—rumors had flown around that JFK himself would be coming to New Haven for the Harvard Game. The rumors seemed plausible enough since the president was known to be devoted to his alma mater. What if he'd actually come? The remainder of twentieth century history might have played out differently.

In May 1965, a year after I graduated, Alice and I were married.

I attended my fifty-fifth Yale Reunion in June of 2019.

As usual faculty members gave lectures, their subjects ranging from the U.S. Constitution in the age of Trump to the relevance of liberal arts in the contemporary world. The university offered splendid food and drink. Campus tours showed off its new buildings, featuring its latest two residential colleges. I was struck by some of my classmates' recent achievements, particularly impressive since we all were in our mid-seventies. One of them had embarked on a round-the-world motorcycle trip. Another had hiked the Appalachian Trail in its entirety. Another, a pilot, had come out of retirement to fly a converted DC-10 to fight forest fires in the Western United States.

Some things went beyond the usual. The reunions always hold a memorial service for classmates who'd died since the last one. In the past, services included personal reminiscences by a classmate close to the deceased. This year though, they simply read off groups of names between prayers and hymns. Too many had died for surviving classmates to give individual biographical snippets.

Another difference, they offered a smorgasbord of small gatherings to complement the large lectures. Their subjects reflected the age of those attending. Programs included topics like retirement travel, ageing with wisdom, and green burials. The tone of many of them was less than jovial. A common concern: in the face of environmental havoc, political upheaval, and likely pandemics, what kind of world would we be leaving to our descendants?

I enjoyed myself to a point. I enjoyed catching up with old friends as well as chatting with people I hadn't known at all while an undergrad. I enjoyed the lectures and the excellent food and drink. The small groups, too somber to be frankly enjoyable, were nonetheless interesting and relevant.

I cut myself more slack than in past reunions. Before I'd trotted a bit frenetically from event to event, from lecture to lecture, barely stopping to catch my breath. This time I walked more slowly and often alone, allowing my mind to drift. Meandering past the stately buildings, I found myself contemplating Yale's impact on the world, its presidents and Nobel and Pulitzer Prize winners. I walked past the Yale School of Drama, whose students included Meryl Streep, Paul Newman, and Frances McDormand. I walked past the Yale Law School, whose students included William Howard Taft, Gerald Ford, both Clintons, nine Attorneys General, and four current members of the U.S. Supreme Court. How could one school, in the heart of a small and nondescript New England city, have produced so many luminaries in so many different fields?

My ruminations took me back to my own undergraduate years. I remembered a lot of things, most of them inconsequential. The Chapel Street diner open twenty-four hours a day, all year long, where superannuated Greek waiters filled orders with a dash of poetry. *Burger with cheese, makes life a breeze . . . Coffee with cream, makes life a dream.* The inviting, soothing leather chairs of the Sterling Library and the less inviting wooden benches in nineteenth century lecture halls. The Yale Art Gallery with its three thousand-year-old Chinese bronzes and its works of Edward Hopper and Jackson Pollack, where I learned of the solace art can provide to a youth who felt way in over his head. Sally's and Pepe's, best pizza on this side of the Atlantic. All-night conversations with tangents going everywhere. Wondering if I belonged there, wondering at the time and for many years thereafter. Concluding, decades later, that maybe I did.

CHAPTER IV

SOMEDAY YOU'LL BE A WONDERFUL DOCTOR

Growing up, I was indoctrinated with the view that medicine was the noblest and most worthwhile of callings. I didn't *really* believe it, but I didn't disbelieve it either. It was the profession I held in the highest regard, in spite of myself. Becoming a doctor had been my inconsistently held dream since kindergarten. My father, no surprise, had a lot to do with this. He didn't say so directly, but he managed to convey his belief that becoming a physician was the best and most honorable thing you could do with your life. Becoming something else—an astronaut, a winner of the Nobel Peace Prize, the president—would almost measure up, but not quite. (*Someone* had to do the lesser jobs.) He actually gave me a *Grant's Atlas of Anatomy* for my sixth birthday. *Robbie,* he inscribed it, *take a look at this once in a while, and someday you'll be a wonderful doctor. Love, Pop*

Not your typical birthday gift for a six-year-old.

Years later, it occurred to me that jokes about Jewish families revering doctors to the point of the absurd have a certain basis in reality, like the one about the distraught Jewish mother running on the beach in Florida. "Help, help!" she cries. "My son the doctor is drowning!" In the same spirit is Sarah Silverman's line, delivered with her trademark deadpan. "I was raped by a doctor. [pause] What a bittersweet experience for a Jewish girl."

Notwithstanding my on-again, off-again dream of medicine, I had flirted with other possibilities along the way. I often thought about pursuing a PhD in history, still a field that interests me like few others, but I couldn't see myself as a permanent academic. I thought halfheartedly about law school, somewhat notorious among Yalies at the time as a refuge for those who didn't know what else to do with themselves.

On an impulse I interviewed for a graduate program in cinematography, mainly because I liked movies. I believed I might be good at making them, based on no evidence whatsoever. I wanted to write, but despite my youth and naiveté, I knew I'd need a day job. Besides, it dawned on me I hadn't learned enough about the world to write knowledgeably about it. I even gave fleeting consideration to the rabbinate, despite having forgotten most of my Hebrew and despite a penchant for BLTs and shiksas. This notion must have brought tears of laughter down God's cheeks.

As college graduation neared, I continued to veer in the direction of medicine. The biggest problem was that I hadn't taken all of the prerequisites. Having dropped out of the Yale physics course, I needed to take it again, and I needed to take organic chemistry too. I wasn't optimistic about my chances of getting into a medical school in the first place. The number of American medical schools was much smaller then than now. New schools in middle-sized cities like Norfolk, Lubbock, and Duluth have proliferated, but few of them existed when I graduated. Furthermore, they could be highly selective about the candidates they took. Their admission committees were unlikely to jump for joy at the prospect of accepting a history major with so-so science grades.

I thought I might have a better chance of getting into Juilliard and studying the double bassoon.

My father had his own thoughts about my born-again aspirations for medical school. They involved two main considerations. The first, to enable me to take the remaining pre-requisites (and possibly some other science courses, for good measure) in as short a time as possible. The second, to put as much distance as he could between Alice and me.

To the best of my knowledge, he had no inherent dislike of her, at least initially. He and my mother received her in their home politely and even cordially. He didn't object to her as my girlfriend. Or, if he did, he never gave voice to his objection. But the idea of my marrying her went strongly against his grain. A large part of this involved religion.

He rarely attended services other than on Yom Kippur and Rosh Hashanah. His intimate friends included as many Christians as Jews; his closest boyhood friend, in fact, had become a Jesuit. He could eat a pork chop without a jot of guilt. He knew no Hebrew, although somewhere along the line he picked up a smattering of Yiddish. But he had a deep and indelible sense of himself as Jewish. He liked Jewish novelists, Isaac Bashevis Singer and Philip Roth in particular, and he relished the earthy if often wistful strains of Jewish humor. He gave generously to Jewish causes. He enjoyed cuisines from the world over, but his favorite dining spot in Springfield was probably Mort Gottlieb's kosher delicatessen with its three rickety tables in the back.

Another part of my father's objections involved control, and I've already alluded to his controlling nature. He must have realized his control and influence over me would diminish greatly if I were married. All other things being equal, married children are harder to control than unmarried ones.

THE YEAR AFTER I graduated from Yale was a crazy quilt of sharply detailed memories and murky interludes as empty as blackouts.

I took a summer physics course at Arizona State University, at Tempe, where the heat bore down on me like a leaden weight that made my shoulders slump, where I ventured outside as infrequently as possible. The Karmann Ghia broke down in New Mexico when I was driving back to Springfield. While waiting for it to be fixed in the VW place, I met a kind, hospitable couple who invited me to stay with them. They were evangelical Christians, disbelievers in evolution, who took me to a church service where a minister with a mane of thick white hair railed against *those ambassadors of hell, the Beatles.*

When I returned home, tension between my father and me reached a high. Things actually got physical at one point, and I gave him a black eye. This is among my chief regrets, and I'd give a year of my life to undo it. In my defense, I can only say that Robert, at his most obnoxious, could have pissed off Mother Teresa. I should add that I never stopped loving him, even when I couldn't stand him.

I MOVED ON TO Southern Illinois University, in Carbondale. I studied physiology there. I also worked as an orderly in a local hospital: helping nurses, talking to patients, emptying bedpans. At night I drank Apple Jack and Old Grand Dad bourbon, usually alone—they were inexpensive, and they did the trick. I was smoking a pack daily. From there I went to Western Illinois University, in Macomb, where I studied organic chemistry. I roomed with a farm boy whose abiding goal, never reached, was to wake up early enough to go to the breakfast buffet downstairs ("... Gosh durn, I missed it again ...")

I filled out applications to a dozen medical schools, convinced they'd reject me. Meanwhile Alice and I kept in touch by phone and letter. We grew steadily closer, despite my father's efforts to keep us separated, or maybe because of them. I lived for our infrequent weekends together.

As I traversed the country, taking prerequisites at three colleges in two states, I chanced upon an extraordinary piece of good luck. Half a century later, I still can't quite believe the unlikelihood of what happened.

My father's closest friend in Springfield was an ophthalmologist named Bud Weisbaum. While my father talked with Bud one day, he bemoaned my low odds of getting into medical school, and Bud made a suggestion. Another friend of his had a son-in-law, now studying medicine in Dublin. The young man's name was Jack Kearney. "Rob should write to him," advised Bud. "Maybe he could go there."

I did as Bud suggested, beginning a correspondence with a stranger who now made his home on the other side of the Atlantic. Jack provided invaluable information about contemporary Ireland.

About subjects ranging from the Irish cost of living to pubs to public transit. He provided especially useful information about his school, the Royal College of Surgeons in Ireland, better known by its initials of RCSI. Its students came, literally, from all over the world. The largest percentage of them came from Ireland and the U.K, but they also came from Asia, Africa, and the Caribbean. The student body included Americans and Canadians as well.

By way of background, the Potato Famine as well as lesser catastrophes had left the country with a shrunken population. But all of its medical schools had stayed open, and Ireland became one of the world's few nations that produced more doctors than it needed. It could therefore accept a number of students from elsewhere.

RCSI was rather like a large disparate family, a place where almost everyone knew everyone else. Jack Kearney, an affable sort, was on friendly terms with the registrar (ranking dean) of the school, Dr. Harry O'Flanagan. By now Jack and I had exchanged quite a few letters, and I'd made a formal application for admission.

It so happened that Dr. O'Flanagan had grown enamored of basketball, a game just starting to become popular in Western Europe. As Jack knew, he wanted RCSI to have its own basketball team. One day, as Jack and Dr. O'Flanagan sat chatting in the Registrar's office, the doctor mentioned he'd gotten an application from an American named Goodwin. "I know him," said Jack, a half-truth at best since we'd never met. "He's a good man." Then came the coup de grâce. "He's also an excellent basketball player." I was about 5'10", had scant interest in the sport, and had never played it, not even on the schoolyard level. Before I became a fan of the awesome Boston Celtics of the Larry Bird years, I cared no more about basketball than cricket.

"All right, we'll take him," Dr. O'Flanagan decided on the spot.

I received a letter of acceptance from The Royal College of Surgeons in Ireland on St. Patrick's Day in 1965. I would spend the rest of the decade in a country about which I'd hitherto known next to nothing. My patchy knowledge of Irish history came mostly from a course taken on the history and geography of the British Commonwealth, but my knowledge of Ireland's history since its independence was miniscule. I knew the Irish had a proud literary tradition—I'd heard of James Joyce, Oscar Wilde, and William Butler Yeats but hadn't read their works. I knew Ireland was supposed to be snake-free, thanks to St. Patrick, and I knew the Irish had a reputation for heavy drinking. And I'd learned more things from my correspondence with Jack Kearney, the benefactor whom I'd not yet met. The rest of my knowledge of Ireland could have been written on a couple of postcards.

How did I feel about this remarkable turn of events? A mix of relief, intimidation, anxiety, and (to a degree, at least some of the time) hope. I'd almost forgotten how it felt. My life was rife with uncertainty, my self-confidence was wobbly, and I was nowhere near financial independence. Shortly after I received the letter of acceptance, I had a dream of stunning clarity, which I still remember in detail. *I am driving down an ominous road in the Karmann Ghia with no other cars along the way. The road leads directly to the edge of a vast body of water with massive waves crashing against the shoreline. I can't stop the car, and I can't get out, and the car will plunge directly into the surf. Certain I'll drown, I wake up in a panic.*

I didn't need a psychoanalyst to interpret it. The water, of course, was the ocean. Far, far away, on the other side of it, was Ireland.

In May of 1965, I left Springfield for Chicago, and I moved into Alice's flat in Evanston. I don't remember taking leave of the rest of the family, another instance when my sometimes-excellent memory completely failed me. I'm pretty sure I said goodbye to Clara though. I can't believe I'd have left without doing so, I wouldn't have been *that* much of an asshole. I don't remember packing, or what I used for money, or what I planned to do for the next four months before I'd depart for Ireland. All I remember is getting on a train and heading north.

With the help of a family friend, a man of clout who ranked high in the Illinois state bureaucracy, I got a job as a social worker for the city of Chicago. At that point you only needed a bachelor's degree to apply for such a job. It could have been in Nordic languages or ornithology or making potholders; a degree in anything sufficed. Training was minimal, and you were pretty much thrown into the deep end.

I was assigned to part of the city just west of the Loop, an area that included skid row. I made rounds of flophouses with rooms containing only a sink and toilet and a bed of sorts, its mattress about the thickness of the Springfield phone book. The fancier ones might have a battered chair and bureau. Rooms often had chicken wire instead of a solid ceiling overhead. My clients, nearly all males, ranged from their twenties to their eighties, and most of them looked much older than their actual ages. Years of living on the streets, of alcohol abuse and random violence and every manner of deprivation, had left them bent and empty-eyed with coarsened features and a look of defeat. They didn't walk as much as shuffle. Hard to believe they'd once been my age, and maybe they'd even had a jot of optimism about their lives.

Toward the end of May, Alice and I married. A no-frills affair in a downtown city office. The clerk gave us only one piece of advice, *talk it out when things get rough*, before he moved on to the next couple. A half a dozen of them sat clustered in the waiting room. Alice and I uttered the standard words, including a vow to stay together till death did us part. God must have laughed, again, not without a measure of sympathy.

Our slightly less than two years together had included joy, sadness, excitement, despair, and moments of blissful if doubtfully warranted optimism. Despite a conviction that we loved each other, despite my best efforts to suppress the thought, I couldn't help but ask myself: *What the fuck did I just do?*

Why, then, did I marry her? There was no one reason (is there ever?), but several come to mind. To stave off loneliness—my exiles in Tempe, Macomb, and Carbondale comprised the loneliest periods I'd ever known. To please her because I thought that was what she wanted. To thank her for staying with me through good and bad and worse—I felt in her debt. To stick it to my father. The more he tried to undermine our relationship, the more I dug in my heels. Marrying out of spite has to be among the worst reasons to marry anyone, but it's real enough.

There was another reason I married her, to play the rescuer. It didn't take me long to form a picture of her parents as unhappy, mean-spirited, and borderline abusive. In other words, they were parents of a daughter who needed to be rescued. Alice's mother, not yet forty when I met her, had given birth to her while still in her teens. She struck me as a woman who never expected a great deal from the world, and her low expectations proved justified. Alice's father, on the other hand, struck me as a man who'd expected quite a bit from the world and sulked and pouted because most of his expectations went unmet. When I began to practice psychiatry in the 1970s, I heard a senior clinician describe a patient in these terms: "He was angry his whole life because the universe would not reshape itself into one large breast for his sole use." I was immediately reminded of Alice's father.

There was yet another reason why I married her, and I suspect it's one of the reasons she married me as well. Despite our real-world ages, twenty-two and twenty-one, despite our degrees from respected universities, we were a lot more like children than adults. Two children who played at being grownups. At times we gave a fair imitation of adults, and we may have had some other people fooled, but not ourselves. Two children who clung together in the dark, trying not to hear the monsters in the closet as we waited for dawn.

CHAPTER V

CÉAD MÍLE FÁILTE

On a cool September night in 1965, Alice and I brandished our hitherto unused passports and boarded an Aer Lingus 707 at JFK. We were about to depart for Dublin, nearly missing the flight as we struggled with eleven pieces of luggage, as we made last minute purchases and phone calls. On the plane, exhausted but too wound up to sleep, we talked little as the plane made its way eastward six miles above the Atlantic. It would be nice to relate that I left JFK confident and optimistic as I prepared to start an exciting new chapter of my life. It would also be hogwash. Since graduating from college fifteen months earlier, I still worked overtime to fend off self-doubt.

I read as much as I could about Ireland before we left. Despite this, I had at best a rudimentary knowledge of the country. But I did know life would be vastly different from life in the States. My travels had been limited to America, Canada, and the Caribbean, almost all of them with my parents. Looking down at the ocean gave me a sense of its unlimited vastness, a sense of how far we'd be from home. This would be my first time in Europe, and easily the most distant trip I'd taken, and there'd be no parents or old friends to fall back on. Alice and I would only have each other for support, and I wondered if that would suffice.

We would live in Ireland for six years if everything went as planned. The medical curriculum per se was five years, compared to four in the United States, with a mandatory year of the basic sciences before starting medical school proper. Six years, half an eternity, or so it seemed.

We arrived at Dublin Airport, small and a bit sleepy in 1965, about the size of Hartford's Bradley International but not as busy. Making our way through customs with our unwieldy heap of luggage, we encountered a squad of custom officials—unarmed, all male, mostly avuncular, and florid-faced with appealing brogues. One of them, an older gentleman, his uniform stretched tightly across his chest, greeted us with particular friendliness.

"Your first time in Ireland, is it?"

We nodded.

"Well, then. *Céad Míle Fáilte*. That's the Gaelic for *A Hundred Thousand Welcomes*." He gave us a grandfatherly smile.

We changed dollars into local currency and tried to figure out the Irish money; Euros wouldn't come along for thirty years. There were half crowns but no crowns and units of currency for which there was no coin or note. A guinea, for example, equaled a pound and a shilling. They printed paper money in half a dozen colors, including purple. The notes had English and Gaelic writing, the latter full of letters strung in unpronounceable combinations. What does one make of a language with groups of consonants like *nmh* and *chdh* and *mhr*?

We chanced upon a small hotel on Harcourt Street, a few blocks from RCSI. Our room, clean but tiny, had barely enough space around the bed to accommodate all our luggage. But the room had its own bathroom, an uncommon luxury in modest establishments.

Alice went into the bathroom and came out, her hands behind her back. She made a peculiar crackling noise, like pieces of tinfoil being squeezed into a ball. "Do you know what that is?" she asked.

I shook my head.

"It's toilet paper." She brought out her hands and showed me something that looked as if it might be used for shelving.

"Jesus."

The next day brought an unpredictable and remarkable turn of events. We walked into a small travel agency close to where we'd stayed and asked a pleasant-looking woman if she might know of other hotels, less expensive and preferably with larger rooms. We were about to start looking for an apartment, and Jack Kearney had warned me it might take a while to find one.

The woman's name was Barbara Taylor. We struck up a conversation that lasted over thirty minutes. The three of us hit it off easily, as if we'd already known each other. At the end of it, she told us not to worry about finding another hotel. "My husband and I have just moved into a new home. Last year we got married. We hope to have children, but for now we have some spare rooms. I'd love to have you stay with us, and I'm sure I speak for him as well. You could stay as long as you'd like."

Alice and I were stunned. A woman we didn't know an hour ago had just offered us lodging, had extended an open-ended invitation to us. Barbara Taylor and her husband, Iain, would remain among our closest friends for the whole of our time in Ireland, and beyond.

About two weeks later we found a third floor flat on Leeson Street, a twenty-minute walk from RCSI. The walk was no hardship. It took me through one of Dublin's finest parks, St. Stephen's Green. The Green encompassed twenty-two acres of gardens, tree-lined lanes, playgrounds, and ponds, where a number of extremely well-fed ducks swam about. Among St. Stephen's treasures was Henry Moore's modernistic statue of William Butler Yeats, Ireland's Nobel laureate poet, on top of a rounded pedestal. The statue stood in isolated majesty, its rough-textured grayish-green in perfect contrast to the wealth of trees and shrubbery surrounding it.

The furnished flat, plain but adequate, lacked central heating. My life had been so sheltered I didn't know what central heating *was* until I found myself living in a place without it. Jell-O set faster in the bedroom than the fridge, and for much of the year we had to brace ourselves to shower. The goal, to undress in the bathroom at the last possible moment, and dowse ourselves in water that felt slightly above freezing, and get dressed before our fingers and toes turned blue. The flat included a tiny single-coil electric space heater, barely powerful enough to toast a marshmallow. We switched it between rooms as circumstances dictated.

I thought winters in Central Illinois and New England had made me immune to cold weather and found out I was wrong.

My parents did me the much-appreciated service of saving almost all my letters. Then, ten or fifteen years later, they gave them back to me. Excerpts of these letters appear herewith:

I'm taking the standard pre-reg [first-year] program of physics, chemistry and biology. My weekly load is eleven lectures and four labs, so I can't complain of overwork. Biology is by far the most interesting, taught by a pleasant old fart who's also the school librarian. So far he has focused on anthropology—Australopithecus, Neanderthals, etc.—fascinating, but I don't grasp its relevance to medicine...

Physics and chemistry are slanted toward those with no previous experience with science. I especially look forward to the chem labs, mainly because of the heat of Bunsen burners. Classes are conducted formally. Lecturers wear their academic robes, [and] you must dress decently for all lectures and labs. Tie and jacket for men, dresses for women...

There are five Americans in my class, from Yale, Georgetown, Rutgers, Villanova and Boston College. We reminisce about things like hamburgers made of beef and college football games on Saturday... Now that we're reasonably settled, Alice and I spend part of the weekend exploring Dublin and environs. The Irish countryside is, indeed, beautiful. We spent last Sunday hiking through County Wicklow, directly south of here, in an area that looks a lot like the Wisconsin Dells...

Despite the initial disappointment of having to go through pre-reg, I've found a great deal that's worthwhile in the RCSI system. I've talked at length with students farther along than me, and I [gather] that a med student's life is very different than it is in the States... they tell me that relations with faculty are truly collegial during the clinical years... busywork is minimized. Despite the lack of fretting over constant exams and quizzes (your grades come down to two exams per course per year), most students work hard...

I really like the RCSI crowd. Their backgrounds make up quite a mosaic. There's Jack P., a successful gentleman-farmer from Wales, starting pre-reg at thirty-five with a B.A. & M.A. from Cambridge in economics. Roma J., finishing up this year, comes from Lebanon by way of Trinidad, occasionally appears on Irish TV as a Calypso dancer. Tom T. was at West Point for two years before transferring to Georgetown, where he majored in biochemistry. He did research for Burroughs-Wellcome before coming here ...

I WASN'T EXAGGERATING ABOUT the diversity of my classmates. I would meet classmates with names like Deva and Dola, Sichi and Stale (pronounced *STA'-leh*). They came from around twenty countries, converging for six years on this rain-swept edge of Europe. Some of them, especially some of the older ones, had backgrounds that didn't suggest the likelihood of a medical career. One of them had worked for years in a Dublin bank, another for the Guinness Brewery. A woman in the class ahead of me had managed a theater in Oslo. A woman in the class behind me paid her way through RCSI as an Aer Lingus flight attendant. Every Saturday, so went the story, she flew to New York or Boston, and every Saturday night she flew back to Ireland.

While I got on well with classmates for the most part, at times I found myself in a new role for me, an American on the defensive. Hard to believe this, but I came to Ireland believing the U.S. was the world's darling. Admired, respected, well-liked if not frankly loved.

While such an assumption might now seem strikingly naïve, it made more sense in the context of the times. America had been the crucial player in winning World War II, which had ended only twenty years before we arrived in Dublin. Not only that, it had been instrumental in rebuilding a devastated and demoralized Europe. American music, movies, clothing, cars—American culture in nearly all its facets—had taken the world by storm. But now I had classmates who held a different notion of my country. They regarded it as a bullying colossus that supported dictators and vile regimes from Spain to South Africa, from Iran to Indonesia. A place that supported anyone, however bloodied his hands, who made anticommunist noises. A place that mouthed platitudes about racial equality but still kept a sizeable number of its Black citizens poor and powerless.

I became variously angry, flummoxed, and dismayed to hear such views. It further dismayed me to have to acknowledge to myself that some of these views had merit. But the overwhelming majority of my classmates regarded my fellow Americans and me as individuals rather than citizens of a country they may have disliked and distrusted. It's also worth noting that my own view of my country underwent significant changes as the Vietnamese morass worsened, as the voices of the1960s became ever more strident and divisive.

SO MANY THINGS, BIG and small, that were new to me. The food, for instance. Fish and chips, served in grease-laden pages of a newspaper, which sat in your gut like a bowling ball. Pizzas made with catsup, vegetables cooked to the point where they looked pureed. Kum Tong, Dublin's sole Chinese restaurant at the time, where they served chow mein with cauliflower. Getting used to Irish turns of phrase. *I'll knock you up at half eight*, i.e., *I'll come by for you at 8:30*. Or, *don't get your knickers twisted*, i.e., *don't get upset*. An extraordinary and creative array of insults. Among the worst of them: *Your people took the soup!* which means, *Your forbears took charity during the Great Famine. They went to Protestant church services, where they sang a few hymns and received bread and soup for their trouble.* Many of their countrymen thought it more honorable to starve to death.

Getting used to the rain—it rained at least part of every day for what seemed like months on end—and the gunmetal skies. Getting used to a telephone system that worked roughly sixty percent of the time. Getting used to a country where the Catholic hierarchy still called most of the shots, where they'd made birth control illegal although they used oral contraceptives for "menstrual irregularities." It was said that Ireland had the highest rate of menstrual irregularities in the world. Getting used to a country where divorce did not exist and censorship was the norm. A country where priests provided spiritual guidance, marriage counseling, financial advice, and whose words often carried more weight than the law, especially in rural parishes. This was twenty years before scandals rocked the Church, before Irish mothers grew reluctant to let their children spend time alone with men of the cloth. A small indicator of how things had changed: When I went to Dublin in the late 1990s, I used a men's room at the airport. In it, I found a machine selling condoms.

Getting used to people rife with contradictions, who laughed in the face of their brooding history, and their gift for living in the present. They regarded the past as a string of tragedies and the future as too murky to dwell upon. So that left you with the present by default.

PERHAPS THE STRANGEST THINGS to get used to, and among the

most attractive, was how the Irish regarded time. Ireland, *the land of time enough*, its population often called it.

There was time enough to go to plays by Oscar Wilde, George Bernard Shaw, and Samuel Beckett. Student tickets made them cheaper than the movies. Time enough to cruise Dublin's wealth of bookstores and the open-air stalls that lined the Liffey River. In doing so, I found books I wouldn't have discovered otherwise. Books about the Famine and the Irish Civil War. Novels by writers I'd never heard of, like James Plunkett's *Strumpet City*, perhaps the best thing written about Dublin and its inhabitants since James Joyce's *The Dubliners*. Among my favorites, Brendan Behan's *Borstal Boy*, the memoirs of a quintessential Irish rogue who died a cirrhotic death at forty-one. "I only drink on two occasions," he faux-defended himself, "when I'm thirsty and when I'm not." There's a story, of unproven veracity, of Behan's parting sally to the nursing nun who tried to make him comfortable as he lay dying. "Thank you, Sister. May all your sons grow up to be Bishops."

You were *supposed* to use time for your own purposes. Where else did a medical school give you an hour and a half for lunch? Where else did a medical school arrange hiking jaunts and encourage you to play field hockey and rugby? There was time enough to frequent pubs and partake of the Guinness, the Harp lager, and the crack—that is, the conversations that spun and swerved in all directions and the accompanying wit and wordplay. The Irish might well be the best verbal stunt pilots on the planet.

There was time enough to explore the far-flung corners of the country. Ireland, about the size of Indiana, can easily be traversed by car and rail. In the course of six years there, Alice and I saw a great deal of it. We walked the perimeter of Staigue Fort, in County

Kerry, a circular stone behemoth that measures ninety feet across and twenty high, built around the sixth century A.D. without mortar but still standing. We made it to the wilds of Donegal, in the country's extreme northwest, with its 2,000-foot cliffs and thundering surf that pounds its beaches, where there's nothing but the raw Atlantic between you and Iceland. We hiked along the Giant's Causeway, across the border in Northern Ireland's County Antrim, where 40,000 columns of molten lava have coalesced into hexagonal slabs as high as forty feet. Surely one of the world's most dramatic landscapes.

While Alice and I saw much of Ireland, it wasn't hard or expensive to get to the U.K. The ferries went there frequently, as did flights to London and the smaller English cities. My most memorable trip took place in 1970. A friend and I took the ferry to Wales. From there we made our way southeast on my motorcycle, a 50cc Yamaha. Then we took another ferry to the Isle of Wight, where we joined about 400,000 or 700,000 of our new best friends. Estimates of attendees varied wildly.

We'd come together for a Rock Festival, often referred to as the British Woodstock. Among the individuals and groups featured: Joni Mitchell, The Who, John Sebastian, The Doors, and Emerson, Lake & Palmer. A slew of others, performed as well, but my memory of the event was compromised by fatigue, snatches of sleep, and a contact high. My friend and I weren't smoking ourselves, but we didn't need to. A marijuana haze hung swirled over us like a grayish-purple mantle. One of my most vivid memories of the event was Jim Morrison, then at the height of his fame and popularity, as powerful a performer as I've ever heard. His voice was a hypnotizing demagogic rasp, a voice that might have sent mobs to the barricades, a voice gripping enough for the Nuremberg rallies. At a break between songs, he had this to say—*We want the world, and we want it now.* A ridiculous statement considered half a century after the fact, but at the time he made it sound altogether reasonable. Our due, pure and simple.

༄

As much as I liked Ireland and the Irish, I was no stranger to homesickness, especially during the first year there. An odd mix, the things missed. Although never sports-crazed, I missed the World Series and college football. Never a foodie, I missed pizza made catsup-free and seafood that transcended fish and chips. Never addicted to TV, I missed *Jackie Gleason, Get Smart,* and *The Ed Sullivan Show.* I missed reliable telephones. Say what you will about AT&T (they had no competition then), their phones worked.

And I definitely missed feeling warm from time to time.

༄

After pre-reg, I launched into the medical curriculum proper. One of my letters home began as follows:

There's no question about it, I'm in medical school. The anatomy professor's introductory statement was, "You have until Saturday to learn the bones of the lower limb." He then proceeded to kick out three students in the first five minutes. One for talking, one for yawning, and one for coming three minutes late. The last of these was prodded out by a femur against his belly.

My schedule for the first few months will be as follows—three lectures a week in physiology and biochem, and three lab sessions or practicals. The rest of the time will go to anatomy, either demonstrations or dissections. In December we start lectures and practicals in histology,

[with] *embryology in the spring. There are weekly anatomy quizzes, which should make for an active fall.*

Winter has coincided with the commencement of classes [it was only October, but Ireland gets cold early]. *The wind whips, the rain drips, and so much for sunshine until April.*

∼

THE ANATOMY COURSE DESERVES special mention. First, you must imagine the dissecting room. It was long and wide, as high-ceilinged as a Victorian railway station with thirty or forty stainless steel dissecting tables laid out and boxes of skulls and bones along the wall. A small amphitheater with hard raised benches for lectures and demonstrations made me think of Rembrandt's painting of an anatomy lesson. A spiral staircase led to faculty offices. Just before a lecture, the professor descended from the mountaintop, his white coat flowing. If he'd carried a stone tablet in each arm, he would not have looked out of place.

∼

MIDWAY THROUGH MY THIRD year at RCSI, my classmates and I took The Halves. These comprised ten days of written and oral examinations in anatomy, physiology, and biochemistry. If you passed, you went on to pathology, microbiology, and the clinical subjects. If you didn't, you took the basics again until you did.

I passed, and my life became like that of medical students everywhere. I watched autopsies, learned of toxins and pathogens and congenital anomalies. Listened to impromptu bedside lectures, observed operations and occasionally assisted. Started to become familiar with the interpretation of X-rays, lab results, and EKGs. Listened to heart and lung sounds, learned to draw blood and suture, and performed scores of other health-related tasks. Delivered babies. I recall the introductory lecture of one of the OBG professors. "For some of you, delivering your first baby will be a highlight of your professional career, and you'll send the child birthday cards all your life. Others of you will be traumatized enough to get out of clinical medicine altogether and take up full-time research."

Apropos, the teaching was frequently enlivened by memorable digressions and one-liners. During a practicum in the RCSI Pathology Museum, the lecturer pointed to a syphilitic skull— "The poor man must have been to England."

When I think back on the RCSI experience, I remember it as a fascinating blend of tradition and modernity, of state-of-the-art medicine against (at times) a nineteenth century backdrop. When you walked into the main building, uniformed porters greeted you. Doctors and students alike paused in late afternoon for tea and biscuits in the teaching hospitals. Surgeons were called Mister, not Doctor. This stemmed from a kind of inverse snobbery, originating in the days when surgeons were regarded as more like glorified barbers than professionals. The new technologies were quickly making their way to Ireland, and several of our professors were researchers as well as clinicians. Many had trained in premier hospitals on both sides of the Atlantic. Visiting lecturers and honorees during my time there included Christiaan Barnard (the first surgeon to perform a heart transplant) and Michael DeBakey, among the world's best heart surgeons.

An incident that nicely sums up the juxtaposition of past and present in the RCSI experience: One day I was part of a group making neurosurgical rounds. The Q and A was brisk, the teaching excellent, the discussed technologies up to date. Tom, one of my American classmates, nudged me and pointed out a window. About twenty sheep wandered aimlessly on the street below while a lone man tried to move them along. Upstairs, everything was as contemporary as Aer Lingus's new 747s; downstairs loomed a scene as old as Ireland itself.

APART FROM CLASSMATES AND professors, I grew close to a number of people with no connection to RCSI. Carey Donaldson, a quiet American from Georgia with a quick wit and a bone-dry sense of humor, lived in the flat adjacent to us. Carey enjoyed going into Dublin's restaurants and ordering grits, completely unknown in the country. On one occasion the waitress returned apologetically from the kitchen. "The chef apologizes," she told him, "but we're all out."

A classical musician, a trombonist who played in the Raidió Teilefís Eireann (Irish Radio and Television) Symphony Orchestra, Carey spent innumerable evenings with Alice and me in his apartment or ours or with us in one of several pubs within walking distance. We were often joined by Herbert and Anne Kupers, who lived upstairs. Herbert was German, a linguist and philologist who spoke quite good Italian to go with his fluent German, French, and English. Later, when he returned to Germany, he taught himself Turkish in order to communicate with an influx of Turkish immigrants. Anne was French, the daughter of a career naval officer. After their Irish sojourn, the Kupers split the year between Karlsruhe, near the German-Swiss border, and Anne's family home in Normandy.

I should add that despite Herbert's near-perfect English—I've only heard him make one grammatical mistake since I met him—we've had some enthralling discussions about the nuances of English usage. Such as trying to convey to him the difference between *horseshit* and *bullshit*.

To date the friendship of the Goodwins, the Kupers, and the Donaldsons (Carey married shortly after returning to the States) has lasted well over fifty years. In varying combinations we've gotten together in New York, New Orleans, Ottawa, Bruges, and perhaps ten other places on both sides of the Atlantic. Getting to know Herbert has been particularly enlightening. About seven years older than I am, he is old enough to remember growing up in Hitler's Germany. He told me about his parents, liberal socialists, warning him that under no circumstances should he repeat in school the things his parents said at home, lest his parents be taken away and shot. He also told me this, during the campaign of 2016, "I see expressions on the faces of the people at the Trump rallies, and they frighten me. They're the same expressions I saw in pictures and movies of people at the Nazi rallies."

I came back to our flat one Saturday evening with several friends. Alice had taken a solo weekend trip, so I had the place to myself. There'd been a dinner at a teaching hospital for some occasion or another—there was always an occasion. I went upstairs and knocked at the Kupers' door. "I have a few visitors," I said, "and I'd like to take whatever alcohol you have on hand. I'll reimburse you tomorrow, and I'll do my best to keep the noise down." Herbert and Anne obliged, as I knew they would. I left with a nearly full bottle of Irish whiskey and half a dozen Guinnesses. After thanking them profusely, I turned to them. "This place makes a person unfit to live anywhere else."

They agreed.

Alice and I made other friends with no connection to RCSI.

Kevin and Jane were Irish Americans from Boston. He studied veterinary medicine, which provided a number of anecdotes, such as how Kevin lost his wedding ring—*"up a cow's ahss."* David was a Welshman pursuing a PhD in chemistry, Henry was a carpenter. But our closest non-RCSI friends remained Barbara and Iain Taylor. We shared dinners, birthdays, and New Year's Eves. On one such occasion Iain, a Scotsman, from Aberdeen, introduced us to haggis, a traditional Scottish dish and a memorable addition to our book of life experiences. Its ingredients include sheep's pluck (heart, lungs, liver, and tongue), diced and cooked in the sheep's stomach with onions, oats, and spices. It's better than it sounds, especially when accompanied by abundant Scotch.

There was a book's worth of memorable encounters. One of them involved an Aer Lingus pilot.

Alice and I returned to the U.S. almost every June. Our summer jobs would pay for a good part of the subsequent year's expenses, and subletting the flat brought in extra money. One summer we sublet it to the pilot, Desmond. It worked out nicely. Des was getting married in the fall, and he needed a place of his own for several months. As often happened, the business transaction turned into a social occasion, accompanied by Guinness.

Des and I struck up a conversation, in which I mentioned my lifelong fascination with flying. My first flight, in an Ozark Airlines DC-3, had been among the highlights of my early childhood. "I have to say, Des," I said as I recounted this, "I envy you. One of my childhood dreams was to become a pilot."

Des looked at me with a strange expression, quizzical, with a hint of wistfulness. "Funny you should say that. Myself, I always dreamt of becoming a doctor."

So, even in Ireland, the grass is always greener . . .

~

THE YEARS PASSED, MUCH more quickly as the end came into sight. And all of sudden, there it was—June 16, 1971. *Conferring*, the RCSI term for graduation.

We marched, two by two, through a wood-paneled hall lined with parents, spouses, significant others, friends, and faculty, with flashbulbs popping like firecrackers. That evening, the Conferring Ball at the Dublin Intercontinental. As the night rolled on, a recognition wormed its way into the joy, relief, and camaraderie—*this was it*. The party was almost over, and after the hugs and handshakes and promises to keep in touch, we would disperse to the dozens of countries from which we came. We would experience the inevitable mix of success and failure, joy and sorrow, gains and losses, but we'd never recapture these six extraordinary years. There'd be no more jaunts across St. Stephen's Green between classes or impromptu pints of Guinness in pubs only steps from the college. No more study groups as we quizzed each other on the anatomy of the wrist or the workup of a child with a fever of unknown origin. No more sharing of tales from our homelands that spanned the world. *This was it.*

It wasn't paradise. You never got used to the rain, not fully, nor to the short cold winter days when daylight dwindled to roughly seven hours. Many students had a firsthand look at a kind of grinding poverty hitherto unknown to them. They saw thin-faced children who looked perpetually hungry and adults in their twenties who lacked teeth because their diets lacked calcium. They saw beggars in every city and in many of the villages. There were strikes—bakeries, buses, and even banks. When the bank strike was finally settled, as I wrote in a letter to my parents, they began to process a backlog of checks totaling four billion pounds, a good number of which bounced.

And there was this: The Irish Republic had remained fairly quiet throughout our time there, but violence and political upheaval lingered constantly nearby, like storm clouds threatening a picnic. Bombed out parts of Belfast, over the border, looked like pictures of London during the Blitz. One of our few trips to Northern Ireland was for a wedding. Michael, a Catholic classmate from the Republic, married Mary, a Protestant girl from the North. A lovely affair, notwithstanding barbed wire in the streets less than two miles from the church. The first time I'd ever seen barbed wire in other than an agricultural context.

I GREW TO LOVE Ireland dearly, and I regard my time in the country as one of the great blessings of my life. (Yet another part of my connection with it: in November 1970, Alice gave birth to our son there. Thomas Brendan Clare Goodwin had dual citizenship. His parents were Americans, so he was too, but he was also an Irish citizen by birth. So we finally had a bona fide Irish relative.)

The birth of a son and the conferring of a medical degree, two of the happiest events I've known, in the same year. A fabulous end to the Dublin experience.

Leaving Ireland when I graduated in 1971—returning to an America with its myriad schisms and alienations, with Vietnam still a quagmire—was one of the hardest things I ever did. Apropos, Vietnam left me with a kind of survivors' guilt. My age would have made me just right for the draft. But while my contemporaries fought and died in the jungle while protests raged, often returning home to be cursed and spat on, I lived safely half a world away. I availed myself of the pubs and plays and excursions throughout the country and a thousand impromptu get-togethers with friends and classmates. Not to mention, earning a medical degree in the bargain.

Even so, leaving was the proper thing to do, and I knew it. Despite my cherishing of the Irish sojourn, and despite my own country riven by every sort of animosity and angst, I learned in Dublin that I was indelibly American. I might fantasize about staying in Ireland for the rest of my life, but in my heart of hearts I knew I'd return to the country of my birth. The country, familiar to me in a way no place else could ever be. The country I would always love despite all the unlovable things about it at that time.

It was time to go home.

CHAPTER VI

THE DEFAULT PSYCHIATRIST

Fast forward: in September 1996, I returned to Ireland with a surfeit of goodwill and buoyant expectation. I'd come for the Royal College of Surgeons Reunion, Class of 1971. Astonishingly, impossibly, a quarter of a century had passed since my graduation from medical school. The merest eye blink.

Attendees arrived from New York and Nigeria, from Sydney and Singapore, from the southern Caribbean and above the Arctic Circle. A classmate, Tore, held a chair in pediatrics in Tromsø, Norway, at the northernmost medical school in the world.

They'd done all kinds of things in their professional lives. One of them, Jack, had worked in India with Mother Teresa, tending to some of the most deprived and wretched people on the planet. Per Egil, a Norwegian neurologist, had spent many years with the United Nations and was back in Oslo, where he lived with his wife, Molly, a classmate from the Cayman Islands who'd become a psychiatrist. Michael had become a Park Avenue rheumatologist, and Colin practiced in the hinterlands of South Africa. Some, originally from India and the Far East but succumbing to the lure of Ireland, had returned and now lived and worked there.

Apart from classmates, I reconnected with professors and administrators. Among these was a fire hydrant-shaped Irishman, his unruly gray hair veering off in all directions, named Seamus Gallen. Dr. Gallen, a gruff but extremely kind gentleman in late middle age, served as a superintendent (dean) of students. We chatted, bantered, and caught up a bit, and then Dr. Gallen said something that intrigued me. "I knew which of you would become psychiatrists from the day you started here." He pointed a near-accusatory finger at me. "You were one."

"Oh? What tipped you off?" As I recall, none of us were smoking cigars or wearing *I Love Freud* buttons.

Dr. Gallen shrugged. "I don't know, there was just something about the lot of you." He named several members of my graduating class, from three different continents, all of us shrinks now. "I was right, one hundred percent."

THE CONVERSATION PROMPTED ME to reflect on my own choice of specialty. No straight line, my road to psychiatry. I had other serious interests along the way, most seriously with pathology. I liked its scope, encompassing no less than all the illnesses and injuries that might beset the human organism, from a burn to a bunion to a brain cancer. In its breadth, it reminded me of history. I liked how pathologists sought answers to questions that flummoxed other doctors. *His surgery went well, his vital signs were perfect, and they planned to discharge him in a day or two. So, why did he die?* Or, *she was fifty, no relevant history, nondrinker, nonsmoker, no cardiac problems, no headaches, no anything. One night, she went to bed and*

never woke up. Her husband found her, cold, in the morning. What happened to her?

I don't regard myself as ghoulish, but autopsies intrigued me. I enjoyed the give and take between pathologists and students, the impromptu quizzes. *What does this liver tell you about her? What do you make of its color and texture?* The Q and A worked both ways, of course. *Why didn't he have cardiac symptoms when his coronary arteries were almost completely blocked? Or, it looks like there's nothing wrong with her esophagus, and she had no neurological disorder that we know about, so why couldn't she swallow?* A well-conducted autopsy can become an excellent teaching tool. Medical students can *see* diseases, not just read about them. They can also enhance a student's knowledge of basic anatomy. In freshman anatomy the cadavers have died weeks or months prior, and they've literally been pickled. Often they barely look human. In this, they differ sharply from the subjects of autopsies, who lived and breathed a few days or even hours earlier.

Apart from the peculiar pleasures of the morgue, I enjoyed the lectures. I remembered one professor, Paddy Bofin, in particular. Dr. Bofin served as Dublin's coroner. A courtroom veteran who'd testified before scores of juries, a born performer, he held forth with dramatic gusto as he paced all the while. A true spellbinder. Dr. Bofin was also an expert on neuropathology. He showed slides and specimens of arcane brain tumors with names like ependymomas and oligodendrogliomas. He made you think about going into neuropathology yourself, even though it's unlikely you had a prior interest in it.

But I had sufficient insight to know I preferred the living to the dead. I also balked at the prospect of spending most of my professional life in a lab—preparing reagents and fixing slides, peering into microscopes, playing with microtomes and spectrometers. I'd never been much of a lab rat. And something else, I never got used to autopsies on infants and children. A child's demise struck me as so fundamentally unnatural, so *wrong*, that I never managed to assume a clinical detachment about it. Nor, truthfully, did I want to. If this made me a wimp, so be it.

Another flirtation turned out to be emergency medicine. My favorite rotation as an intern was the ER. I liked its pace, its immediacy, and especially its variety. You never knew what a given day might bring. A law professor, say, a woman with an IQ of 145, suddenly unable to remember the names or ages of her children. Or a firefighter temporarily blinded by smoke and pulverized debris. Or a man of unusual preferences who shoved a lightbulb up his ass and couldn't get it out. Such a patient presented himself to my father, during *his* internship in the 1930s.

I might have applied for a residency in emergency medicine if they'd existed then, but no hospitals offered them until two years after my internship ended. Over time I came to regard that as a blessing. The epidemic of drug abuse completely changed the face of emergency medicine as drug-related injuries and illnesses began to account for an increasing percentage of ER patients. They came in hoards—heroin addicts with swollen crimson arms, with cellulitis from shooting up; wives and girlfriends beaten to a pulp by coke-crazed men. Teenagers in comas after combining cinnamon schnapps with half a bottle of Xanax. A fragile looking woman who weighed 115 pounds, who'd used Ecstasy and now required three men to subdue her. Potheads who drove stoned, pulled out of their wrecked cars with multiple broken bones, twisted limbs, and mangled faces.

There were briefer flirtations. I liked surgery, to my surprise. Never a child who whittled or built model airplanes, I was pleased to learn my fingers could do quick, deft things. Still, I knew I'd never be more than mediocre as a surgeon. I'd assisted at enough operations to see the best ones, the ones who could practically tie knots in spider webs. Furthermore, I wondered how I'd fare with a steady diet of repetitive procedures. Three hundred gall bladders, a thousand hernias.

I rather liked my father's specialty of dermatology, an attractive mix of medicine, surgery, and even psychiatry. The skin is a great template for a variety of illnesses including, for instance, obsessive compulsive disorder. If you wash your hands a hundred times a day, you're apt to have dermatologic issues. The problem was my father, who would use every trick in his considerable arsenal to persuade me to join his practice. Which would conceivably result in mayhem. In fact, our relationship had improved markedly through the years after a guerilla war that waxed and waned throughout my adolescence and lasting until the Dublin years. But that improvement would melt away like an ice cube on a waffle iron if we worked side by side.

I thought about neurology, and pediatrics, and general practice. There were things about all of them I found attractive, but none of them seemed the proper fit. God may not have laughed out loud at these deliberations, but He may have chortled in passing.

And always, in the background, lurked the psychiatric option.

AFTER THE CONVERSATION WITH Dr. Gallen, I recalled an incident from the late 1950s during my sophomore year at Springfield High School, an incident that hadn't crossed my mind for decades. One of my friends was Felix, a sensitive youth enamored of the theater, especially with costume and set design. Better dressed and groomed than most of his peers, bored by sports, but otherwise unremarkable. One day he told me that he was gay.

To be gay was unquestionably *not* all right in the America of 1957. This was twelve years before the Stonewall Riots, about twenty years before the American Psychiatric Association decreed that homosexuality wasn't a disease after all, and almost sixty years before the Supreme Court legalized same-sex marriage. At best, homosexuality in 1957 meant you might be taunted, mocked, and ostracized. At worst, it meant you might lose your job, your freedom, or your life. The case of Matthew Shepard might have been the most notorious murder precipitated by sexual orientation, but by no means was it the first.

Felix correctly sensed, however, that he could talk to me about his situation without risking mockery or scorn, without risking that I'd pass judgment or end the friendship. You could say Felix provided my first introduction to psychiatry. I was fifteen at the time.

Before Felix came out to me, however, I was already intrigued by why people behaved as they did and how they got the way they were. My attraction to history, which started well before I majored in it, fed into such questions. Why did Lincoln become the greatest president and Hitler a monster? There existed a few odd similarities between them. They both had nasty fathers and doting mothers (a stepmother too, in Lincoln's case). Both of them had known early trauma. Both of them had ambitions well beyond the isolated small towns where they grew up, high native intelligence (although of very different kinds), and a gift for swaying others. Why, then, had their lives diverged so totally?

When I started to read fiction, questions of behavior and motives continued to intrigue me. What made Holden Caulfield so depressed and alienated? Throughout my formative years, few books had more impact on me than J.D. Salinger's *Catcher in the Rye*. Philip Carey in Somerset Maugham's *Of Human Bondage*: why had he developed a paralyzing obsession with a dreary, selfish, unattractive waitress in a relationship from which he got nothing except pain and humiliation? Among the characters who fascinated me most was Cathy, in John Steinbeck's *East of Eden*. A genuinely evil figure, her malice was compounded by diabolical patience. What was *her* motivation? I often thought of Cathy decades later when working in correctional settings. A colleague once said of hardcore psychopaths, "The temperature drops five degrees when they enter a room." In Cathy's case, it might have dropped by ten. Steinbeck himself wrote this about her: "I believe there are monsters born in the world to human parents . . . and just as there are physical monsters, can there not be mental or psychic [ones]?"

In high school, I also read an introduction to psychoanalysis. I didn't understand all of it, or maybe most of it, but it definitely held my interest. I read another book from my parents' library that held my interest even more, *The Fifty-Minute Hour*, by a clinical psychologist named Robert Lindner. Written in 1955, the book consisted of case histories. They must have had an impact on me since I remember some details of them sixty years after I read about them.

My first exposure to psychiatry at RCSI proved inauspicious.

At the time, Dublin had a massive fortress of a psychiatric hospital called St. Brendan's, a place you could imagine with turrets, a moat, and an underground dungeon. Most Dubliners knew it as Grangegorman, named after the suburb where it sprawled on a site that eventually grew to seventy acres. Initially it served 250 lunatics, the official name for psychiatric patients in its earliest days. At its maximum capacity it may have held ten times that. Opened in 1815, it wore its age poorly.

On my first day there, a nurse conducted me and the patient, a largish muscular man, to a small bare interview room about twenty yards from the nurses' station. She locked the door and promptly forgot about us. Thirty minutes later, the patient grew restless, not bouncing off the walls but fidgety and twitchy. I was growing restless too. Borderline claustrophobic. Trying to keep a calm demeanor, I stood up slowly, careful to avoid jerky motions, and tapped lightly on the locked door's window. No response. Five minutes later I tried again, and five minutes after that. When the nurse finally came to let us out, close to an hour had passed. She gave us a jaunty smile, and I wondered if this was a rite of passage, something the Grangegorman nurses did to all the incoming medical students.

IN 1971, I CAME back to the United States, rookie doctor in Nixon's America. They'd accepted me for an internship at the Hospital of St. Raphael, in New Haven, one of Yale's teaching hospitals.

Initially I felt overwhelmed. I suspect most new doctors feel the same if they're honest about it. I'd done well in medical school, much better than I'd done as an undergraduate. Apart from the books and lectures, I'd earned my bones on the wards, OR, and morgue.

Even so, I'll always remember the first hour of the first day of my internship. At the time St. Raphael's still used an overhead paging system, and they paged me by name. I was now officially Doctor Goodwin. *Christ,* it hit me like a slap in the face, *they mean* me *and not my father!*

Not an easy year, but I enjoyed it. I enjoyed the camaraderie with other interns, the residents, and a few of the attendings. Almost as diverse in their geographic origins as my RCSI classmates, they hailed from Mexico and Greece, Japan and Pakistan, and half a dozen other countries. I enjoyed the improvement in my clinical skills and my increasing self-confidence. I enjoyed the surge of adrenaline when the ER buzzed. And let's be honest about this, I enjoyed the sexual smorgasbord laid out before me. Perfect timing; it seemed that all the women I met were on the pill and no AIDS yet. Perfect timing; occurring at a point when my marriage was stressed to the max, when Alice and I moved farther apart by the day.

Two decades later, in private practice, I had a session with a high school French teacher five years my junior. She reminisced about the easy-come, easy-go zeitgeist of the late 1960s and 1970s. "The political excitement . . . the music, the movies . . . the drinking and drugs and promiscuity . . . *God,* I miss it!"

To my credit, I remained the stolid professional. I didn't stand up and high-five her.

I enjoyed the internship despite the notoriously long hours and chronic sleep deprivation. (I would learn that I could fall asleep standing up in an elevator, if only for a matter of seconds.) I enjoyed it despite seeing illnesses and injuries that comprised the stuff of nightmares. Mrs. Gray, for instance, a woman of forty-six with intractable scleroderma. The origin of the word is Greek, meaning *hardened skin.* An autoimmune disease, it can lead to an abnormal collagen coating that invades and surrounds skin, connective tissue, blood vessels, and muscles, as well as internal organs. Symptoms can be protean, from pulmonary hypertension to kidney failure to blindness. At its worst, it renders patients trapped and immobilized in the coffin-like confines of their own anatomy, unable to make the smallest movement without excruciating pain. And Mrs. Gray had it at its worst. To try lifting a cup of tea to her lips might mean ten minutes of torture.

Unsurprisingly, I learned a tremendous amount about diagnosis and treatment and people in general. But one of the most important single things I learned concerned medication, and it has stayed with me throughout my professional life. The incident leading to this occurred around 3AM in mid-July. A call summoned me to a nurses' station. The nurse asked me to see an elderly Italian-American gentleman named Salvatore Rossi who'd had prostate surgery the previous morning.

Mr. Rossi wasn't doing well at all. He yelled and groaned, he writhed and bucked, he kicked at the air. They had him in restraints after he tried to pull out his IV and catheter. I glanced through his chart, checked his vital signs, and tried unsuccessfully to talk him down. I decided to give him intravenous Valium.

Here's the thing about most intravenous (IV) meds, especially the psychoactive ones: they need to be given *slowly.* Your brain does not like surprises. I should have taken the syringe and emptied it into his IV milliliter by milliliter, over the course of a minute or more, carefully observing how Mr. Rossi reacted to it. Instead, I emptied the syringe in one rapid push, in an action that took less than two seconds.

Valium, like other drugs of its class—Klonopin and Xanax, among them—depresses respiration. Mr. Rossi, moreover, was seventy-six. Even without his postop pain meds (and their interactions are highly significant), he would have been much more susceptible to the effects of it than a young or middle-aged adult. So when the Valium hit him, he promptly sat up in bed and froze. He moaned, and inhaled deeply, and then stopped breathing altogether.

I did a quick mental review of CPR. I also speculated on the nice career in medicine I'd almost had. I also asked myself, *God Almighty, what did I just do?*

"Do you want me to call a code?" the nurse asked.

"Not yet. Let's give him a few more seconds."

Salvatore Rossi did, in fact, have the thoughtfulness to resume breathing. Very slowly and shallowly, but breathing is breathing.

So, what are the take-home points here?

The first and most obvious one: Treat medications with respect. Practically every medication, prescribed or over-the-counter, can have side effects and bad interactions with other agents. Practically every medication can be problematic and possibly fatal if wrongly used.

A second and related point: It's very easy to do a patient harm. Maybe you can't help everyone you treat, but you don't have to make someone worse. Before I left for medical school, my father told me something that should be etched in the brain of every health care professional, a Latin phrase that dates back two millennia: *Primum non nocere.* First, do no harm.

A third point: Do everything you can to stay out of a teaching hospital in July and August. The internship and residency years traditionally start on July 1, and interns and first year residents will provide much of your day-to-day care. You'll recall that this incident happened in mid-July. Do *not* have elective surgery in these months. Wait until the brothers and sisters have more experience under their belts.

A fourth point, truly sobering: All health care professionals do every procedure, from a psychiatric session to a root canal, from simple suturing to a liver transplant, for a first time. The people they (literally) practice on are called patients, and the debt that those in the healing professions owe them is unpayable. Amazingly, most of them survive.

A final point: Medications can be remarkably effective. You'll recall that Mr. Rossi calmed down right away. Indeed, I almost calmed him down for the rest of eternity.

When I reflect on my internship, more than forty years after the fact, a jumble of memories and images return to me. Drinking bitter dregs of coffee, the remains of what might have been brewed ten hours earlier; smoking in defiance of the fire marshal . . . taking amphetamines to keep me aglow during thirty-six hour shifts. . . scribbling thousands of hand-written notes . . . trying to draw blood from a drug addict with no usable veins left . . . telling someone that a spouse of thirty years has died . . . telling parents that a child's operation has gone well . . . doing a spinal tap for the first time; willing my hands not to shake . . . waiting in the not-so-lonely confines of the hospital's on-call rooms . . . enduring a tug-of-war between the adrenaline rush and the exhaustion . . . feeling like a medical student when it started and a doctor when it ended.

Meanwhile, I continued to meander down the road toward psychiatry, despite a mother lode of ambivalence about it. I had interviews throughout the East and the Midwest. The most memorable of these took place in Topeka, Kansas, at the Menninger Clinic (it has since relocated to Houston). The clinic paid for airfare, two nights at a Holiday Inn, and all meals. I had at least half a dozen separate meetings with senior staff psychiatrists, residents, and nurses; I underwent a slew of psychological tests. The people could not have been more welcoming and pleasant.

But the trip took place in February. Just before my arrival, a daylong blizzard deposited enough snow to cover gas pumps, and the wind whistled banshee-like across the prairie, and the temperature failed to reach above ten. Never—not in the empty stretches of Newfoundland or the jungles of Costa Rica, not on Isle Royale National Park, surrounded by Lake Superior—never, before or since, have I considered the sense of isolation I felt in that February blizzard in Topeka. I toyed with the notion that the ancients had been right after all, and the world *was* flat. If I walked away from the Holiday Inn and kept going in a straight line, I might fall off the edge of it.

No way was I willing to spend three years there, however welcoming and pleasant they might have been.

LOOKING BACK ON IT, with the clearer eye of hindsight, I committed to psychiatry for two main reasons. First, I believed it would hold my interest more than any other specialty. Second, my intuition told me that over time I'd become good at it.

A lesser factor, my family was the perfect template for a future psychiatrist. There was just enough psychopathology to intrigue me but not enough to scare me off. A close family friend once said the following, apropos of my siblings and me. "If one of you hadn't become a psychiatrist, your parents would have had to adopt."

In the end I only completed one residency application, to the Institute of Living in Hartford, commonly referred to as the IOL. It was regarded as one of the premier private psychiatric hospitals in the country. Formerly best known as a sanctuary for the rich and famous, it used to pick up celebrity patients in one of its new Packards. The hospital maintained a fleet of them for just that purpose. Apart from the excellence of its clinical care, it had also done groundbreaking psychiatric research. I learned all this through Dick, an RCSI classmate who'd graduated a few years before me. We'd kept in touch, and Dick was just about to complete his second year of residency there.

Dick raved about the place. The quality of its teaching and supervision, the diversity and challenge of its patients. The beautiful grounds, the friendliness of the staff. *Go there if possible*, my friend counseled me. *You'll find no better psychiatry residency anywhere.*

So I filled out the application, and I dithered for two or three weeks before I got around to mailing it. By the time it arrived, the IOL had filled its residency positions.

Winter had given way to spring, the internship year would end on June 30, and I had no other irons in the fire. No Plan B. From time to time I felt surges of panic.

Alice saved the day. "Write them back. Tell them you're disappointed, and ask them to reconsider your application if one of the people they accepted changes his mind."

That was, in fact, what happened. Someone decided not to go to the IOL after all, so I slipped in, taking their last slot at the last possible moment, by the skin of my teeth. And so I embarked upon a career in psychiatry, more or less by default, despite near-successful attempts to sabotage myself.

CHAPTER VII

THE COURT OF LAST RESORT

You'd never describe downtown Hartford as a place of great beauty. The state capitol, impressive in a fussy sort of way, features Gothic Revival arches and fancy flourishes, although the passing years have left its white marble with a grayish tint. There's a park nearby and a scattering of government edifices: some stately, others drably utilitarian. There are office buildings, stores, restaurants, a few hotels, and an excellent art museum. None would be candidates for *Architectural Digest*.

In its midst, with perfect lawns broken up by a wealth of trees, sits the IOL. Technically it's now a part of Hartford Hospital, which bought it in 1994, but most people still refer to it by its old initials. Cynics have referred to it as the Substitute for Living, but it had another, more respectful nickname when I began a residency, The Court of Last Resort. Their patients might have come after unsuccessful treatment with a score of mental health professionals within and outside the United States. They might have taken a cocktail of psychiatric medications; they might be veterans of electroconvulsive shock treatment (ECT). They might have been hospitalized elsewhere a dozen or more times.

The IOL took some getting used to. Not exactly stuffy but quite formal, unlike the more casual hospital setting where I interned. Case in point, the dress code called for tie and jacket, and one day I got a quiet reprimand for wearing an ascot.

It was also as hierarchical an institution as you'd find outside the Vatican. You saw this clearly at Morning Staff, also known as Matins, the meeting that took place every weekday in an imposing chamber that doubled as the main dining room. The layout consisted of four long parallel tables with a shorter head table at a right angle to them. The psychiatrist-in-chief held court at the main table, flanked by two or three other senior psychiatrists and one or two charge nurses. At the head of each of the longer tables sat the chief of section. All patients and psychiatrists were assigned to one of four such sections. Next to him (always *him;* no female section chiefs) you found the staff psychiatrists, and next to them the residents. Along the walls and in the back were parked other nurses, directors of various recreational and therapeutic activities, administrative personnel, and whatever medical students who might be doing psychiatric rotations there. You could determine an attendee's presumed importance by where he or she sat with roughly ninety-seven percent accuracy.

At 8:55, not 8:53 or 8:57, a charge nurse rang a small silver bell and called the meeting to order. She proceeded to read out names of patients admitted, transferred, or discharged, and she also recounted notable events occurring since the prior meeting. *Mrs. Trout was transferred from Thompson II* (the most restricted female unit) *to Brigham II* (less restricted). *Judge Minnow was discharged home from Cole. Mr. Carp was transferred to Hartford Hospital with dyspnea and substernal chest pain.* More interesting came a recital of admissions, in which the assigned doctor gave a synopsis of the new patient's relevant history. *Miss Salmon is a thirty-nine-year-old executive secretary presenting with panic attacks, agitated depression, and paranoia involving the CIA. She has four prior hospitalizations in New Jersey and New York City, has taken three different antidepressants and had two courses of ECT.*

Some synopses caught the attention of those present more than others. I remember one that went like this: *Mrs. Herring, a forty-four-year-old housewife from Indianapolis, had her first psychotic break in college. She has lengthy periods of lucidity but experiences command hallucinations during relapses. During her most recent relapse, her hallucinations told her to kill her two children, and she obeyed them.*

I WAS ONE OF seven new residents. We'd gone to medical school on both sides of the Atlantic—St. Louis and Albany, Dublin and Ghent. Three of our fathers were doctors, one had owned a men's clothing store, and one had been an abusive alcoholic. Fred, older than the others, was an Italian American who'd gone to medical school late. A born raconteur, he had a knack for delivering memorable anecdotes. My favorite concerned his account of dating the daughter of a high-ranking Mafioso while a medical student in Italy. Fred, the girl, and her parents were having dinner at one of Rome's best restaurants when mother and daughter went together to the powder room. The father—Mr. Corleone, let's call him—turned to Fred. "So, how do you like my daughter?"

"I like her very much, sir. She's a wonderful girl."

Mr. Corleone nodded. "If you want to marry her, you're all set. You'll pass all your courses with high marks, I'll help you get started in private practice, and the two of you will lack for nothing." He paused before continuing. "If you *don't* want to marry her, you will leave the table now and never see her again."

At which point Fred stood up, thanked him, and left the restaurant.

I couldn't resist asking him, "Were you sleeping with her?"

Fred nodded.

"What would her father have done if he'd found out?"

"He would have killed me. That is, if I'd been lucky."

THE RESIDENTS SOON BONDED. A good thing, since we could use the mutual support. It wasn't just a matter of adjusting to the formal and hierarchical nature of the place. Aside from that, we didn't know what we were doing. All of us had a general medical background with rotating internships under our belts, and suddenly we were seeing quite different patients from those familiar to us. The histories were more complicated, less straightforward, and often much longer, sometimes going back for decades. Symptoms could be vague and inconsistent. A schizophrenic man might hallucinate, but only in certain circumstances. A woman with incapacitating panic attacks might be free from undue anxiety at other times. Diagnosis could prove difficult, and you didn't have lab results or X-rays to fall back on. Before newer antidepressants and antipsychotics came along in the 1980s and beyond, the older drugs were relatively few. And they often had devastating side effects and didn't work well in the first place.

The residents also had to get used to the glacially slow pace of improvement and recovery, which might take months or years or not happen at all. As one of them put it, in general medicine patients usually had the decency to die or get well.

We had formal presentations by staff psychiatrists about diagnosis, psychiatric meds, and the mental status exam, analogous to a physical exam in general medicine. We learned about the law as it applies to mental health with an emphasis on confidentiality. There was also discussion of the circumstances under which confidentiality could and should be broken: dangerousness to self or others, and the grayer area of "grave disability."

We learned about the bewildering array of psychiatric theories from the arch-Freudian to the cognitive-behavioral. We learned about neurotransmitters and brain receptor sites, a field still in its infancy. We learned about group and family therapy, hypnosis and ECT. We went to case conferences, and within a few months we presented cases of our own.

Formal presentations are critical parts of residents' education, but even more important is supervision. Part of this comes down to the nature of psychiatric treatment. During my residency and for a long time thereafter, psychiatrists were expected to do therapy as well as manage medications. But psychiatric treatment—that is, the talk-therapies—varies from treatment in other specialties in a key respect: it's ultimately private. Surgical residents assist at operations before they take over themselves, and senior clinicians usually remain available if there's trouble. It's similar with medical residents. They work in ICUs and CCUs and perform liver biopsies and endoscopies with attendings at hand before they're on their own. But no one sits in on a first-year psychiatric resident's first session with a patient.

Of course residents could record sessions (videotaping them had yet to become widespread) but mainly we discussed sessions with a supervisor after the fact. Accordingly, relationships with our supervisors assumed great importance.

Enter Erik Linnolt.

I FIRST MET ERIK when I applied for the residency. The IOL had applicants come for a series of interviews, and Erik was one of several senior clinicians who spoke with me. A still-youthful man in early middle age, a native of Estonia, he went to medical school in Sweden in the 1930s. After general practice in Western Canada, he came to the U.S., studied psychiatry at the IOL, and stayed on as a member of their staff. He spoke heavily accented but fluent English.

Everything about him seemed pointed. His thin sideburns that curved inward over his cheeks; his thin pointed nose. The cigarillos he smoked, which he aimed at me as we talked, jabbing with them to emphasize his points. And his speech, especially his speech. His questions were blunt, direct, and concise. He seemed to enjoy catching those questioned off guard.

He had opinions about everything—the goddamn bureaucrats who badgered him with paperwork, the goddamn staff meetings he had to attend, the goddamn politicians (Republicans and Democrats alike; he had no bias). His idiosyncrasies emerged quickly, even in the course of our initial meeting. For example, the way he periodically stood up and left peanuts on the windowsill for squirrels who knew they had a good thing going.

When I returned to New Haven after the interviews, I told Alice about meeting Erik. "If I do go there, I hope to God I don't get supervised by him." No doubt God laughed. Erik, of course, became my first supervisor.

Erik did what none of my other supervisors did; he overlapped the supervisory meetings with his own patients' sessions. Such was the case on my first day of supervision. Erik introduced us to each other. "Mr. Frobisher," he said with portentousness, "this is Doctor Goodwin. He is [dramatic pause] . . . an *expert* in your disorder."

Dr. Goodwin had been a psychiatrist, so to speak, for all of three hours.

"Doctor Goodwin," Erik went on, "this is Mr. Frobisher. He is [another pause] . . . a *mental cripple!*"

Nonplused by the introduction, I made a reasonable, all-American response. I offered my hand, not knowing that Mr. Frobisher was obsessive-compulsive with a crippling germ phobia. He pulled away, cowering, trying not to cry out, as if I'd offered him a viper.

Erik threw back his head and emitted what I'd come to know as his characteristic laugh, a clipped series of guffaws.

I soon learned that Erik's gruff façade was precisely that, a matter of façade. He proved to be an excellent listener, both to his own patients and to me. His advice was calm and thoughtful, his interventions well-reasoned. He was kind with an excellent if off-center and often raunchy sense of humor. To my surprise, I began to like him. But the real turning point took place about eight weeks later when I arrived one day for supervision. At the time it was possible to take two years apiece of a psychiatric and neurological residency and become board-certified in both. What, I asked, did Erik think of the idea?

Erik took several moments to frame his answer. "It's the worst goddamn idea I ever heard," he finally proclaimed. *Goddamn*, I'd already surmised, was one of his half dozen favorite words. "I have always believed that neurology is the most depressing specialty," he went on. "A neuron is dead or it is not. If it is dead, there is nothing you can do to revive it. If it is not, it will probably recover on its own."

His tone changed, and in a flash he became solicitous. "Now, the reason you bring this up is that you are disenchanted with psychiatry. *This* is what we need to talk about." The time was 11:45. "I suggest we have lunch off campus, and we will continue the discussion there."

The response took me aback. That was exactly why I'd asked the question. And the chance to talk about it in a restaurant, as opposed to the staff dining room, was exactly what the situation called for. The lunch marked a turning point in our relationship as far as I was concerned. I told Erik about my ambivalence toward psychiatry and my doubts about whether I was really suited for it. I told him about my frustrations with it, which I'd barely acknowledged to myself, much less to anyone else. And Erik sat patiently, letting me talk, throwing in an occasional comment or question but mainly listening.

MORE THAN FIFTY YEARS after our supervisory sessions, I still recall some of them verbatim. Erik might make his points with characteristic directness, sometimes with a joke or anecdote. Once, very early in our time together, he asked me about a patient's treatment plan. I spewed it out hurriedly and unrealistically. *These are the goals for this week, and these will be the ones for next week,* and so on. When I finished, I waited for his critique.

"You want to do too much, too soon . . . you're moving too

goddamn fast. You remind me of the story of the young bull and the old bull. They come to a pasture with ten cows in it. 'Let's jump over the fence and fuck one or two of them,' the young bull says. 'No,' the old bull says. 'Let's walk slowly through the gate and fuck them all.'"

Erik viewed the world with a jaundiced eye, although his cynicism, like his gruffness, was mainly a matter of façade. He had a keen eye for the world's absurdities but was adept at finding humor in situations not inherently humorous. "A cop found one of my patients in his car by the side of the road jerking off," he told me, "and he gave the man a goddamn *parking ticket!*" But his supervision could convey a deep empathy and an awareness of excruciating pain. In one session I told him about a schizophrenic girl I was treating, no longer psychotic but now in the midst of a near-suicidal depression. Sobbing, with as powerful a show of despair as I'd witnessed, she said, "I'm too lonely to go on living. In the whole universe I don't have *one friend!*" I told Erik I'd been blindsided by her outburst and had no idea how I should have reacted to it.

"Perhaps you should have told her, 'now you do,'" said Erik quietly.

Reflecting back on this incident, I realize that many therapists would disagree with such an intervention, especially the hardcore Freudians. Therapy isn't friendship, they might point out. A patient needs an empathetic silence and insight, they might add. Nonetheless, I feel it would have been an absolutely appropriate and potentially comforting thing to say, and I'm sorry I hadn't thought to say it at the time.

TOWARD THE END OF my first year of residency, I took a week's vacation. That led to another memorable exposure to the Linnoltian style. Whenever IOL psychiatrists took time off longer than a weekend, they made temporary reassignments for their patients. I asked Erik to assume the care of a patient of mine named Gordo, a high school junior.

Gordo was a beefy young man, six feet tall and weighing about 200 pounds. His life had become a misery because of persistent, intractable, and crazy-making homosexual obsessions. They plagued him from the time he woke up until he fell asleep, and rarely was he altogether free from them. Never would he describe them to me, but he mentioned them in every session. He hated everything about homosexuals and homosexuality, making it clear he found nothing the slightest bit appealing to him about such people and their practices. His obsessions angered and tortured him but also confused him since he had no idea how or why they came about. He'd never been sexually abused, had never known anyone gay except for a few classmates whom he studiously avoided. He volunteered that he found girls sexually attractive but he'd never had a girlfriend, and I speculated that there could have been something pro forma about these claims. The Selective Serotonin Reuptake Inhibitors—Prozac, Zoloft, and the others—might have helped him considerably but they wouldn't be on the market for another decade, and Gordo showed no improvement with the meds currently available. Our sessions went nowhere. I likened his dilemma to the wheels of a cart stuck in mud.

I looked forward to having Erik take over for a while, wondering what approach he'd take with him. More importantly, I wondered if Erik could help him. If so, how? There was also a hint of challenge in the mix. *Okay, Grandmaster, let's see what you can do with him.*

In our first meeting after I returned, I couldn't wait to ask Erik how he'd made out with Gordo. "Well," he began, "I think he might have liked me. In our first session I let him talk about girls and football and things like that. In the second one, he started in with this goddamn homosexual stuff."

"What did you tell him?"

"I said, don't worry about it."

I couldn't believe what I was hearing. "They're ruining his life," I replied, "and you told him *not to worry about it?*"

Erik nodded. "And then I said [dramatic pause] . . . *the world is full of fairies.*"

I could only shake my head. *If* I'*d said that*, I thought, *Gordo would have shoved my desktop stapler down my throat.*

"How did he react?" I asked finally.

"He laughed. I did too." With that, he launched into his customary clipped guffaws.

It began to dawn on me that you can say practically anything to a patient if you do it nonjudgmentally, and preferably with humor, and you get the timing right.

OUR FRIENDSHIP ENDURED WHEN the supervisory year ended and long afterward. Erik and I met for lunch at grinder shops and four-star restaurants; we went out with our wives and a few other IOL couples to plays and concerts. We met in Atlanta and Toronto when the American Psychiatric Association held annual meetings there. Our friendship encompassed life-threatening illnesses and major surgery, my divorce and second marriage, and the death of Erik's wife of more than forty years.

Our conversations went well beyond psychiatry. We talked about

Estonia, a country about which I knew nothing before we met, and how a small Baltic nation had struggled between the twin terrors of Hitler's Germany and Stalin's Russia. We talked about Erik's travels throughout the world and his returning to his homeland after the Soviet Union disintegrated. We talked about politics, which both of us followed with keen interest. Our friendship included the administrations of eight presidents, from Nixon to Obama.

We talked about books and art and Grand Slam tennis tournaments. Erik told me about studying medicine in Stockholm and setting broken bones and delivering babies in a small town in British Columbia. I told him about my time at Culver and Yale and in Dublin. While I grew to have reasonable confidence in my therapeutic skills, I still ran into difficult situations through the years. I discussed such situations with Erik every now and again, not so much for advice per se, but to use him as a sounding board. The feedback he gave was invariably useful.

I learned more from him than anyone I've ever known, apart from my parents. Our friendship went on until 2015 when Erik died at the age of 95.

One night, on my birthday, Erik was having dinner with Judy and me. He was in his mid-eighties at the time.

He interrupted himself in mid-sentence. "I want you to have something to remember me by," he said. With that, he took off a ring he always wore. It featured a ruby set in gold with two tiny diamonds on its periphery. He gave it to me, and I was initially too taken aback to thank him.

I wear the ring every day. A wonderful, beautiful gift, but unnecessary. There's not the smallest chance I would ever forget him.

The timing of my residency, from 1972 until 1975, was fortuitous in that it preceded the era of managed care. Among other things this meant that hospitals, including mental hospitals, could keep patients beyond the rock-bottom minimum, and they usually did. In fact, the IOL routinely kept them for weeks or months as opposed to days or sometimes hours. Residents therefore had a chance to learn long-term therapy with some very sick people. Suppose the patient is a bipolar alcoholic with a histrionic and passive-aggressive personality disorder and a history of childhood sexual trauma. It's unlikely that a four or five-day hospitalization will do much for her. But if she's treated as an inpatient for a matter of months, you might have a fighting chance to help her. And if you're starting out, moreover, you can learn a tremendous amount from her.

We should acknowledge that the IOL, like other hospitals, not uncommonly abused this freedom. Patients often stayed long after they might reasonably have been discharged. The IOL also had a geriatric unit that was essentially custodial. These units housed patients, sometimes for years, who should have been in nursing homes—patients for whom there was no real chance for clinical improvement. One senior psychiatrist privately admitted to another resident that such patients were good for the hospital's bottom line.

At the IOL, I treated high school dropouts and PhDs, schizoid loners and the famous and glamorous. I saw the wife of one of the two dozen most powerful men in the country and the daughter of one of Hollywood's best-known actresses. My patients proved educational in unexpected ways. They included Father Dowling, an alcoholic pedophilic sociopath. It speaks to my naiveté that I found it hard to believe a priest could warrant these diagnoses. My parents had brought me up with a strong respect for the clergy, and I met Father Dowling almost two decades before revelations of abuse shook Catholicism to its core.

Another patient, Phoebe Polk, proved educational in a different way.

I met her one day as I walked into the IOL's most structured female unit. To get to the nurses' station I had to pass through a large square sitting room, about forty feet on each side. I barely noticed a thin-faced waif of a girl, who couldn't have weighed more than a hundred pounds, sitting silently with her head bowed.

She gave no indication she'd seen me. Obviously she had though. In a split second she flew off her chair and brought me down with a tackle worthy of the NFL. This was a girl who looked about as threatening as a monarch butterfly. I was too surprised to be frightened.

Phoebe did me no harm. A swarm of nurses and aides rushed out, simultaneously subduing and comforting her. A few weeks later, by which point she was certifiably sane, she apologized profusely. She remembered tackling me, although she had no idea why. But she did do me a service, in a sense. Never again would I take my personal safety for granted in a professional setting. Not in my private office or the correctional facilities where I later worked. Not even in the nursing homes where I consulted. Violent residents weren't common there, but they weren't rarities either. An agitated man of eighty—a onetime lumberjack, for instance—can still pack a wallop.

As I got to know them, I learned that IOL psychiatrists had some interesting stories of their own. One of them, a psychiatrist-in-chief emeritus, was involved in the psychiatric examination of several of the Nuremberg defendants, the Nazi elite tried for crimes against humanity after World War II. One had been a nun before she went into medicine. At least two served in Vietnam. One was an accomplished artist whose paintings sold for four and five figures. I found it hard to understood how so talented a man had summoned the drive and wherewithal to go to medical school. One of them eventually went through gender reassignment surgery. One of them, a fellow resident named Sam Silverman, has been a close friend and confidante for nearly half a century. He has also been indispensable as an unpaid editor and beta reader.

Apart from Sam, the resident with whom I formed the strongest connection was Sulaiman Marikar. A native of Sri Lanka, Sulaiman had as broad an array of interests as anyone I knew there, from boxing to writing poetry to creating the hottest and most peppery meals imaginable. Tall and thin, often wearing a sarong, he liked to hum Tamil songs to himself while he cooked. He maintained an affable manner and upbeat outlook in spite of a history of life-threatening health problems. In 1976 he was diagnosed with an extremely rare heart condition, an intraventricular aneurysm. After surgery at the Mayo Clinic, he appeared to be making an excellent recovery. A few years later, he had a stroke. Again, he appeared to recover fully.

Notwithstanding all this, Sulaiman married, fathered two daughters, built a successful private practice, and appeared to enjoy his life with a special appreciation (enhanced, no doubt, by surviving two near-fatal conditions). In 1987, however, he collapsed and went into abrupt and irreversible cardiac failure. He was forty-four when he died; his younger daughter was three weeks old.

Fifteen years after I left the IOL, another alumnus made a shocking reappearance in my life. Walking through a corridor in the Hartford Jail—by now I'd started working for Corrections—I spotted an inmate with a vaguely familiar face, but the man's name eluded me. It came to me a few moments later: Barry Steiner. Dr. Steiner was part of a group of residents two years ahead of me. We greeted each other awkwardly. Barry, in the midst of a venomous divorce, had been arrested for not paying alimony and child support.

The staff psychiatrist who had the biggest impact on me, apart from Erik, was Charlie Boren. A fellow Midwesterner who grew up in Poseyville, Indiana, he'd completed an IOL residency after medical school in St. Louis. Joining the Navy, he returned to the IOL upon his discharge. After climbing the hospital's ladder—staff psychiatrist, chief of section, director of medical education—he became the last psychiatrist-in-chief before the facility's merger with Hartford Hospital. Despite the interminable hours he worked, he had an open-door policy. Most residents made ample use of this for both impromptu consultations and more personal issues. A gifted and enthusiastic teacher, he gave classes to residents and IOL alumni alike. He also ran an intensive review course, invariably well-attended, for the psychiatric board exams. I don't know how many attendees actually passed their boards through the years, but I wouldn't be surprised if we all did.

Ranking high on the list of the IOL people most important to me was a priest. Father John Kiely, head of pastoral counseling, was one of the best known and best liked people at the Institute. Certain individuals have a quality impossible to define, and even describing it can be elusive. Whatever it is, however, it makes you feel better in their presence; they have about them a comforting aura. Father Kiely was such a man. An attentive and accepting listener, he made himself available to everyone who sought him out. No matter if you were Catholic, Jewish, Muslim, or atheist; he was something of the caretaker's caretaker. No matter if you had a child in trouble, or your marriage was on life support, or you lost a parent; Father Kiely found time for you. In fact, I turned to him in all those situations.

On top of everything else, he had a sharp, quick wit. Once we'd arranged to go to lunch. I was driving, and I swerved abruptly to avoid an overturned trash can in the street.

"Jesus!" he exclaimed.

"Oh, ye of little faith!" I responded.

"Listen, Rob," he said without missing a beat, "you work your side of the street and I'll work mine."

Long after I finished my residency, I met with Erik, Charlie, and Father Kiely for breakfast every six or eight weeks. Our venue was a diner, no more than a step above a greasy spoon, a few blocks from the IOL. Conversations might touch on an unusually vexing patient, or Mel Gibson's *Braveheart* or Emma Thompson's *Sense and Sensibility*, or the latest absurdity in Washington—on anything. Serious topics were leavened by frequent jokes, and Father Kiely was not above laughing at the ruder ones. (He also told a few himself, to wit—*Question:* What did they find in Jeffrey Dahmer's kitchen? *Answer:* A refrigerator that seats six.) Erik told one during John Paul II's long tenure, which Father Kiely particularly enjoyed. *Question:* What do you call a Polack in a funny hat? *Answer:* Your Holiness.

The breakfasts made for one of those traditions not fully appreciated until they're gone. This particular tradition lasted until the late 1990s when Charlie and his wife moved to a retirement community in New Hampshire. It was also around this time that Father Kiely noticed a black splotch beneath a thumbnail. He died of a melanoma eighteen months later. More people came to his funeral than to any other I've attended, before or since.

A NUMBER OF RESIDENTS sought therapy in the course of their training, myself among them. I knew I'd do this sooner or later. I knew my relationship with my father, although much improved through the years, was a formidable piece of unfinished business. I knew I had a tendency to sabotage myself, to turn into my own worst enemy. My marriage foundered, and I knew I was as much to blame as Alice, if not more so. I did things even though aware they'd likely prove to be mistakes. Despite doing well in medical school and in my internship, despite a growing awareness I was becoming a competent psychiatrist, I couldn't rid myself of a sense of my own inadequacy. I slept fitfully, and I often didn't fall asleep until close to dawn.

I began to see a psychiatrist named Rebecca Solomon.

Dr. Solomon was a psychoanalyst in private practice. She was also a senior staff member of the IOL, where she'd attained a near-legendary status as a teacher and supervisor. At one time or another she taught psychiatry at the Yale School of Medicine, held a high position in a major psychoanalytic association, and edited its journal. A white-haired woman with blue eyes that seemed to miss nothing, she possessed a youthfulness that belied her fifty-five or sixty years.

I had a certain reverence for psychoanalytic theory, as well as for the encyclopedic breadth of Freud's own knowledge. Aside from developing his earth-shattering theories, you have to admire a man familiar with great literature from Sophocles to Shakespeare to Goethe, a man familiar with philosophy and art, and who still found time to master eight languages.

In spite of this, I had more than a hint of skepticism about analytic orthodoxy. About the universal applicability of such concepts as castration anxiety, penis envy, and primal scene-induced trauma. Moreover, I was skeptical about the vaunted silence and passivity of the analysts. Erik Linnolt, Charlie Boren, and most of my other mentors favored an interactive approach that made better sense to him. They had a repertoire that went beyond *Uhm hum, go on,* and *tell me more about that.*

Why, then, did I choose Dr. Solomon? For one thing, her seminars impressed me. Erudite, with a world of experience, she also struck me as down to earth and possessed of abundant common sense. She maintained what I regarded as an exemplary balance between personal warmth and clinical objectivity. And (the main thing, really), she struck me as someone I could talk to.

I met with her twice weekly for about two years. The sessions touched on all the important facets of my life. My parents. My recurrent angst throughout my time at Yale and beyond. My marriage, with all its disarray, and the growing dissatisfaction on both sides. Becoming a father myself, and my uncertainty that I could do the job right. My intimate relationships, my intermittent depression. My doubts still—*still,* even when well into my residency—that I belonged in psychiatry in the first place.

Apart from her crucial aid in helping me make sense of my life, she also taught me a tremendous amount about the therapeutic process. The use of silence: when to interject yourself and when to wait someone out. How to make the most of patients' dreams, a skill that's more than a historical footnote; a relevant interpretation can still help people. She also taught me a lot about confrontation. In one memorable session when I became evasive and enamored of my own verbiage, she looked me in the eye and delivered a verdict. "Bullshit!" That was, indeed, what I'd been giving her, and she'd called me on it. Furthermore, it occurred to me, *if she can say this to a patient, so can I.* She reinforced what I'd already learned from Erik. *You can say nearly anything to whomever you're treating if you have a solid relationship with the patient and you get the timing right.*

Freud viewed therapy as successful if it enabled patients to love and work. I agree, but I'd presume to add two more criteria. Therapy should enable patients to come to terms with their demons, whatever they may be, and to assume responsibility for their lives. In my own case, Dr. Solomon made those things possible. I consider my time with her to have been invaluable. More than worth the considerable pain and money it cost.

I WAS THIRTY-TWO WHEN I left the IOL. After weighing other options, a move to New Hampshire or New Jersey in particular, I decided to stay in Connecticut and start a private practice. Was I prepared for such a step? Yes and no.

On the one hand, I believed my training had been solid. I couldn't have asked for better supervision, not just from Erik and Charlie but from other IOL clinicians. I'd learned about the various therapies, I'd worked with groups and families as well as individuals. I knew how to prescribe the psychiatric meds currently available, and I knew when to refer to a neurologist or another specialist—an important consideration in that a number of medical illnesses can present with psychiatric symptoms. I knew something of the interface of psychiatry and the law. I'd learned about the assessment and treatment of psychiatric emergencies. My residency included a rotation through Hartford Hospital, which involved a good deal of time spent in its teeming ER.

On the other hand, I knew little about the nuts and bolts of real-world psychiatry. About such things as how to publicize the opening of a practice and how to keep medical records—the IOL had a whole department that took care of this—and how to obtain malpractice insurance. I knew little about something as basic as how and where to order prescription pads. My father helped quite a bit, but there's a world of difference between psychiatric and dermatologic practice. The IOL staff psychiatrists provided information too. Still, I had to acquire much of this information on my own, mainly through a process of trial and error.

There was also the matter of money. One evening, pen and pad in hand, I sat down and figured how much I'd need each month. My estimate of living and car expenses and my percentage of rent for a shared office. Health insurance since the IOL's excellent coverage would no longer be available to me. And, in the wake of the failure of my first marriage, I'd have to factor in alimony, child support, and legal fees. Also travel expenses if I wanted to see my son. Alice had custody, and she'd moved to Texas with him.

When I added up the figures, they looked like the expenditures of a small nation.

I couldn't contemplate the possibility that I'd fail in private practice. At the same time, I found it hard to believe I'd succeed.

CHAPTER VIII

SURVIVING DIVORCE AND REMARRIAGE, MORE OR LESS

Judy and I slammed into each other's lives with all the subtlety of a head-on collision of two locomotives.

We met at a time when I should have felt better than I did. As noted, I'd done all right as a medical student and intern. Despite a lingering ambivalence about psychiatry, I found the field fascinating. Most of the time I was glad I'd chosen it as a specialty. I had a strong support system at the IOL—Erik Linnolt, Charlie Boren, and Father Kiely, first and foremost. My fellow residents and I had coalesced into a close-knit, empathetic group. The sound and fury relating to my family of origin had already diminished, even before I began to meet with Rebecca Solomon. Still young, just under thirty when my residency started, I enjoyed good physical health despite a lack of exercise and smoking. I wouldn't quit until the early 1980s.

My marriage was another story. Alice and I had drifted apart, ever since ... since when precisely? The marriage had been under siege from the onset. For starters, there'd been family issues, financial constraints, and our own immaturity. No honeymoon, figuratively or literally.

The drifting apart worsened around the middle years of our stay in Ireland. Both of us loved our time there, full of cherished people and memorable events. A trip to the magnificent Cliffs of Moher in County Clare, several weddings of my classmates, seeing a play by Brendan Behan or George Bernard Shaw. An evening of Guinness and good talk in a pub, an impromptu gathering with Carey Donaldson and the Kupers. In terms of how the two of *us* were doing though, the Irish adventure proved a mixed blessing. The wealth of interesting and pleasurable things occurring made it easy for us to avoid taking a hard look at our own relationship.

During the last two years of our time there, Alice resumed her education. She took graduate school courses in Irish literature and history, which would eventually lead to a PhD. Our separate academic lives provided another means by which we avoided dealing with each other. I had my work, she had hers. When we did deal directly with each other, a conversation could turn snarky in a flash. We sniped and criticized, we gave little comfort to each other. Both of us used words adeptly, and—like most married couples—we knew the quickest and most effective means to get under each other's skin.

Sometimes I marvel that we had so many friends. We couldn't have been a lot of fun to hang around with.

I LEFT IRELAND IN June of 1971 while Alice stayed on for three more months with our son, not yet a year old. When she did come back to the States, she missed Ireland fiercely, probably more than I did. I typically put in a sixty-hour week as an intern, and I didn't have time to miss Ireland as much as she did.

Her own life was exhausting too. We co-rented a large house

in Branford, on Long Island Sound, twenty or thirty minutes from the hospital, and we only had one car. If she needed it, which was usually the case, all three of us had to leave the house together by six thirty. Then, unless I worked all night, she'd have to pick me up, rarely before seven or eight.

There were other distractions from the marriage. As noted in an earlier chapter, I didn't make a fetish of fidelity.

That we stayed together as long as we did was due largely to our son. Thomas Brendan Clare Goodwin, better known throughout his childhood as Toby, was bright, attractive, charming, and frankly doted upon. The first child, the first grandchild in both families. A cheerful toddler with a ready smile and a booming laugh. Also effortlessly funny, as children tend to be. When we were in a restaurant one day, a pleasant older gentleman walked by. "What a nice little boy!" the man said. Toby considered this. "Sometimes I'm nice," he replied, "and sometimes I'm hideous." On another occasion a few years later, when he was learning to read and write, he was swimming in a pool with his Aunt Lisa. The water temperature was not to his liking. He wasn't a particularly loud child but his voice carried well. "Lisie," he complained, "my p-e-n-u-s is cold."

"What did you say?" I asked my sister when I stopped laughing. "Nothing. I swam away and pretended I didn't know him."

I WAS MORE INVOLVED in Toby's early life than my father had been in mine. Generally speaking, paternity in the early 1970s differed vastly from what it was in the mid-1940s. My mother told me he'd changed my diaper precisely once, "and he did such a half-assed job that I never asked him again. I suspect he did it that way on purpose."

She also told me she couldn't remember him ever reading to me, although he was always an avid reader himself. By contrast, I read to Toby when he was still a baby.

Toby was good company, and I didn't have to work hard to enjoy him. I took him for walks in parks, and on errands, and to movies. Also to fast food places. This led to an event that could have been disastrous. One Sunday morning, when Alice slept late, I brought him to a Dunkin Donuts. I left him strapped in his car seat while I went in to buy donuts and hot chocolate. Leaving the shop, less than five minutes later, I saw the car drifting backward onto a busy boulevard. Toby had undone his straps, wriggled out of his seat, climbed over the driver's seat, and gotten the car out of gear.

He wasn't hurt. The car, a behemoth of a 1968 Chevy, hit another car with enough force to spin it around 180 degrees. But its bulk absorbed most of the impact, and it was heavy enough to remain upright. A compact would probably have been overturned and demolished. By far this is still the most frightening thing that ever happened to me. It brought to mind, yet again, the inexorable fragility of life. It also brought to mind the nightmare, which most parents banish for the sake of their sanity, the possibility of losing a child.

As much as Alice and I loved and enjoyed him, we bestowed on him a surfeit of attention and affection, some of which we might have directed toward each other. It might have benefitted all three of us, including Toby.

Such was a snapshot of my life at the point when Judy and I met.

She had a round Irish face framed by reddish-brown hair and dark blue eyes, almost black, that looked at you as if you were the only person in the world. A near-sashaying walk that dared you to ignore her, not that I tried to. The attraction was immediate and mutual. I believe the old Freudian cliché that falling in love might be compared to a manner of psychosis. "I want to understand my psychosis but not be cured of it," I told Rebecca Solomon in one of our sessions.

Among the many hitches I knew we'd face in a long-term relationship: Judy had two daughters. No doubt she viewed my son as a similar hitch. We put these facts in a basket, usually ignored, where we kept the rest of our doubts and reservations. As Scarlett O'Hara might have said, we'd worry about it tomorrow.

I had a pretty clear sense from the onset that our relationship would have dramatic consequences, and I was right. Among the things I learned in the course of it (some of them quite obvious, others less so):

An affair like ours is as exhausting as it is exhilarating. Apart from being forty years too old for it now, I'd never go through it again, I couldn't, *even if I wanted to.*

In the course of it such things as logic, common sense, and practical considerations melt into an insignificant puddle. However, such a puddle does not stay insignificant forever.

Disengagement from a once-loved spouse or partner can be much harder than anticipated. Residual feelings can be considerable.

Guilt, for many of us, can be deferred but not extinguished. In the course of our supervisory sessions, Charlie Boren liked to make use of the legend of the Pied Piper of Hamelin. One of his favorite sayings was an admonition, "The Piper will be paid." To which I'd add, "Yes, and the interest can be considerable."

The extraordinarily difficult transition from a no-holds-barred affair to a viable long-term relationship may be conveniently put aside in the short run but not forever.

Jean-Paul Sartre summed it up nicely. "We are our choices."

Another quote that has some relevance here—from George Washington, of all people. In 1795 he wrote this to his step-granddaughter: "Beware of an involuntary passion . . . In the composition of the human frame there is a great deal of inflammable matter."

I've likened the next few years to a long ride on Space Mountain at the Magic Kingdom. Taking a rollercoaster ride is one thing, but taking it in the dark is something else.

Around the midpoint of my residency, Alice and I separated. The IOL owned a three-story house on Maple Avenue, one of the streets adjacent to it. Within it, modest apartments were available to residents at modest rates. One of them became my home for the balance of my residency. Sam Silverman, also newly separated, had another apartment. Sulaiman Marikar, not yet married, had a third.

I compare the sojourn on Maple Avenue to a poorly edited home movie of the type popular before camcorders and smartphones. A dark, choppy movie, shot almost entirely at night, with a jumble of intersecting plotlines. Judy and Toby made frequent appearances. Alice made appearances too, less frequently. Toby, just shy of four when his parents separated, seemed to be dealing all right with the separation. But I very much wanted that to be the case, which may have skewed my vision. The apartment was furnished with beanbag chairs, a makeshift bookcase of bricks and boards, and two lava lamps. A few tables and a bed, and a small black and white TV set with uncertain reception, a small kitchen. A film noir ambience prevailed.

I can't remember many other details since I wasn't there very often. In addition to the usual work at the IOL, I was now moonlighting at a hospital in Massachusetts. Sometimes I made four or more round trips there in the course of a weekend. I worked primarily in their ER, well-patronized by the suicidally depressed, decompensated schizophrenics, and agitated demented patients brought from local nursing homes. Illicit drugs were beginning to affect the landscape too. Cocaine and heroin had yet to become widely used, but they were hardly rarities. Bad trips from psychedelics occurred commonly though. I also met with patients hospitalized on their psychiatric unit. A few of the attendings were loath to come in on weekends.

Later, toward the end of my residency, I began to moonlight at a state-run facility in Connecticut that housed residents with profound cognitive impairment. Some couldn't walk or talk or were permanently incontinent. Their meds consisted primarily of tranquillizers and anticonvulsants, since controlling their outbursts remained a chief concern. Violence toward themselves was also a concern, and many of them wore padded helmets because they might spend hours banging their heads against a wall. In addition to handling their neuropsychiatric meds, I did general medical work—simple suturing, prescribing antibiotics for strep throats, ordering labs. During a hepatitis outbreak I gowned up, wore a surgical mask, and put paper booties on my shoes when I made rounds.

Admittedly, my stay at Maple Avenue involved more than overwork and angst. I read to Toby, played with him, and took him out whenever possible. I also took him to eat at the IOL's cafeteria, where nurses fussed over him, which he relished. Judy came over when she could. No easy undertaking since her life was as helter-skelter as my own. We told ourselves things would get better—easier—and sometimes we believed it. Sam and Sulaiman provided companionship and support.

Official psychiatric nomenclature describes a condition known as borderline personality disorder. It's characterized in the *Diagnostic and Statistical Manual of the American Psychiatric Association* (DSM5) by "a pervasive pattern of instability of interpersonal relationships, self-image and affect, and marked impulsivity." In varying combinations, it may include frantic efforts to avoid real or imagined abandonment, alternating idealization and devaluation of significant others, impulsivity regarding sex and substance abuse, a sense of emptiness, and intense and inappropriate anger. I have toyed with the notion that those who are going through a bad divorce or breakup become temporary borderlines, and I acknowledge that this was quite possibly the case with me.

Judy and I juggled work, children's schedules and doctors' appointments—she, too, had started therapy. We met with lawyers. We sought out friends, some of whom accepted the new regime and some who didn't. We drank too much. Sometimes we enjoyed each other as we used to, and sometimes we brought a new tension and irritability to our times together. A few times we halfheartedly broke up. In the midst of all this, I started a private practice, lest everything else become too humdrum.

We couldn't remember what it was like to be well-rested.

On a spring afternoon in 1976, returning from a seminar on Hilton Head Island, Judy and I waited at the Charleston airport for the flight back to JFK. By now we felt decades older than the passion-blinded couple who'd fallen in love a mere three years earlier. In a word, we felt battered.

Over miniature bottles of bourbon, the way they sold hard spirits at the airport then, we decided to get married. We set a date for four months hence.

⁓

MARRIED LIFE PROVED MUCH harder than expected, and we never expected it to be easy. Scores of changes to get used to. I now had a second wife and two stepdaughters, she had a second husband and a stepson. We went about the daunting business of moving into the new home we jointly owned. There was the matter of combining possessions, of determining what to keep and what to discard. In addition to a private practice, already burgeoning, I saw hospital patients and consulted at a nursing home. I put in fifty hours a week now, sometimes closer to sixty, and Judy had to adjust to my schedule. She also worked part-time in my office.

We came from radically different backgrounds. Revealingly, the wedding cake displayed a Star of David and a shamrock. Our tastes were worlds apart in music, movies, furniture, and especially food. Judy favored standbys like meatloaf and macaroni and cheese; I liked Szechuan and sushi. Once, at a local deli-restaurant, I ordered borscht, gefilte fish, and a chocolate egg cream. She ordered tomato bisque, chicken pot pie, and a cup of tea. As the waitress left our table, Judy asked me, "Do you think she knows which of us is Jewish?" I viewed travel as a blessing while she viewed it as more of a penance.

We had to get used to each other's myriad quirks and habits. These can be concealed in the course of an impassioned affair or else written off as cute or endearing. But they become less cute and endearing when two people are together for years or decades.

Sloane and Elizabeth, Judy's daughters, were nine and four when we married, and Toby was five. As adults, her daughters became the closest of friends, but as children they turned sibling rivalry into high art. A skirmish might take place at any time, and we could hardly drive to a Wendy's without one. The notorious stresses and pitfalls that arise in the course of building a blended family were much in evidence. There occurred a slew of quiet or not-so-quiet resentments and sullen silences. Sloane and I, especially, took a long time to get used to each other, and Judy often found herself in the middle of an impasse between her older daughter and husband. Elizabeth and I appeared to do better. Despite experience with two younger sisters, I found living with two stepdaughters a foreign country, and learning the language did not come easily to me. No doubt Judy felt the same when Toby came up for visits. When he returned to Texas, she gave a near-audible sigh of relief. I, by contrast, began to miss him as soon as his plane took off.

Two dramatically different and telling events occurred in the first year of our marriage.

The first took place in December when my parents and sisters came to visit. Toby came too, on his maiden solo flight from Texas. A bad omen: Alice didn't bring him to the airport on time and he missed his flight. He arrived on a later one, tired and out of sorts.

Everything about the visit became a debate if not an argument. Which movie or restaurant to go to, which TV programs to watch. We aborted an outing when we had an untimely flat tire on I-84. My father, not at his best, fought constantly with Lisa and Lolly, who added to the *je ne sais quoi* by fighting with each other. He insisted on calling the Christmas tree a Hanukah Bush, to the bewilderment and disapproval of Sloane and Elizabeth. One evening I thought the mood might be made merrier if I built a fire. But I piled on too much wood, and the fire turned excessively hot. Hot enough to crack and shatter the glass siding that formed a semicircle around the fireplace.

The week summarized everything difficult, tense, and frankly wrong about the new regime.

The second event took place the following March when Judy and I threw a St. Patrick's Day party. It was also something of a housewarming, the first time we hosted a major social occasion in our new home. Thirty or maybe fifty of our friends showed up. Hard to tell since it was more like an open house, and people came and went at all hours. A genuinely festive mood prevailed, enhanced by the supercharged bowl of punch we concocted, replenished throughout the night. There was plenty of Guinness on hand as well. Irish music resonated through the house, and a few of the guests did Irish step-dancing in the kitchen. The assortment of people worked out well too. Charlie Boren and Terry Holcombe were there with their wives, and Sam, and the now-engaged Sulaiman with his fiancée. Our old and new neighbors came and several of Judy's girlhood friends from Massachusetts. Also one of my sisters and Judy's brother and sister-in-law.

It was everything a St. Patrick's Day party ought to be, and more. No one seemed to want to leave. A gathering that led us to believe that maybe, just maybe, the worst was over. It is possible that God met our optimism with a cackling laugh.

I wondered, which would be the more accurate harbinger of

our future, the December or March event? One could only hope it would be the latter.

~

Slowly and painfully, we carved out roles as stepparents. Two steps forward and one backward, and often vice versa. There were times when we appeared to be making baby-steps of progress, and other times when we wondered what the hell we'd gotten ourselves into.

There was a scattering of happy interludes—a trip to Cape Cod or the Connecticut shore in the summer, trick-or-treating with Elizabeth at Halloween (Sloane demurred). There were Thanksgivings and Christmases and birthdays that went smoothly, when the blended family actually seemed to be blending.

A dog provided a number of lighter moments.

Lest our lives become too staid and somber, Judy and I added Frisco to the household two years after we married. A mongrel—part terrier, part spaniel, and part sheepdog—Frisco combined the worst of their recessive genes. He had long, unkempt, and usually filthy hair, and attempts to groom him failed utterly. Nothing gave him as much pleasure as rolling in mud, especially after we showered him. He was stupid as sin. When I tried to teach him to retrieve, he only learned to fetch one particular stick; he couldn't generalize to the broader concept of *sticks*. I speculated that another brain cell would have made an even dozen.

Some of Frisco's doings became part of the family folklore. Neighbors kept a crèche on their lawn at Christmas, and one year Frisco tried to eat the Holy Family. Pick-your-own strawberry fields adjoined the house, and every summer people came to them from nearby towns. Frisco perturbed the pickers by sniffing at their nether regions as they bent over. A local cop came to the door when several of them complained. I entertained a vision of Frisco sitting in the back of a cruiser while the cop read him his rights. Although the dog had a generally good disposition (he loved playing with the children, who rode him, listened to him with my stethoscope, and put silly hats on him), he hated cats. This was significant, in that Sloane had a cat named Fifi. The luckless feline was shy and skittish to begin with, and Frisco delighted in terrifying her. She spent most of her time cowering behind the laundry room door while he growled at her from the other side. After she died under suspicious circumstances, I believe she was reincarnated as a box of Tide.

CHILDREN AND STEPPARENTS GREW close, eventually. Rome wasn't built in a day, but once they finally built it, it lasted a while. Sloane and I, long inclined to keep an emotional distance from each other, had put together a viable relationship. By the time she left for college in the mid-1980s we'd grown to love each other, perhaps to our own surprise. The same held true for Judy and Toby.

To date we've remained together for over forty years, to the amazement of others and sometimes ourselves. We have weathered the death of family members, including three parents and one sibling, the death of friends and pets, our children's wild rides through adolescence, my preoccupation (self-absorption?) with psychiatry and writing, Judy's traditional Irish temper, a thousand arguments and squabbles of varying intensity, and life-threatening illnesses. We have weathered the standard narcissistic insults of advancing years. So far, anyway.

I believe the marriage has survived for four main reasons. First, we still love each other despite occasional appearances to the contrary. Second, from the beginning we've shared a gut-deep dread of going through another divorce. Third, we've grown used to each other—grown used to the long, long list of our habits, likes, dislikes, and preferences. We could order a meal for each other, or read a book or hear a joke and know with near-certainty how the other would react to it.

And fourth—in my case, anyway—I believe that if our marriage crashed and burned, the best part of my life would have ended.

Years later, in sifting through the endless assortment of my junk and memorabilia, I came upon a poem written shortly after our marriage. Not deathless literature but a fair capturing of my mindset at the time. Parts of it read as follows:

This time we'll do it right
Clergy blessed,
Guests paying homage not so much to our
wedding as our survival . . .
We are ten years older, no longer children
huddling together
On a raft in high seas
If once we took marriage too lightly
Springtime pranks we played upon ourselves
We think of it too much now
Studying the doubts and risks
Like bugs under a microscope . . .
This time we'll do it right because
The rubble will kill us next time
Will rain down on us like boulders
If we don't

CHAPTER IX

PSYCHIATRY IN THE ROUGH

A conversation that seems of no great importance at the moment can have life-altering consequences. So it was in 1975, two weeks before I finished my residency at the IOL, when Dr. Veeder accosted me after Matins. Ray Veeder, born and bred in the U.K., distinguished and borderline-imperious with his abundant white hair and perfectly tailored three-piece suits, served as the IOL's medical director. A British Army officer from 1939 to 1946, he still looked the part. His quarter century in the United States had made no dent in his English accent.

Ray knew I would shortly be leaving the IOL and planned to practice in the Greater Hartford area. "I'm an advisor to the Whiting Forensic Institute," he told me, "and they could use another psychiatric consultant. Do you think you might have a few open hours?"

"I think so," I replied. I'd be lurching into private practice with two patients and an otherwise empty schedule. If I didn't fill a lot more of my time, and quickly, I might have to start a sideline like walking dogs or driving a school bus. As a last resort I could always work at a McDonald's drive-thru. *Hello, I'm Doctor Goodwin, would you like fries with that?*

I knew next to nothing about Whiting, so Ray filled me in. Better known as WFI, halfway between Hartford and New Haven, it straddled the line between DOC (Department of Corrections) and DMHAS (Department of Mental Health and Addiction Services). It mainly housed those who couldn't be held elsewhere, intractably violent inmates and patients from the state's mental hospitals who posed ongoing danger to other patients and staff. It also held inmates accused of major and well-publicized crimes who underwent extensive psychiatric evaluations. Another group of Whiting residents consisted of patients found incompetent to stand trial or not guilty by reason of insanity.

I went there for a perfunctory interview. It's possible they'd have hired anyone with a medical license, no felony convictions, and a pulse.

I FOUND MYSELF WORKING in a sprawling structure full of security checkpoints, locked steel doors, and windowless corridors. Not an enticing workplace. The plan was that I'd stay there only until I had a viable private practice and gotten on my feet financially. After that I'd have no further dealings with the criminal justice system. God, no doubt, laughed heartily.

Never had I knowingly treated anyone who'd committed a violent crime, nor had I set foot in a correctional facility. I was therefore nonplussed to come face to face with high-profile gangbangers, brutalizers of children, rapists, and stalkers. There was also the occasional serial killer, one of whom came to WFI the first month after my arrival. Wayne Mills—about 5'5", chunky and unmuscular, soft-spoken and bespectacled—looked more like the assistant manager of a struggling Dairy Queen than a murderer. He'd killed his first victim shortly before his sixteenth birthday.

I found WFI oppressive and disheartening but much more interesting than anticipated. Not to mention educational. By that point, I'd seen stark poverty, and hellacious diseases of mind and body, and soul-crushing despair. But I'd had no firsthand exposure to the violently psychotic or to those whose acts made them candidates for death row. I knew a fair bit about evil, or so I thought, but my knowledge came primarily from books. Such knowledge doesn't measure up to talking with someone who has killed people and then recounted the crimes without a scintilla of remorse.

IN THE EARLY 1980s I went from WFI to Corrections, to do consulting work in jails and prisons proper. My first position was at the Hartford Jail.

Jails are different from prisons. You go to jail when you're arrested, whether for shoplifting or felony murder. If you can't make bail, you stay there through your trial. Sentences are short, rarely more than a year. Jails are therefore in constant flux, with inmates who come and go daily. They're a disparate assortment of nineteen-year-olds with no priors and repeat offenders with four-page rap sheets, of a few well-educated businessmen accused of white-collar crimes, and old men with wet brains who think Gerald Ford is still president.

The Hartford Jail squatted along a flat drab stretch of the city known as the Meadows, near the city's railway yards. An overgrown pillbox, it looked as though the architect had tried to create something as bland and self-effacing as possible. If so, the architect succeeded.

The corridors were brighter than those of WFI, with walls of peach and light blue that broke up stretches of grayish-white. Floors gleamed with hundreds of coats of wax. It held 547 inmates when I started there—the number is close to a thousand now. COs and inmates bantered easily, as if some of them were old friends (which might have been the case since their backgrounds were often similar). Not so in prisons, where COs and inmates typically viewed each other with suspicion if not open enmity.

Despite service at WFI, or maybe because of it, I still had qualms about working in correctional settings. This did not relate to danger, which I'd learned to accept as a given. It had more to do with socio-economic factors. Like most of my private patients, I was indelibly middle-class, white, and living in the suburbs. I wondered if I could establish rapport with a clientele so different from myself: the urban poor, in deep trouble, largely Black and Hispanic. I also wondered if practicing psychiatry—that is, doing anything beyond prescribing medications—was really possible. A major goal of psychiatry, after all, is freedom. The freedom from the excess baggage of old conflicts and traumas, from the vice-grip of depression and thought disorder. How, I wondered, could a psychiatrist help patients to pursue such freedom in a place so patently unfree?

In my experience, healthcare personnel who worked in Corrections ran the gamut from professionals as good as you'd find anywhere to quacks and burnouts. An example of the first group was Louise Homicki, the head nurse at the Hartford Jail. She assisted the doctors and dentists who came there, treated minor and not-so-minor illnesses and injuries, did a great deal of impromptu counseling, made up staff schedules, arranged appointments with outside specialists, ordered supplies, and kept track of mountains of paper records. She treated inmates with something akin to solicitude but neither patronized nor coddled them. A kind, tough woman, and harder to sweet-talk than a ghetto loan shark. She had a formidable job, and she did it very nearly perfectly.

On my first day there, Mrs. Homicki brought me to my office in the hospital wing. To call the hospital wing a *hospital* was a stretch. They performed no surgery, not even simple suturing. Diagnostic tools consisted of an unused centrifuge and a box of Ketostix for testing urine. Its cells resembled those elsewhere in the jail, with no resemblance to real hospital rooms. The miniscule office lacked windows, skylight, and—most crucially—a phone. By contrast, in the prisons where I later worked, every office had a phone and a panic button. The office's sole decoration consisted of an incongruous calendar with lush Hawaiian beach scenes.

I rarely spent more than twenty minutes with an inmate, thirty minutes tops. The predominant symptom, by far, was insomnia. Not surprising, in that jails are noisy places where lights don't dim completely. Fear of a physical or sexual assault compounded the insomnia. They didn't occur routinely but they did occur. I soon learned that an element of paranoia among inmates was useful and likely necessary. As the civil rights activist Eldridge Cleaver wrote in the 1960s, "It's not paranoia if they're really out to get you."

I saw other symptoms in countless combinations. Many inmates were depressed to varying degrees, and no small percentage of them were psychotic. In two typical weeks I saw a wider range of psychopathology than in two months of private practice. It wouldn't have been unusual to treat a suicidally depressed chronic schizophrenic with neurological problems from repeated head trauma and considerable cognitive impairment. Problems with substance abuse compounded the picture. "What drugs do you use?" I routinely asked. A common answer, "Whatever I could get."

It was at the jail where I met my second serial killer, Michael Ross—his real name; his case became a matter of public record. Michael was convicted of raping and strangling women, most of them in Eastern Connecticut. His victims of choice were in their teens and early twenties with long dark hair. It wasn't lost on me that my stepdaughters fit the bill exactly. By chance my assignment to different facilities paralleled Michael's transfers to the same ones, and our relationship lasted almost a decade.

As a result of Michael's second trial, in which I testified as an expert witness—they reversed the first verdict on technicalities—he was sentenced to die. After eleven years of incarceration, he received a lethal injection in 2005, becoming the first inmate executed in the state since 1960. His death was basically a suicide enabled by the state since he'd relinquished all appeals. Most likely he could have stayed alive until Connecticut did away with capital punishment altogether in 2012.

An articulate man of well above average intelligence, he may have been the only Ivy League graduate in the U.S. to receive a death penalty (Cornell, Class of 1981). He talked openly about his crimes, at times with a narcissistic flair, but at other times with what may, in fact, have been regret. I found it hard to decide if it was genuine.

Years later though, when I met with Michael in prison, I came to believe it was. He'd begun to receive Provera, a synthetic female hormone normally prescribed for contraception and various gynecological symptoms. It also acts as a testosterone antagonist and can be used to treat certain male sex offenders. In Michael's case it worked well. He described its effect in this way: "My thoughts about rape and murder were like living with a college roommate who had the stereo on, full blast, twenty-four hours a day. With Provera I could still hear the stereo but as if it was at the end of a long corridor, far away from me, with the door shut."

Provera may cause hepatic damage, however, an uncommon but serious and potentially fatal side effect. Michael's liver enzymes began to rise, and they discontinued it. He was willing to sign a waiver releasing the state from all liability if he went into liver failure, but they wouldn't reorder it. He requested another medication, depot Lupron. They didn't want to give it to him either on the grounds that it was too expensive; there was no generic equivalent available at the time. Michael threatened to sue in order to get it, and the state gave in. His position was clear; "I want to die like a human being and not a wild animal. And that's what I am, a wild animal when I have those thoughts."

At the other end of the inmate continuum was Norman Funk. Only twenty-two when I met him, he'd already had five priors, always for misdemeanors—disorderly conduct, criminal trespass, petty theft, and the like. A typical scenario: he got drunk, began to yell and scream in a donut shop, refused to leave, and got arrested.

Tall, pale, and obese, with a goofy half smile and an IQ of about 80, he was not unlikeable. Though he professed to hate jail, I suspect he felt pretty comfortable there. The COs regarded him almost fondly, like a big oafish dog who snaps once in a while and pees on the curtains but is basically good-natured. He caused few problems in general population except for his suicidal gestures, such as trying to slash his wrist with the bottom edge of a tube of toothpaste. "Goddamn, guess I fucked up again, Doc," he said when we met afterward, flashing his goofy half smile.

Diagnostically, it's easier to say what he wasn't than what he was. He wasn't psychotic, depressed, or unduly anxious. He wasn't bipolar or autistic. He didn't have an organic brain disease or a seizure disorder. Although usually drunk when arrested, he wasn't even clearly an alcoholic. He made me think of a term discarded from earlier psychiatric nomenclature, *Inadequate Personality Disorder*. For whatever reasons, such a person's ability to cope effectively with the world for any sustained period approached nil. Put more simply, he was three enchiladas short of a Mexican banquet.

I thought it likely Norman Funk would spend most of his life behind bars, probably for offenses no more serious than creating a ruckus in a donut shop.

PART OF MY JOB was to determine if an inmate might be malingering. The benefit of feigning insanity is clear-cut. While a stay in the state hospital system is no picnic, it's still preferable to time in Corrections. Once there, the ex-inmate will pull himself together and be probated to a community mental health center, or so he hopes. He could thereby lose freedom for months instead of years or decades. Of course this can backfire, a point made forcefully in *One Flew Over the Cuckoo's Nest*.

It's more difficult than you might think to feign insanity convincingly. The speech and mannerisms of a true psychotic—the sharp breaks in the middle of sentences, the random laughs and grimaces as he responds to hallucinations, the rapid-fire mood changes—would tax the efforts of a gifted actor. To stick a banana in your ear and say that aliens from outer space are after you does not suffice.

Elliot Winkler's crazy act was much better than most. A few

weeks after his arrest, his behavior began to change drastically. Hitherto fairly sociable, he secluded himself in his cell, mumbling incoherently as he paced and postured. Hitherto fairly calm, he jumped menacingly whenever someone approached him.

I first met Elliot after his transfer to the hospital wing. Sitting on his cot in yellowed underwear, his long hair unkempt, he lived amidst a clutter of bits of food and clots of toilet paper although COs described him as fastidious when first arrested. Attempts to talk with him proved fruitless. At times he rambled about Hitler and Charles Manson, but mainly he didn't talk at all. Once though, when he did talk, he told me that voices instructed him to rid the world of Blacks and Jews. For the most part he sat perfectly still, but every so often he yanked himself off the cot and circled aimlessly around his cell. A third-year medical student might have diagnosed him as a paranoid schizophrenic.

The next week a medic approached me. "Listen, Doc, I think Winkler's faking it. I overheard him on the phone with his lawyer yesterday, and he was clear as a bell. But as soon as he saw me, he started that garbage about Hitler and Manson."

"If he's not crazy, he should be on Broadway. It's the best imitation of a psychosis I've ever seen."

"Talk to him again. You might be surprised."

The next time we met, Elliot launched into his usual routine. I interrupted him in a neutral tone. "Mr. Robertson thinks you're trying to con us. He heard you on the phone with your lawyer."

No response. I pressed further. "'You spoke completely normally,' he said."

Still no response. "It must be hard to keep up this act."

Elliot's face changed. The grimacing stopped, and his eyes began to well up. He lapsed into a long silence. "All right," he said finally, "I'm not crazy. I can't stand the idea of going back to prison, that's all. I'm only twenty-five, and I've already spent three years there. I've been raped, I've been ripped off too many times to count. I'll do okay on the street for a while, but then I go back to drugs and get arrested again. I'm not crazy but I need help. I need to find out how to stay clean . . . how not to make such a goddamn mess of things." He was crying now. All traces of craziness had vanished.

Elliot went back to the general population. Eventually he entered a residential drug treatment program, so he avoided another stint in prison after all. I don't know if he managed to stay clean and steer clear of subsequent incarcerations. When you work in Corrections, it can be hard to impossible to get follow-up data on your patients.

I still marvel over his portrayal of a psychotic, a performance worthy of Leonardo DiCaprio or Bryan Cranston.

I worked at the jail for three years, although I did another stint there in the late 1990s. I estimate that I saw a thousand inmates, or maybe twice as many. In addition to native-born Americans of every race and background they included Poles and Jamaicans, Mexicans and Cambodians, an Ethiopian and an Israeli. They included illiterates and a few with postgraduate degrees and a few with IQs worthy of Mensa. They included burglars and computer programmers, a host of teenagers and at least one septuagenarian.

As noted, some of my inmate patients had a significant number of prior arrests. In my more dour moments I judged the sociopaths to have become more sociopathic, the schizophrenics crazier, and the Norman Funks more inept at life, but I regarded them as otherwise unchanged. Moments of therapeutic triumphs occurred as frequently as harvest moons. I should note, however, that at times I felt the same about some of my private patients.

I had to remind myself that in psychiatry, as other specialties, one may help patients without curing them ... that, given the presence of severe and usually multiple diagnoses, any gains were worthwhile, however small and short-lived ... that every so often my inmates flirted with insight and even with the unprecedented notion they might make positive changes in their lives.

I DON'T KNOW IF DOC still functions the same way, but it used to move its personnel around quite a bit throughout the state. At one point or another, I pinch-hit in five other jails and prisons. When I left the Hartford Jail, however, I worked primarily at Connecticut's largest facility, in Somers, now known as the Osborn Correctional Facility (OCI).

It housed about 2,500 inmates when I started there. A city within itself, it spread over 900 acres. The complex included administrative offices, classrooms, a chapel and library, a greenhouse and baseball diamond. It also had a helipad. Its workshops turned out products as varied as dentures and grandfather clocks. Conjugal and family visits took place in an adjacent trailer park.

At the time, Osborn was a Level 5 facility (maximum security). Considerations of security were evident from the time you parked your car. Above you, rolls of razor-sharp barbed wire topped off two rows of cyclone fencing. You had to go through three separate checkpoints before you made it to the belly of the beast.

I worked mostly in the mental health unit (MHU), but periodically

I made rounds. Accompanied by a nurse or social worker, I traversed the most restrictive cellblocks. Any inmate could approach me with any manner of complaint or request:

"—you got something to help me sleep? Half the time I'm awake till dawn."

"—that stuff you gave me for depression ain't workin' . . ."

"—my sister, she's dying of AIDS. I need to talk to someone about it."

"—hearin' voices again . . ."

"—my cellie snores like a pig. Can you get me some earplugs?"

Of course not all inmates availed themselves of mental health services. The dialog might also go like this:

"How are you doing, Mr. Brown?"

"Get outta my face, motherfucker."

In the MHU, I often saw inmates nonstop from the moment I arrived until I left. Self-referred for the most part, they also came to me by way of COs or medical personnel. As in the jail, inmate visits didn't last long, almost never more than twenty minutes. They focused on meds—what worked and what didn't, or was a dosage too high or low, or did they cause side effects. Discussion might have touched on other things, albeit not at length. I recall snippets of inmates' backstories, such as how one of them was conceived when his mother had been raped at fourteen. Sometimes—not commonly, but not rarely either—inmates brought up their offenses. One such instance was when an inmate, serving time for vehicular manslaughter, told me how a much-loved girlfriend had died in an accident caused by his drunk driving. As in the jail, inmates might flirt with insight. An extraordinarily simple statement—*Maybe you don't have to botch everything up the way your father did*—can elicit a new way of looking at his life. "I never thought about it like that," he might say. He might realize, sometimes for the first time, that he had options.

But more than a few inmates sought MHU appointments for reasons unrelated to psychiatry. They might have sought them because they wanted meds that enabled them to glide through their sentences in a mindless haze. Or because their lawyers thought it would impress the parole board. Or because at least it would get them out of their cells for half an hour or so—because it would break up the staggering monotony of serving one's sentence. Loss of freedom, loss of privacy, and a constant threat of violence may be the three things inmates hate most about prison, but boredom and monotony would come in close behind.

When I began to work at the Hartford Jail in the early 1980s, AIDS was just becoming widely known. By the time I came to Somers though, it had burgeoned into a full-blown and highly publicized epidemic. Since inmates could not be tested for it against their will, the exact incidence within the DOC population remained uncertain. But at least three percent of inmates were thought to be HIV-positive, probably a low estimate. This was of more than passing interest to DOC psychiatrists since ten to fifteen percent of HIV-positive patients presented with neuropsychiatric problems (confusion, low-grade dementia, hallucinations, and delusions) before showing other symptoms. At autopsy, over ninety percent of patients who die of AIDS will have evidence of central nervous system involvement.

Most of the lifesaving and life-prolonging drugs weren't yet available, so a diagnosis of AIDS was a de facto death sentence. Beyond the anger and depression the diagnosis entailed, there might be an existential concern. *I want to do something useful before I die.* Not easy to address, especially when the patient faced decades of incarceration, and his chances of release before he died might be minimal to nil.

───

PEOPLE HAVE CONSIDERABLE, IF morbid, curiosity about prisons, similar to their curiosity about train wrecks and tsunamis. Consider the popularity of movies like *The Birdman of Alcatraz* and *The Shawshank Redemption*, consider TV shows like *Oz* and *Orange is the New Black*. They often asked me what it's like to work in one. Some of the more common questions follow—

Were you afraid there? Answer: Not as a rule, but that warrants qualification. Those who work amidst potential dangers need to maintain a delicate balance. They can never be unmindful of these dangers, but they're ill-advised to dwell on them. A measure of healthy denial is appropriate. *I will keep my eyes open and take no unnecessary risks, and chances are I'll be okay.* No doubt this mindset also proves useful to police officers, firefighters, coal miners, and window washers on skyscrapers. Apropos, I learned to have great respect for the instincts of COs. If one of them said, "You'd better look out for Joe Green today . . . the guy just doesn't look right to me," I'd have been an imbecile to ignore it.

An inmate attacked me precisely once in over twenty years. We had a decent relationship, or so I thought. My attacker, Hal, a chronic schizophrenic kept marginally sane by large doses of antipsychotics, was a large but slow man serving life after killing his parents and the family dog. When I told friends and relatives about him, almost all of them had the same reaction. "*The dog?* Why the hell did he kill *the dog?*"

Periodically Hal took breaks from medication, after which he promptly decompensated. Once when he did this, he took a swing at me. I swerved to the side; no harm done. At the time I played a lot of racquetball, and I had good reflexes. A useful reminder, though, about the dangers of complacency.

Are inmates treatable? Answer: Yes and no. Almost any psychiatric ailment you can find outside a prison, you can find within it—from bipolar disorder to body dysmorphic disorder (a morbid preoccupation with real or imagined flaws in your appearance), from panic attacks to posttraumatic stress disorder. Meds that work outside can work inside as well. Even sex offenders, a notoriously hard group to treat, might be helped. Through the years, OCI pioneered work with them, involving a combination of meds and group therapy.

We should note, however, that many inmates have no interest in treatment or wish to change in any meaningful way. And some inmates—surprisingly few, but memorable out of proportion to their number—struck me as not merely untreatable but genuinely evil.

How has working in a prison changed you? Answer: First and foremost, it gave me a heightened appreciation of personal freedom. The freedom to take a walk on an autumn day, to get in the car and see a friend on the spur of the moment. The freedom to do something as simple as throwing a football around with one of my grandsons or dallying over a second cup of coffee on a Sunday morning. Imprisonment means losing control of your life to a degree most people would find inconceivable. Being told when you can leave a place (your cell) and when you must return to it; when you can eat and shower; when you can use a phone. And even the freedoms you do have might be stripped from you in a heartbeat.

Apart from that, it made me much more aware of the dark side of human nature. Given my interest in history, I'd learned something of atrocities through the ages, from the Roman treatment of early Christians to the Salem witch trials to the Holocaust. But to find myself dealing directly with committers of horrific acts took my knowledge of the dark side to a different level.

Lastly, it has led me to believe that those who've committed absolutely heinous crimes are still members of the human race, with all the hopes and dreams, all the good and bad memories and baggage that entails. The worst of us can show flashes of humanity. A well-known example: Hitler could be very nice to dogs and children, as long as the children were Aryans.

Inmates receive treatment from qualified health care professionals and often take medications costing thousands. They're sent to outside hospitals as needed, sometimes by helicopter. In other words, they may receive care that many law-abiding citizens can't afford. How could you defend this? Answer: I couldn't. How could I? It's one of about a hundred reasons why an overhaul of American health care is overdue.

Are there times when you wished you'd never set foot inside a jail or prison? Answer: Of course. I was known to get tired of the panorama of razor-sharp barbed wire and cyclone fencing, tired of the security checks, and especially tired of the dour ambience. Beyond that, I heard things that were sickening, things I'd never tell anyone else because no one else should have to hear them.

Still, I would work in Corrections again if I had it to do over. It was endlessly interesting, and I believe it made me a better psychiatrist to have done it. I also feel the work I did was useful. At times.

I can sum it up in thus—I'm very glad I did it and equally glad to be out of it.

CHAPTER X

A DAY IN THE LIFE

As I began to think seriously about writing a memoir, I read—or reread, or listened to—twenty-five or so of those of others. Not an onerous undertaking. The list included books by Nobel Prize winners (Ernest Hemingway, Elie Wiesel), comedians (Tina Fey, Amy Schumer), and a nun who worked with Death Row inmates (Sister Helen Prejean, *Dead Man Walking*). Other authors included a psychiatrist stalked by a lovesick patient (Doreen Orion, *I Know You Really Love Me*), a pilot of 747s (Mark Vanhoenacker, *Skyfaring*), and a recovering sex and porn addict (Erica Garza, *Getting Off*). *The Bright Hour* by Nina Riggs is an unforgettable one, relating Ms. Riggs's living with metastatic breast cancer. A beautifully written book, poignant and life-affirming and—hard to imagine, but true—extremely funny in places. She didn't live to see its publication.

Among the most interesting and enjoyable was Anthony Bourdain's *Kitchen Confidential*. Bourdain's life experiences included working his way up from a scrubber of pots and pans to a master chef, running restaurants, writing crime fiction, producing TV shows, and going through rehab for heroin addiction. He literally ate his way around the world. The treats consumed include the still-beating heart of a cobra. He filmed a TV episode in Beirut when a war between Israel and Lebanon broke out, and he dined in Vietnam with Barack Obama. Bourdain's suicide left me, like many of his admirers, disturbed and mystified.

In *Kitchen Confidential,* Bourdain devoted a chapter to a typical working day. Doing a mental tally of supplies, the forequarters of lamb, the two cases of beef tenderloins. Fine-tuning the specials, like steamed cockles with chorizo. Sautéing, grilling, grinding, caramelizing. Overseeing an army of sous-chefs, waiters, busboys, and dishwashers. Soothing ruffled feathers. Tasting entrees, taking aspirin. The whole package.

I liked the idea and decided to borrow it. What follows, accordingly, is a rendition of a typical workday in my own life, occurring roughly between 1985 and 2005.

THE PROFESSIONAL DAY BEGINS at 7:45, at the Willow Grove Nursing Home and Rehabilitation Center, a few towns away from where I live. Of the dozen nursing homes where I worked through the years, Willow Grove is one of the two or three best. The staff tries hard to keep residents stimulated and involved. They offer gentle yoga, Scrabble tournaments, and concerts from orchestras and choirs of local high schools. They've painted rooms in soothing hues; they serve bland but tolerable food. The place doesn't smell of urine or feces, and old people aren't parked in front of TV sets all day, and the staff responds to call bells in a fairly prompt fashion. None of these things are true in other facilities familiar to me, where you wouldn't give your dog the food they serve, and bodily smells affront you as soon as you walk in, and the residents can wait an hour when they call for assistance.

Fabulous doesn't capture the way I feel about going to Willow Gove, but I have found nursing home work rewarding in carefully titrated doses. Residents may have fascinating stories if you take time to listen to them. Through the years I've met the widow of a diplomat—in the course of her husband's career, they lived in six different countries, from the Philippines to Ecuador to Morocco. I've met a veteran of World War I and a nurse who cared for polio patients in their iron lungs in the days before the Salk vaccine. I've met a woman of 103, still bright-eyed and clear of mind, who told me about coming from Lithuania at the age of nine and how she cried with joy when she sailed into New York and saw the Statue of Liberty.

When I consider the more memorable of my nursing home patients, two spring to mind right away. Mrs. Bellamy, London-born, came to America as a war bride in 1945. Widowed for fifteen years, she was in her eighties when she first became my patient. Full-faced and ruddy-cheeked, her white hair tucked into a net and her glasses tending to slip down her nose, she could have been a model for a Toby jug. They asked me to see her for irritability and mild anxiety. Apart from searching for words at times, she showed no significant cognitive impairment. She was lucid, appropriate, and rational except in one specific area: she was absolutely paranoid about the British royal family.

During the first meeting when I asked her innocuous questions about her sleep and appetite she interrupted me in mid-sentence. "Young man [I was fifty-five at the time], I must tell you something." After briefly pausing, she spoke with unmistakable anger and indignation. "The Queen—plays—*baseball!*" Her indignation ratcheted up a notch. "She *catches!*"

In my drearier moments, I've been known to summon up the image of Her Majesty behind home plate with chest protector and shin guards, her handbag over an arm, sending signals to the pitcher. One finger for a fastball, two for a curve, three for a changeup.

Unforgettable for a different reason was Greta Schwartzfeld. Going through her chart at the nurses' station before we met, I noted she was born in 1925 in Germany. She came to America in the early 1950s, gained citizenship, and did office work for half a century.

I introduced myself, and we shook hands. She spoke fluent English, her German accent still evident. Then, about ten minutes into the interview, I asked her a question I hadn't planned to ask, but the question came forth with a life of its own. "Did you ever see Hitler?"

"Oh, yes," she replied. I couldn't be sure, but I thought her eyes brightened. "In fact, I shook hands with him! We *loved* him, you know." She paused, a bit too long. "But we realized later that he was very bad."

So it was that I found myself a handshake away from a figure of consummate evil.

NURSING HOME WORK CAN be useful. Being heard can be useful to a person of any age, of course, but it goes beyond that. A depressed octogenarian can respond to treatment as well as a depressed teenager if you get the meds and dosage right. There's also the fact that about forty percent of Alzheimer's patients have psychotic symptoms. They can become terrified and miserable when they think others sneak into their rooms, intending to steal from them or assault them. A miniscule dosage of an antipsychotic can bring about marked improvement in their quality of life and renewal of their peace of mind. Apropos of Alzheimer's, as of this writing you can't cure it, but you can prescribe meds to slow it down. In other words, you can buy time.

The work can be challenging. I believe geriatrics is the easiest part of psychiatry to do badly and the hardest to do well. You can come into a nursing home and ask a few questions, overcharging Medicare in the process, order a low dose of Prozac or Risperdal, and be done with it. Or you can take your time going through the charts, often large and heavy enough to serve as doorstops. You can do a detailed mental status exam, a task that may take most of an hour. There's an array of physical illnesses that cause psychiatric symptoms, from multiple small cerebral infarcts to a urinary tract infection to pulmonary disease. Patients can't think straight if their brains don't get enough oxygen, an obvious point but commonly overlooked.

Medications and their interactions can cause symptoms too. Assume an elderly patient takes seven meds (in fact he may take twice as many). The possible interactions are seven times six times five, and so on. The total number of possible interactions exceeds five thousand.

My visits to Willow Grove usually include consultations on their Alzheimer's Unit, locked and isolated from the rest of the facility. At its onset, Alzheimer's can be mild and fairly subtle, but the Unit houses patients well past that stage. They need total care, from feeding to maintaining basic hygiene; they might laugh or cry or lash out violently for no reason. They may no longer recognize their children.

One of my patients was a distraught old man. *"I don't know who I am! I don't have any money!"* he yelled despairingly throughout the day. "Your name is Laurence Smith," the nurses tell him, over and over, with a patience I can only marvel at, "and you don't need any money here." Mr. Smith would calm down for a few minutes, and then the cycle would start over. In my view, the staff in such units fall into one of two groups, saints and burnouts.

I've come to terms with my own mortality, or at least I think I have. But the prospect of extreme old age frightens me considerably, a direct result of my time spent in nursing homes. In the course of working there, they've frequently asked me to see suicidal patients. I've talked with them, trying with them to devise ways of finding meaning and purpose and maybe even pockets of enjoyment in their remaining days. But these exercises often left me feeling hypocritical. More than a few times I've prayed silently as I left a nursing home, *Please, God, let me die before it comes to this.*

～

IN MID-MORNING, AFTER STOPPING for the third or fourth cup of coffee of the day, I arrive at the office where I see private patients.

Psychiatrists often subspecialize. They focus on geriatrics, substance abuse, eating disorders, and other areas. I, by contrast, have always been a generalist. Some of my patients have functioned at a notably high level, as doctors and lawyers and vice presidents of major corporations. Others have barely managed to totter through life, not unlike Norman Funk.

They may have had a dozen hospitalizations with another one possible at any moment. Some come to me with relatively clear-cut problems—panic attacks or depression, an ageing demented parent, or an unmanageable fifteen-year-old. Others may have a plethora of disorders and issues. Some developed paralyzing posttraumatic stress disorders from military service or chronic physical or sexual abuse. A job exposing a person to repeated horrific scenes can also lead to PTSD. In a session with a retired undercover cop, he voiced the opinion that anyone in law enforcement for over a year was more likely than not to be afflicted with it.

Most of my private patients are completely rational, but a few have been flagrantly psychotic. The old conventional wisdom held that a third of schizophrenics do well, a third get by with varying degrees of impairment, and a third improve minimally if at all. With more effective medications and earlier diagnoses, the outlook is brighter than it used to be, but you can still find plenty of patients in the last two groups.

One of the most fascinating phenomena in psychiatry is the patient with a circumscribed psychosis. In other words, someone who is psychotic but only in one narrow area. Mrs. Bellamy would fall into this group, given her rage against the baseball-playing late Queen. The delusion may be extremely specific, and it may be life-ruining. Consider Wallace Barnes.

Dr. Barnes, an internist, had just turned forty-five when we met. A local hospital referred him for follow-up care after three weeks as a psychiatric inpatient. His background was by and large unremarkable. He grew up in Canada, in Thunder Bay, Ontario. An exemplary student, he received his undergraduate and medical degrees from the University of Ottawa. He completed an internship and residency in Toronto.

During his internship, while on an oncology service, he treated a woman in her late seventies with advanced stomach cancer. She received chemotherapy intravenously, but the rest of her treatment was palliative. One night Wallace made a mistake in setting up her IV, administering too high a dose of the cytotoxic agent. A nurse caught the error, and they set up a new IV; no harm done. The patient died two weeks later, unsurprisingly.

Wallace finished his residency, subspecialized in pulmonary medicine, and married a successful caterer. The couple moved to America, became naturalized citizens, and had a son and daughter. Together with two other pulmonologists, he established a thriving practice.

Fifteen years later, for no discernible reason, he began to dwell on a patient he'd treated while an intern, the elderly woman with stomach cancer. He became convinced that his mistake had killed her, and terrible things would result from this. Her family would sue him and take everything, and his own family would become destitute, and he might even face criminal charges. He'd lose his medical license. His citizenship would be revoked, and he and his family would be deported back to Canada. But he wouldn't be allowed to practice there either. His wife, blaming him for their misfortunes, would divorce him. His children would have nothing to do with him. The family would be in ruins.

No one could reason with him, not his wife or his friends, not his partners or his pastor. His depression worsened, and he became suicidal. His hospitalization led to minimal improvement.

By the time we met, he'd already been on a number of medications, none of which had brought about much benefit. Somewhat despairingly, I tried an older and rarely used antipsychotic called pimozide. I remembered hearing that one of my colleagues found it useful with a circumscribed psychosis. Fortunately, it proved useful to Dr. Barnes. His thoughts about having killed the woman diminished and finally disappeared. His life reverted to what it had been, for the most part.

Another instance of someone with a solitary delusion occurred in a quite different context. For several years I was in a group that determined competency to stand trial. The format was as follows: a psychiatrist, psychologist, and social worker met with an inmate or a defendant out on bail. A competency exam should not be confused for an NGRI (not guilty by reason of insanity) evaluation. It focuses on three areas. Did those accused understand the charges against them? Did they have a basic knowledge of the legal system—what the judge did, what was the role of a witness, what did it mean to make a plea? Finally, could they work with an attorney who defended them?

One day, the team was meeting with a woman accused of possession with intent to sell. She did beautifully, sailing through the examination like a law student. Then, out of the blue, she asked the team, "Do any of you have Negro seizures?"

Taken aback, we asked her what she meant. She went on to tell us how Black people have the power to reach out invisibly and squeeze someone's genitals, thereby causing intense sexual arousal. She said this matter-of-factly, with no indication of an intent to deceive us.

The team members conferred among ourselves and said no, we hadn't had these seizures to our knowledge. She continued to sail through the rest of the exam, and we found her competent.

This brings up another point. Psychiatric work is usually serious and sometimes heartbreaking, but a sprinkling of lighter moments may punctuate it. Sometimes it comes when patients embark on a losing battle with the English language. When a man described his candlestein affair, for instance, or a police dispatcher told me how she found her DWI humbilizing. Humor may be intentional or otherwise. Mrs. Flugleman, a private patient, provided an example of the latter.

Bernice Flugleman, a hand-wringing woman in her early fifties, had recently married her second husband. There was trouble in paradise, and mainly the trouble involved sex. During our fourth or fifth meeting, Mrs. Flugleman provided more details. She recounted a conversation with her husband. "He said he wanted oral sex, he said everyone was doing it now. 'Melvin,' I said, 'I don't care what other people do, as long as they don't shove it down my throat.'" She told me this with no hint of attempted humor or irony. I nodded, biting down hard on my index finger.

When I passed on the story a few days later to Sulaiman Marikar, also in private practice then, he trumped me. He told me about a patient who announced to him, with utmost seriousness, "Doctor, I'm going to *lick* this problem with oral sex!"

Apropos of unintended humor regarding sex, there was a story that made the rounds about a teenage girl who came into a local emergency room. Taking her history, the nurse began to ask about her intimate relationships. "Are you sexually active?" the nurse asked.

"Not really," the girl answered. "Mostly I just lie there."

IT WILL SHOCK NO one that the subject of sex comes up often during psychiatric sessions. Despite the many facets of the sexual revolution—the availability of birth control, the surfeit of porn, the *anything goes* attitude to which many individuals give lip service—sex has yet to be turned into a carefree garden of earthly delights. By the time I'd been in practice a year or two, I thought I'd heard it all. From the perpetrators and casualties of infidelities, and from those who lusted after children, domestic animals, or shoes. From professional types, pillars of the community, who'd compulsively masturbate in public, and from the vice president of a major insurance company who liked to wander late at night in 24-hour supermarkets with his penis out. From men and women driven to the brink of suicide when their love affairs ended badly.

Whenever I thought I'd heard it all, though, I'd invariably find out I was wrong. Permutations of sexual acts, and their complications and consequences, approach the infinite.

There are also those who forego sex altogether, or who try to, or who are supposed to. At some point in the early1990s, within a period of eighteen months, I had these three patients:

Mr. A., a devout Catholic, felt devastated and betrayed on learning that his much revered uncle, a monsignor, had systematically molested his two sisters and four of his female cousins.

Ms. B., an accountant of forty-five, came to me after her discharge from the IOL. She'd been treated there for five weeks after a serious suicide attempt. The precipitating event was when her lover, a priest, broke off their affair of more than two decades.

Father C., a kind and placid man, had led a double life. By day he was the pastor at one of Hartford's larger churches. By night he cruised gay bars, where he found scores of transient partners. He'd just learned he was HIV positive.

The juxtaposition of these patients, seen within the same brief span, led me to conclude that celibacy works poorly for most people.

In the course of my professional life, from the 1970s until well into next century, I saw fewer patients traumatized by the Church's stance on sexual matters. Part of this no doubt relates to societal changes about sex, about what's viewed as normal and permissible and what isn't. I imagine the personality and temperament of Pope Francis has brought an additional softening. Still, I had plenty of patients, mainly older ones, who never got past the idea of sex as deeply disquieting. Timothy Mooney, for example, who spent most of his childhood in a Catholic orphanage in Maine. Mr. Mooney, a construction worker and World War II vet, had fought hand-to-hand in the islands of the South Pacific. Not a wimp, in other words. He was in his seventies when I treated him. Once, when we discussed his time in the orphanage, he talked of running to confession immediately after masturbating, praying he wouldn't get hit by a car and die before receiving absolution. He literally trembled when he told me about episodes like this, which had occurred six decades earlier.

From time to time I hear things that go beyond conventional experience and logic. Again, consider the stories of three patients. None of them were remotely psychotic, or hysterical, or given to flights of fancy. If anything, they were all unimaginative and rather phlegmatic.

Mrs. D., a retired librarian, came for treatment after the sudden fatal coronary of her husband whom she'd known since college. When I questioned her about her background, she told me about an incident from her childhood. "We lived in New York City. My grandmother, whom I adored, had died a few months earlier. I was seven. One day I was crossing the street in a hurry. As I left the curb, almost running, a car ignored a stop sign and careened around the corner. A hand pushed me backward and out of the way, hard enough to knock me off my feet. There was no one there. The car would have crushed me like a bug. My grandmother saved me, I don't have the slightest doubt about it."

Mr. E., the manager of a Credit Union, came to me after his wife left him. In his second session, he began to talk about his family of origin. For years he'd been estranged from his brother. "He got mixed up with heroin and cocaine, and his life went down the drain. He'd get violent. We lost track of how many times he was arrested. We did everything we could for him, but nothing worked. We even went to the exorcism."

Mr. E. went on to describe it. The vile smells, different from any he had known. His brother speaking in a voice completely unlike his own, an inhuman voice in an unintelligible language. The coup de grâce: his brother's levitation, a yard into the air. There were no hidden wires or platforms, no trick mirrors. "I don't expect you to believe me," concluded Mr. E. "I'm not sure I believe it myself. But I was there, and it happened."

Among the most impressive stories was that of Ms. F., a semi-retired attorney of sixty-two. She came to me because of a recurrence of panic attacks that had plagued her since her twenties. A recovering alcoholic, she told me what led to her sobriety. *"My father, an aunt and uncle, and two grandparents were all drunks. I knew I was becoming one myself, but I rationalized it away. I'd done well in college and law school, even made the law review. I'd never had alcohol-related crises like accidents or DWIs. I could quit anytime, I told myself, but I didn't want to."*

Then she told me about her son. *"He was eighteen. Drank a lot, but he kept his grades up, just like me. When I told him I was worried about his drinking, he sneered at me. 'Who are you to tell me about drinking, Ma?'"*

She stopped to wipe her eyes. *"He died a month after his high school graduation. His car bounced off a guard rail, fell down an embankment, and rolled over. He broke his neck. His blood alcohol was twice the legal limit."*

Ms. F. felt doubly devastated. Not only did she lose a son, but she knew her own drinking had set a terrible example for him. Her drinking accelerated—she drank throughout the day and most of the night. She could barely get out of bed, much less work. Her marriage was on the rocks.

She took a few moments to collect herself. *"Then, one night around Thanksgiving, a half a year after his death, I dreamt about him. It was like no dream I'd ever had, it was clearer and more realistic. I could make out every detail of his dress and appearance, every facial blemish, every scuffmark on his sneakers.*

"'So, Ma,' he asked me, 'what have you been doing since I died?'"

"'Nothing,' I told him. 'I just drink.'"

"He looked at me and smiled, a warm smile but sad too. 'Is that all my life meant to you?' And that was it, the dream ended."

She never drank again. No AA, or rehab, or helping hand from mental health professionals, or medications. She simply stopped, remaining sober for twenty years when I met her.

Just a dream? And if not a dream, what? My own view is that Shakespeare had it right, as always. *There are more things in Heaven and Earth . . . than are dreamt of in your philosophy.*

AT 5PM I LEAVE my office for the Laurel Ridge Recovery Center (LRRC), an outpatient treatment facility, the satellite of a private psychiatric hospital in another New England state. Its clientele consisted largely of dual diagnosis patients, namely those with substance abuse problems compounded by other psychiatric illnesses.

For roughly forty years, insurance companies and HMOs have progressively cut back on reimbursement for inpatient services for drug and alcohol problems. This, despite an estimated cost per annum to the American economy of $225 billion, a conservative figure. Not to mention the human toll. The lives ruined or ended prematurely because of illnesses and injuries due to substance abuse, the domestic violence and fractured marriages. Addiction-related murders, suicides, and incarcerations.

But insurance companies and HMOs have been somewhat more willing, or at least less unwilling, to pay for outpatient treatment. They also pay more willingly if the alcohol- or drug-addicted have other psychiatric disorders, which is more often than not the case. Hence, the burgeoning of facilities like LRRC.

Alcoholism and drug addiction are democratic phenomena, which may affect anyone from presidents to skid row derelicts. The clientele at LRRC mirrors that diversity. While consulting there, I saw high school students and retirees, high school principals and career criminals, a retired naval officer who served on nuclear submarines, an ex-nun and a stripper.

Most of what I did consisted of med evaluations and management. My LRRC patients had a full range of comorbidities, i.e., other conditions, ranging from Asperger's Syndrome to trichotillomania (the compulsive pulling out of one's hair). Many had cognitive loss caused or worsened by years of substance abuse. And predictably, they had an array of physical problems. Many had residual effects of injuries incurred when they were drunk or high. Cardiac, pulmonary, and digestive disorders. Neuropathies characterized by burning pain in their extremities. And predictably, patients with varying degrees of liver impairment. Your liver is a remarkably resilient organ, but that resilience has its limits if you continue to drink a fifth of vodka or a twelve-pack daily.

Some of my LRRC patients survived injuries and illnesses they had no business surviving. The hospital admitting clerk who'd had several episodes of massive upper GI blood loss from esophageal hemorrhaging. The petty criminal beaten in the head with a brick when a drug deal went bad, a beating that left him in a three-week coma. The abruptly suicidal woman who threw herself out of a car going seventy. And this, among the more unusual suicidal acts I've heard about: A man had a life-threatening allergy to bee stings. Despondent after his fourth or fifth unsuccessful stint in rehab, he went to a meadow on a sunny spring day without his EpiPen. He meandered through the meadow for two hours waiting to be stung, but he wasn't.

I did other things despite managing medication. I attended staff conferences, helped to compile treatment plans. I gave presentations open to the public on topics pertinent to addiction. One of the more important and often enlightening things I did was to meet with family members of LRRC patients. It's widely known that denial is commonly a feature of alcoholism and drug abuse. *Yeah, I drink a lot, but things aren't so bad*, a man might say, sounding altogether believable. *I provide for my family . . . never had a DWI . . . never fired, never even came in late. Besides, I was never violent.* Then his wife might tell me how he ruined holidays and birthdays with obscene outbursts and drunken gibberish, how he terrorized the children and pets, and how he only kept his job because of times she pleaded with his boss to keep him.

Among the LRCC patients I remember clearly are two women. The first was a Latina named Daniela Flores, striking with her dark eyes and abundance of shiny black hair. She had a lovely smile, but it never quite concealed a core despondency. Dr. Flores, an honors graduate of Georgetown before she went to medical school in Syracuse, had been a resident in trauma surgery. She'd lost her residency because of abuse and theft of opioids, and now she faced the possibility of losing her medical license. Her husband left her, returning to their native Chile with their four-year-old daughter. In effect, her treatment at LRRC was her last chance to redeem her family, career, and self-respect.

I've often wondered what became of her. I hope she got herself together, returned to medicine, and made a go of her marriage and family life. But it wouldn't shock me to learn she wound up on the streets.

But I do know what happened to Karen Cole. Karen, in her mid-thirties, owned a thriving arts and crafts store. Unmarried, she'd never lacked for men, often juggling two or three of them at a time. Tall, blonde, and buxom, she wasn't as classically beautiful as Daniela but made up for it with cheerfulness and skillful flirting. She was, to make use of an old phrase, a live wire. Always a heavy drinker, she'd gotten into trouble with amphetamines and cocaine as well.

Entering treatment largely because of pressure from her parents and one of her boyfriends, she took it half-seriously at best. She prematurely dropped out of the LRRC program, and no one there heard from her again.

Eight years later, I consulted part-time at a community health clinic in another town. The clinic's facilities included a respite unit, a kind of short-term halfway house that also served as a shelter. Its residents were impoverished, homeless, and severely impaired. One Monday morning, glancing at a list of the weekend admissions, I noticed her name. I'd always liked her and looked forward to seeing her again.

The woman I reencountered was a stranger. She looked more like seventy than forty-three. The thick blonde hair was thin and gray, the animated blue eyes had turned filmy and lifeless. Her formerly smooth complexion was splotchy and pitted. Well-dressed when we met before, she wore rags. But the most striking change was a lack of facial expression. Before, she'd been vivacious, given to mild histrionics. Now, her face had become a frozen mask. She registered no pleasure, pain, disappointment, or any other emotion. Toothless, she wore no dentures. Before, she talked at length and liked to go off on overly detailed tangents. Now, a typical sentence consisted of three of four words.

After our meeting, I took my time going through her intake chart. Waitressing after losing the arts and crafts store, and then clerking in a 7-Eleven. Fired from there, she started turning tricks. Her medical history included hepatitis C, several bouts of pneumonia with one episode of respiratory failure, and pelvic peritonitis from a ruptured ectopic pregnancy.

She didn't remember having met me, nor did she remember her period at LRRC. She could provide only the barest details and the vaguest generalities of the last five years. "I've been here and there . . . had treatment in different places, can't think of their names, been in different hospitals, can't say how many . . .

had a couple of arrests . . ." When I asked about her hopes and expectations, she drew a blank.

You'd be hard-pressed to come up with a more dramatic example of the worst that substance abuse can do. A socioeconomic downdrift, a deterioration of mind and body. Arrests, isolation, degradation, loss of hope. Karen Cole demonstrated all of it.

―

At twenty to eight, I left LRRC. Judy and I would have a late dinner while we shared snippets of our day. A TV program, maybe two, and a half hour of reading, and we'd go to bed.

Lying there, I might consider whether or not to take a Xanax—sleep had long ago become an iffy proposition. And I'd probably reflect on the workday just concluded. I liked my work, and by and large I liked my clientele. The bell curve comprised my sole knowledge of statistics, but I thought it covered nearly everything. It certainly covered how I felt about my patients. At one end were those I loved, whose sessions I looked forward to, whose terminations saddened me. Some of them I would have liked to sleep with (a line I never crossed. Among other considerations, I had a sentimental fondness for my medical license.) At the opposite end of the curve were those I couldn't stand. The abusers of spouses and children, the worst manipulators and the remorseless. In fairness, some of them would have been hard for Jesus Christ himself to cotton to. But the overwhelming majority of my patients were somewhere in the middle. That is, people I liked and cared about.

I'd helped a lot of them, or so I hoped. A desire to be useful was a basic part of who I was. I knew my limitations—I couldn't compel people to get better, or make them overcome the obstacles that kept them from getting better, or protect them from the consequences of their own bad judgment. I had no illusions about my omnipotence or omniscience.

Despite my initial and long-lasting ambivalence about a psychiatric career and my not-so-subtle attempts to sabotage myself, despite my flirtations with other specialties along the way, I was glad I'd chosen it. More than that: glad I'd stayed the course. Most of the time.

CHAPTER XI

THE LONG SHADOW OF TODD KILMER

He was tall and gawky, a shade over six feet, scarecrow-thin, his hair halfway between brown and blond. His gray eyes beheld the world with an avoidant fearfulness, as if he wondered what new source of hurt awaited him. He appeared younger than his age of seventeen, notwithstanding his height, and he looked scarcely old enough to shave. On meeting him, I thought immediately of Ichabod Crane.

The boy's name was Todd Kilmer. His previous psychiatrist referred him to the IOL for long-term hospitalization six months after I began my residency, and his case had been assigned to me.

Decades later, I still recall details of Todd's story. He grew up in Western Massachusetts, an only child. Although quiet and tending to isolate, his childhood sounded ordinary enough. He made good if not spectacular grades, liked math, and built model airplanes. No behavioral problems at home or in the classroom. Teachers made modestly approving comments on his report cards. *Polite and respectful . . . excellent handwriting . . . steady worker . . .* He had the usual childhood diseases, from which he recovered fully. His only surgery had been a tonsillectomy.

The Kilmers, while not rich, lived comfortably. They didn't travel much, but they skied in the Berkshires and made frequent summer visits to Cape Cod. Todd liked these excursions, to a point. "He could take them or leave them," said his mother. "He wasn't enthusiastic about them, but he wasn't enthusiastic about much of anything." He didn't strike his parents as unhappy, although he didn't enjoy life as much as they wished.

His parents acknowledged no serious mental health issues of their own. A schizophrenic great uncle in their extended family, two alcoholic cousins, and that was it.

Todd began to change in junior high school. He pulled away from his few friends. Always a solid student, he struggled to make passing grades. He lost interest in skiing, and in spending weekends on the Cape, and everything else. He spent most of the time in his bedroom. "We pleaded with him to watch TV with us, at least," his mother said. "Nothing doing, he wouldn't budge."

"He came down for meals," his father added, "but you knew he didn't want to. He ate as quickly as possible and went upstairs again."

Their GP gave Todd vitamins and pep talks but nothing changed, so he sent the boy to a psychiatrist. Mainly Todd sat in silence when they met, though he did acknowledge thoughts of killing himself. They admitted him to the psychiatric unit in a local hospital. When he failed to improve, they transferred him to the IOL.

DURING OUR FIRST ENCOUNTER Todd answered questions politely but tersely, completely without elaboration. I asked routine questions.

When did his depression start? Despite it, was he able to enjoy things, even to a limited degree? Did he tend to blame himself for things that really weren't his fault? Had school or family problems contributed to it? Had he been abused or bullied? What would it take to make him happier? More friends? A girlfriend? Bad form, at the time, to ask a male about a boyfriend. I tried to get him to talk about the things he used to like—model airplanes, skiing, trips to the Cape. Most of his answers consisted of *Yes, no, I don't know,* or *I'm not sure.*

I came to dread our sessions. Not because I disliked Todd—I didn't—but because they were so strained and dreary, so lacking in interaction.

But Todd did improve, more than I'd anticipated when I began to see him. The yes and no answers gave way to short sentences. The sentences became longer, and sometimes self-revealing. He spoke about his parents' tacit but high expectations and his doubts that he'd fulfill them. He talked about his social awkwardness and never knowing what to say to people. "But I didn't feel it mattered what I said. I didn't think they'd like me anyway." He believed he was different from them in some ill-defined but basic way, and he always would be.

Medications helped too. In the days before the more effective and better tolerated ones, before Prozac and Wellbutrin and the rest, there were far fewer choices. Available ones had side effects that ranged from mildly unpleasant to life-threatening. These included weight gain, drowsiness, blurred vision, and constipation. They could cause nausea or ruin your sex life. In high dosage they could cause fatal cardiac arrhythmias. Despite all that, they might actually help you feel better, at least sometimes. So it was with Todd.

He made use of the IOL's ancillary programs, attending classes in arts and crafts and photography. He frequently worked out in their gym. Attending group therapy sessions, he mainly sat in silence, but once in a while he hazarded brief comments. Occasionally his parents came in for family meetings.

Todd's eye contact became more the rule than the exception. Every so often he would even smile. A small, poignant smile, but a smile nonetheless.

Over time, he appeared to gain a modicum of self-esteem and self-confidence. While he'd never become a social butterfly, he did seem more comfortable with others, or at least less uncomfortable with them. He acknowledged that working out regularly helped him to feel better about himself ("for once I don't feel like a weakling,") and he vowed to remain physically active after his discharge. He looked forward to resuming high school classes, especially in math and science. Beyond that, he began to think about college, and not solely due to his parents' expectations; the idea began to appeal to Todd himself. "I think I might be good at engineering, especially something to do with airplanes." It was the first time he gave voice to the possibility that he might be good at anything.

After three months, Todd was discharged. I walked with Todd to the IOL's main lobby, where his parents awaited him. We shook hands all around, and the Kilmers headed home.

ONE MORNING, THE FOLLOWING October, John Donnelly summoned me to his office. Dr. Donnelly was the IOL's psychiatrist-in-chief, a man in his mid-fifties who conveyed a prison warden's sternness, a chain smoker with darting dark eyes behind thick glasses. He was not an unkind man, but he did have extraordinarily intimidating eyes. More than anyone I've known, John Donnelly's gaze sent this message, *Don't even think about trying to bullshit me.*

I felt a bit queasy. The psychiatrist-in-chief didn't summon residents for casual chats.

"Sit down," Dr. Donnelly ordered me, parking himself behind his massive desk. "I thought you should hear it directly from me," he said as he lit a Parliament. "Todd Kilmer killed himself yesterday."

I jolted upright in the chair. At first I couldn't speak. "What happened?" I finally asked.

"I don't have the whole story yet. His mother was too upset to tell me much. She said he'd done well, or so they'd thought, until mid-summer. But then he became quieter, the way he was before, rarely leaving his room. His psychiatrist increased his imipramine, and he seemed to be getting better. But yesterday his mother came home from work and found him dead. He hanged himself."

Shaken, I entertained a jumble of thoughts. *Why? He was all right when he left here. Or was he? Guess he wasn't. What must this be like for his parents? If only, if only—if only* what? *Suppose he'd stayed here another month, or even another week; would it have made a difference? Christ, what a waste!*

"I'm so sorry," I said. Not much, but that was all I could manage.

Dr. Donnelly rested his cigarette in the ashtray. "I went through his chart, and I read your notes. As best I can tell, you did everything you could for him. But sometimes that's not enough. Is it the first time this happened to you?"

I nodded. "We had close calls during my internship when I

rotated through the ER. And we had DOAs. But I didn't know them, I hadn't spent hours with them."

We talked for five or ten more minutes about Todd—his background, his time at the IOL, and what we knew of his life after he returned home.

"Try not to blame yourself," said Dr. Donnelly when we fell silent. "Are there any other parts of this you want to bring up about him?"

"I can't think of anything right now."

"If you do, come see me again."

We took leave of each other. Pausing at the door, I turned to him. "If you find out any more about what happened to him, please share it with me."

Dr. Donnelly said he would.

I walked slowly to my own office. Ordinarily a brilliant fall morning in New England, with trees turning orange and maroon, would have lightened my mood and quickened my pace, but today I barely noticed them. I recall thinking, *this has to be the ultimate therapeutic failure.*

MY EXPOSURE TO SUICIDES of people I knew personally has been limited. The first occurred when I was ten. Dr. Bruce, a general practitioner, the father of a classmate, lived close to us in Springfield. I remember him as friendly and soft-spoken with an abundance of red hair. A World War II vet, a family man, an outdoorsman who liked to hunt and fish. One night he shot himself. The official story held that it happened accidentally while he cleaned a hunting rifle, but the real story soon made the rounds. What I recall most clearly about the incident was how Paul, the doctor's son, turned inward.

He'd hitherto been outgoing. He was popular, a good baseball player, an active participant in class. When he returned to school two weeks later, he accepted condolences with a nod and a mumble. His classroom participation never went beyond the barest minimum. The next year his mother and the children moved away.

The second one occurred when I was in my teens. At Springfield High School I had an English teacher named Mae Woodard. Demanding and easily irritated, she was nonetheless popular with students. She had a knack for making old poems and plays alive and relevant. Miss Woodard provided my first introduction to Shakespeare, *The Merchant of Venice*, and she had the class memorize pieces of it. I still recall a few of them. *Hath not a Jew eyes? Hath not a Jew hands, organs, senses, dimensions, affections, passions?* And this: *The quality of mercy is not strained / It droppeth like the gentle rain upon the plains beneath . . .*

People said she loved a man killed in World War I and never got over it. Periodically she stopped coming into school, stopped doing just about everything. The psychiatric unit of one of the city's two hospitals repeatedly admitted her. During one such admission, she went to the hospital's roof and jumped off.

This one troubled me more than Dr. Bruce's. I'd sat in her classes, had heard her expound on Shakespeare and Milton with unmistakable enthusiasm. Despite her cantankerousness, I liked her. And she'd thrown herself off the roof of a seven-story building.

But the suicide that touched me most was that of Rachel Silber, a beautiful woman, a cousin by marriage. She could be charming if it suited her purposes, especially with male admirers. At some point she grew tired of her husband, a salesman who wore ill-fitting suits, smoked cheap cigars, and never earned much. She divorced him, and four years later she married a well-off older gentleman. Six years after that, the second husband had a fatal stroke.

For the first time in her life Rachel attained financial security. But she was also in her late fifties now, and alone. The number of male admirers dwindled as the years took their toll. While still a good-looking woman, she'd morphed into a good-looking *older* woman. Her expensive clothes and jewelry were nice enough, but they couldn't undo the ravages of time. The smooth skin now leathery from hours on the beach, the liver spots, the bags beneath her eyes. Her ageing brought narcissistic insults but little accompanying wisdom. One day, a few weeks after her sixty-fifth birthday, she took all her sleeping pills *before* she slit her wrists in a bathtub. Hard to question her intent.

A college junior at the time, I meandered through my memories of her. Rachel, splashing around with me in Lake Michigan . . . calming me down when we got stuck on the top of a Ferris wheel at the Illinois State Fair . . . playing Chinese Checkers with me. The truth is, I had a schoolboy crush on her.

AT LEAST THREE HUNDRED of my patients, a conservative estimate, attempted suicide at one point or another. How many of them truly hoped to die is debatable. Sometimes the answer appears clear-cut, as with a woman who took five aspirin tablets, called her husband to inform him, and told him not to feel bad about it. At the other end of the continuum was an inmate who killed his wife before turning the gun on himself. He jerked his arm at the last minute, and he only succeeded in blowing away his mandible and the lower half of his mouth.

Like most psychiatrists, I've learned ways to try to assess a patient's suicidality. Mainly they involved four questions, asked repeatedly and with different wordings. *What are your hopes and expectations? To what extent do you see your life as possibly improving?* For those who came close to attempting suicide but didn't: *What kept you from it?* For those who did attempt it: *Are you glad or sorry you're still here?* While useful, such questions aren't foolproof. Assessing suicidal intent, like assessing a potential for violence, can be problematic. Those who make such assessments are often wrong, with dire consequences.

Three of my patients, apart from Todd Kilmer, committed suicide while I treated them or shortly thereafter. The first was an alcoholic assistant dean at a local college. He'd lost two wives, one to breast cancer and another in an auto accident. No children, his parents deceased, estranged from his siblings. "I didn't know it was possible to feel so alone," he told me a few months before he drove into a bridge abutment at high speed.

The second suicide was a lesbian in her thirties. Feeling trapped in a dead-end job, often entangled in abusive relationships, she lacked family support to fall back on. Her mother told her once that she'd rather see her dead than gay. Talking to the mother afterward, I refrained from noting that her wish had been granted.

The third, a man of forty-five who'd wrestled with depression since his teens, told me he wouldn't do it but took comfort in owning a handgun, just in case. Just in case, in fact, turned out to *be* the case.

ONE OF THE SUICIDES that touched me most did not involve a patient. Ada Verronne was a neighbor, a few years older than Judy and me.

Every two or three months we went out to dinner with her and her husband, Bert. Appearing comfortable together, they seemed contented with their lives. Bert had a thriving local printing company. The Verronnes drove late-model cars, owned a near-mansion, and often traveled. Hawaii and the Caribbean were favored destinations. We noticed that Ada drank heavily but never displayed slurred speech, an unsteady gait, or other signs of drunkenness.

When Bert left her, neither I nor my wife saw it coming. Nor, it seems, did Ada.

A few months later, she phoned me late one Saturday night. Her two daughters were spending the weekend with their father, and she was alone. "I've just taken a handful of sleeping pills," she told me. "Do you think you could come over?"

Her speech and gait were normal, as usual, when I followed her to the den. A depleted bottle of Scotch sat next to an empty bottle of Quaaludes on the coffee table. Quaaludes, one of the strongest sleeping pills ever made, was arguably the worst of them against stiff competition.

I spent more than two hours there. Finding powdered mustard in her spice rack, I mixed it with warm water and got her to drink it. After she vomited, as we sat in the den, she told me what had happened. Bert had met a younger woman for whom he'd done several printing jobs, and he fell for her. He covered his tracks well, and Ada had no inkling of their affair until the day he moved out.

Ada, just old enough to remain untouched by Women's Lib and its new possibilities, had married Bert shortly after their high school graduation. A onetime secretary, she hadn't worked since the birth of their older daughter. Her life revolved around her family. Bert was the only man she'd ever been with. Sometimes they argued about her drinking and she'd cut down temporarily, but she admitted that she found it hard to drink in moderation.

I did what I considered the right things. I listened to her, let her give voice to her sadness and her restrained but unmistakable fury. I suggested that perhaps calling me meant she didn't want to die after all. I got her to talk about her daughters and the obvious pride she took in them. The older one was a high school soccer star, the younger one hoped to go to Annapolis—the Service Academies had recently begun to admit women. I asked what effect she thought her suicide would have on them. I suggested that a psychiatrist might help her through this. Knowing her too well to take her on myself, I gave her the name and number of a trusted colleague, and she promised to call him. I spoke to her gingerly about AA, suggesting she go to a few meetings. She told me in a lukewarm manner that she'd think about it. "The thing is, I don't do well in groups, unless I've been drinking."

Repeatedly she assured me that she wouldn't try to kill herself. She sounded genuinely grateful that I came. "You saved my life," she said when she hugged me just before I left.

Judy and I woke up to sirens the next morning. Ada's best friend had called to check on her. Getting no answer, the friend went to her house. She found Ada dead on the floor of the den. She'd finished off the Scotch, and a second bottle of sleeping pills sat empty on a table.

Having been the last person to see her alive, I've continued to wonder what might have happened if I'd said or done something differently. If I'd called 911 as soon as I'd gotten there, for instance. Or if I'd stayed longer, or even stayed for the rest of the night.

A RATHER SPECIAL CASE involved Dr. Elkins. He was a resident at Willow Grove, the nursing home with which I'd had the longest association.

Harry Elkins was only seventy-three, but you'd have guessed him to be in his mid-eighties. He had a host of medical problems, from cluster headaches to osteoarthritis of both hips to plantar fasciitis. The most serious of these was renal failure due to his chronic intractable hypertension.

Overweight, he didn't wear the extra poundage well. His hypertensive ruddiness had given way to grayish pallor. His slow, unsteady gait reminded me of the Thorazine shuffle, almost a rarity as newer and better drugs came along. A tremor made it hard for him to sign his name.

He was angry about almost everything. Angry with the ex-wife who left him a quarter of a century ago—he'd never remarried. Angry with his son and daughter ("they parked me in this dump, the goddamn ingrates"), and with the nurses and aides who answered his call bell too slowly. As the founder of one of Connecticut's premier orthodontic groups, he'd become enraged and wounded by the neglect of his former partners. "I treated them like family, I made them all rich men, and *not one* of them has come to see me here!"

Dr. Elkins' anger rested on a bedrock of depression, but he had all manner of side effects on every antidepressant I ordered. He also complained of terrible insomnia and deemed sleeping pills useless. "Didn't sleep a wink," he routinely complained, although his snoring could be heard by residents two rooms away.

Everything about Willow Grove stoked his ire. The bland monotony of his low-salt diet. A mattress too hard, a pillow too soft. The activities, which he called mind-numbing pap. "Not my idea of fun," he groused, "to be in some goddamn singalong with a bunch of braindead nitwits who can't remember the words to *Jingle Bells*."

⁓

WHEN I CAME TO Willow Grove one morning, the medical director and nursing supervisor awaited me. "We have to talk about Harry Elkins," the director said.

"Oh?" I expected them to talk about his refractory depression and the need to try another medication.

"He wants to stop dialysis," the nursing supervisor informed me.

I took a moment to digest this. "So, he wants to die. To commit suicide by refusing life-sustaining treatment."

They both nodded.

"Tell me about the legal implications."

"Well, the courts have held that that's his right," the director said, "assuming he's competent to make such a decision. Of course it's a big assumption. It will mainly depend on your evaluation."

From time to time I've made weighty determinations. To write or not to write Physician's Emergency Certificates, which in effect might deprive patients of their freedom. To establish a conservatorship for patients with dementia in cases involving large sums of money. To determine if a criminal defendant was competent to stand trial. To inform the State that I suspected child abuse, a decision which might put a child at risk but might also break up a family. But this particular decision was a first for me.

The next day I returned to Willow Grove. I'd set aside over an hour for a meeting with Dr. Elkins. As soon as I walked into his room, his change in demeanor struck me. The usual anger was conspicuous by its absence. So, too, his litany of complaints. The man seemed a picture of calm.

"I suppose you've heard about my wanting to stop dialysis," he said, "and I suppose they sent you to evaluate me. To see if I'm in my right mind."

"Something like that."

"Go ahead. You won't find me the least bit crazy. You won't even find me depressed." Dr. Elkins smiled, the first time I'd seen him do so.

I conducted as thorough an evaluation as I've ever undertaken. I asked standard questions about depression and anxiety and indications of thought disorder (none existed). I asked how he'd arrived at his decision. "I came to it gradually, over the course of weeks, or maybe a month or more. It wasn't a spur of the moment sort of thing, if that's what you're thinking."

I did a cognitive assessment, everything from naming the last five presidents to performing simple calculations to interpreting proverbs. "What does it mean," I asked him, "if someone says, 'you can't tell a book by the cover?'"

"It means appearances can be deceptive. It means you may think I'm a senile old fart who only needs a bunch of high octane antidepressants to fix him up, but you'd be wrong."

I learned more about his life in this meeting than in all our previous times together. He talked about growing up in Maine, "on a farm so isolated that we were forty-five minutes from a restaurant, even a fast food place." About getting married while still in dental school, and the couple's happiness despite having to stretch every dollar. "It was a big deal to see a movie every three months or so." He talked about his daughter's near-drowning on a trip to Lake

Champlain and a son who won a statewide high school science fair. And he talked about his death. "An optimistic agnostic, I guess you could call me. I've never been religious, but I believe that whatever happens is for the best.

"I expect you to find me psychiatrically competent," he concluded, "but if you don't, I've asked my lawyer to get another opinion." Not a threat but a statement of fact. This proved unnecessary though. Dr. Elkins showed no evidence of cognitive impairment or undue anxiety. He was much less depressed than he'd been on the day we met. His competency, as best I could tell, was unassailable.

Harry Elkins spent his dying days in peace, to all appearances. He said *please* and *thank you*, words he'd scarcely used since coming to Willow Grove. He never complained, he never lapsed into self-pity. Several nurses cried when he slipped into a terminal coma, including ones who couldn't stand him a few weeks earlier.

ONE NIGHT, CLOSE TO two generations ago, I sat in the library of my parents' home in Springfield. My favorite room—wood-paneled, large enough to house numerous book shelves but still cozy. I sat with my father's rifle, which I'd loaded. Dr. Goodwin was no gun nut, but he did enjoy duck hunting with his friends.

I placed the barrel of the rifle against different parts of my body. My site of choice was my chest. If I did decide to kill himself, I didn't like the vision of my brains splattered on the wall.

I'd graduated from Yale four or five months earlier but viewed my time there as a failure. I'd made decent grades in some classes but more than a few had been mediocre, and I withdrew from some because I thought I'd fail them if I didn't. At one point or another, I'd been in perhaps a dozen organizations, clubs, or activities, from the Yale Daily News to intramural soccer to Hillel, an informal organization of Jewish students. I'd even joined the choir of a Catholic church, St. Thomas More. Not that I thought about converting, but I liked to sing, and I knew I wasn't good enough for Yale's choral groups.

As noted, I'd decided to take most premed courses *after* I graduated but had little interest in them. I also doubted a medical school would take me anyway. But I'd apply, however pessimistically and half-heartedly—the line of least resistance since I lacked the interest and motivation to try anything else. A terrible reason for trying to launch a medical career, but so it was.

I'd been with Alice for over a year. I was sure I loved her, as sure as I could be of anything, but felt unready to commit to her. An insistent voice in my head told me that to marry her would be a mistake, but I couldn't imagine *not* marrying her.

I didn't like myself, or my life, or my chances for making sense of it.

A telling detail from that period concerned my handwriting. As a rule, it was legible, and the letters of average size. But as my morale deteriorated, it became cramped and tiny. The letters looked like this, and you practically needed a magnifying glass to read them.

I sat with the rifle by my side for an hour, maybe more. And then I unloaded it, placed it back in its oaken case, and went to bed.

Looking back on this incident, half a century later, I asked myself the same questions I'd asked my patients.

What were my hopes and expectations? I didn't have a lot of either, but I hoped that maybe I'd figure out what to do with my life.

Unlikely, but not out of the question. And I hoped I'd eventually feel better than how I felt just then. Hard to imagine that I'd feel much worse.

To what extent did I believe my life was subject to possible improvement? I knew it was, but the knowledge was walled off somewhere, just beyond my reach. I was in a relationship, albeit something of a roller-coaster, with a woman of importance to me, and I had other people in my life who cared about me, and a degree from an excellent university. I knew these things, but knowing something and believing it can be vastly different.

What kept me from it? A fear of death, the great void, the supreme unknown. The possibility of things improving, however slight. The unfairness to others in the family. To my three younger siblings who looked up to me, who'd be shaken and maybe lastingly traumatized by stumbling upon the bloodied remains of their brother. To my parents. Especially to my grandmother asleep upstairs, in her late eighties, who didn't deserve an event like that to contaminate her final years.

Another factor: As down and discouraged as I was, at least I had the sense to appreciate how fortunate I'd been in life. Good physical health . . . the auspicious circumstances of my birth; a concerned family . . . a chance to travel . . . an education at first-rate schools. I knew there were countless people in the world who would have killed for such a life. To remove myself from it would have been profoundly ungrateful, and I abhorred ingratitude.

I knew these things, whether or not I wanted to.

Am I glad or sorry I'm still here? At last, an easy question. I'm unabashedly glad I went on living. Appreciative of my marriages, both of them, for all their potholes. Appreciative of becoming a father, stepfather, and grandfather. Appreciative of friendships made, travels undertaken, books read, plays and movies seen. Appreciative of doing work that held my interest, work that made a difference in people's lives. I would have missed all of it, and more.

I should note that one year later, *just one year*, I'd started medical school in Ireland. Dublin was cold, and parts of it were dreary, and the poverty was as unavoidable as the rain, and the phones worked haphazardly. I've alluded to the Irish cuisine, mainly uninspired (it has since improved markedly). Even so, in a few months I'd already begun to love the place.

I should also note that Alice and I were married the following May. The marriage would fail but we didn't know it then, and at times we were actually fairly happy with each other.

My life, in short, was incalculably better than it had been that autumn evening when I sat alone, my father's loaded rifle by my side.

As I consider all this, my thoughts drift back to Todd Kilmer, fixed permanently in my mind as a tall, gawky seventeen-year-old, scarecrow-thin, who scarcely looked old enough to shave. The boy who'd skied and spent weekends on Cape Cod and built model airplanes, who'd sentenced himself to death for crimes unspecified. The boy who'd had as much of a lasting impact on me as any single patient I've ever had. If he'd lasted one more year, I wondered, might his life have improved as well?

I'd never know, of course, and that was the heart of the matter.

CHAPTER XII

NIRVANA UNIVERSITY

It continues to bemuse and intrigue me how the most unlikely flukes and coincidences can have profound and life-changing results. God must get quite a charge out of this phenomenon. He certainly arranges it often enough.

On a frigid December night in 2006, for example, I went to a promotional drug company dinner. You might question the morality of such events. On the one hand, you can learn a lot at them, and not just about newer medications. There's often useful give-and-take among those in attendance. I also admit that I like the chance to socialize with colleagues whom I see infrequently. The practice of psychiatry can be isolating, and I may have little contact with people other than patients in the course of a workday. On the other hand, it's hard to defend a practice of bestowing filet mignon and grilled sea bass on mainly prosperous doctors at high-priced restaurants as the cost of drugs increase obscenely. But I do go to them periodically, despite occasional twinges of conscience and a sense I'm engaging in a manner of whoredom.

On this particular occasion I found himself sitting next to Dr. H., a casual friend who practiced near the main campus of the University of Connecticut. At the time I held a halftime position as medical director of a community mental health agency. I likened the position to serving in the House of Lords. Impressive title, big office with a window view on two sides, good salary, but an essentially meaningless job that often struck me as kind of silly. Moreover, my boss was a sour, micromanaging psychologist who disliked psychiatrists in general and me in particular. I should acknowledge that her feelings toward me were fully reciprocated.

I asked Dr. H. if UConn (the University of Connecticut) happened to be hiring psychiatrists to serve their burgeoning student population. I hadn't planned to ask this. "They're desperate for people," my friend replied.

"Would you be able to give me the name and number of someone to contact there?" My surge of excitement made it hard for me to speak clearly, or maybe it was the glass of Pinot Noir I'd just had.

"Sure." Dr. H. gave me contact information for the head of the university's Student Health Services.

The next day I followed up with a phone call to an affable man named Michael Kurland. The day after that, I faxed him my CV. The next week I went for the first of three interviews with varying combinations of potential future colleagues. The interviews went well. The hardest part, to keep from telling the interviewers how much I wanted the job. I refrained from saying, *Goddammit, just fucking* hire *me! I'll be the best shrink you ever had!*

Six weeks later I assumed a position as a halftime psychiatric consultant to Counseling and Mental Health Services, C&MHS, at the University of Connecticut at Storrs. I would work there three days weekly. My colleagues were psychologists, social workers, and APRNs (nurses with advanced training, able to prescribe). I'd be the sole psychiatrist at a campus with over 21,000 students.

It so happened that Judy and I had made arrangements several months earlier to meet Herbert and Anne Kupers and Carey Donaldson for a trip through Belgium and The Netherlands in April, ten weeks hence. We convened in a hotel in Amsterdam. Blurry-eyed and disheveled, we'd flown all night.

Herbert studied me carefully. "Your new job agrees with you," he said, notwithstanding my unkempt and unshaven appearance. "You look five years younger than the last time we saw you."

I LIKED MY NEW colleagues. Many of them had been there for years, a few for decades. One of the psychologists had been an undergraduate at UConn, and she'd come back shortly after finishing her PhD. She'd spent the better part of twenty-five years on the campus. This stability of staff impressed me. By contrast, I've had jobs where the rapid turnover made it hard to remember the names of coworkers. On Friday afternoon you told people to have a nice weekend, and some of them had dropped out of sight by Monday morning. C&MHS had the lowest turnover rate of any place I've worked at. Two colleagues *unretired;* they came back to C&MHS on a limited (per diem) basis.

I also liked the workplace ambience, especially the relative absence of turf issues. These may abound in mental health settings, which can be strikingly clannish. Psychiatrists, psychologists, and social workers are wont to gather in nervous huddles, suspicious if not openly hostile toward other huddles. An especially sharp division may occur between the medical and nonmedical people, with the MDs and RNs on one side and everyone else on the other. UConn didn't work that way, as a rule. If you weren't with a patient, your door was probably open. Impromptu consults and social conversations occurred constantly. There were weekly case conferences with people from different fields contributing on equal footing. The main concern was student welfare, not your commitment to a given discipline or theoretical orientation. Apropos, I soon picked up on something else. People took the work per se seriously, but they didn't take themselves unduly seriously. Mental health types have a way of becoming smitten with self-importance.

A few years after I came to UConn, I chatted with a therapist who'd applied for a position with us. "What's this place really like?" he asked.

"It's Nirvana," I answered. An exaggeration, yes, but still . . .

DURING A COUPLE OF days of orientation, I learned how to use the UConn computer system. "Your emails are *not* private," a presenter stressed. "Don't write anything you wouldn't mind seeing on the front page of the *Hartford Courant* (Central Connecticut's main newspaper)." I learned about options for pension plans and health insurance, I watched videos about ethics and sexual harassment. I was told how to request neuropsychological testing or a medical consult. I learned about referrals to other campus services: The Center for Students with Disabilities, the Center for Career Development, the Ombudsman, a dozen others. And then, within hours of completing orientation, my head awash in new information and procedures, I began to see patients.

Self-referred for the most part, my student-patients might also be referred by other students, parents, significant others, the campus police, or faculty members. After triage, they were seen by me or one of the APRNs if a clinician considered a med evaluation appropriate.

Whatever their route to C&MHS, there were a lot of them. I had a full schedule from the day I started.

They came to me with every symptom and disorder I'd seen in other settings, with the sole exception of dementias. Their mood disorders ranged from despondency over a failed romance to a year-long suicidal depression to a full-fledged manic episode. They had panic attacks and social phobias, anorexia and bulimia, addiction to alcohol and opiates and online role-playing games (RPGs). They had agoraphobia and claustrophobia. They had hellacious histories of trauma, of physical and sexual abuse, of witnessing atrocities while in the military, of surviving natural and manmade disasters. I met with a man who survived ethnic cleansing during his childhood in the Balkans and a woman who lost relatives on both sides of the Syrian Civil War. Some students were autistic, and some were narcissistic sociopaths, and some were high-functioning schizophrenics.

They had incapacitating obsessive-compulsive disorders (OCDs). Their grade point average might suffer because they spent half the day cleaning and rearranging things or attending to personal grooming. Sometimes their OCD symptoms could become a bit bizarre. There's a subtype of obsessive-compulsive disorder called *scrupulosity*, a pathological guilt about moral or religious issues, and it may be accompanied by an overpowering and often inappropriate need to confess. I treated a young man who woke up his parents in the middle of the night to confess that he'd been picking his nose. How would Robert and Eileen have reacted, I wondered, if I'd woken them at 2AM to make such a confession? Another student felt compelled to confess to her boyfriend that she found his father extremely handsome, and she had fantasies about sleeping with him. She had no intention of doing this, but the confession did not enhance their relationship.

While most of my clientele consisted of healthy young adults, I have seen more than a few with a past or current history of serious physical problems. A partial list of them includes chronic ulcerative colitis, Crohn's Disease, leukemia, bone cancer, thyroid abnormalities, congenital heart disease, and insulin-dependent diabetes.

My student-patients have come from all over the United States and at least thirty different countries, from Taiwan to Turkey, from Peru to Poland. Some lived in the world's great cities—New York, London, Rome, and Rio de Janeiro, among others—and some grew up in tiny hamlets in Africa and India. Some were children of privilege, and others had faced the starkest poverty. Their first languages include Vietnamese and Greek, Afrikaans and Creole.

One of the most interesting and challenging aspects of working at C&MHS was dealing with cultural considerations. I've had gay patients from places where same-sex relationships could result in years of imprisonment or worse. I've had a South Korean graduate student who told me a history of mental health treatment would result in automatic loss of his scholarship. Furthermore, it would probably mean that he could never get a decent job in his native country. I've heard scenarios like this one: A student, a first-generation American, had Pakistani parents who ran a convenience store and worked 130 hours per week between the two of them. Their chief motivation, to ensure their children received a college education. They decreed that their oldest son (my patient), the first family member to go to college, would become an electrical engineer, but the boy had no interest or aptitude for engineering. Maybe he wanted to become a physical therapist or high school Spanish teacher. Or maybe he didn't want to go to college in the first place—maybe he wanted to join the Air Force or become a plumbing contractor. In his culture, however, you obeyed your parents, no matter what. Besides, his parents had worked like slaves on his behalf, so how could he refuse to do their bidding?

MY COLLEAGUES INCLUDED PEOPLE of various races, socioeconomic backgrounds, and sexual orientations. As a rule, they didn't flaunt their gay and lesbian relationships, but neither did they hide them. I worked in places where everyone was aware of these relationships but they were never mentioned openly, nor were matters of sexuality mentioned at all. By contrast, glancing at a pair of nicely built female graduate students at a staff meeting, I asked a colleague, "Barry, what's the gay male take on breasts?"

"Well, frankly," my colleague answered, "we wonder what all the fuss is about."

My coworkers have come from South Dakota, South Carolina, California, Puerto Rico, Mexico, Mainland China, and India. They've included a classical violist, an improv comedian, a lawyer turned social worker, and a rabbi turned doctoral candidate in psychology. Their areas of particular interest include cognitive behavioral therapy, existential psychotherapy, substance abuse, treatment of student-athletes, violence toward women, and eating disorders.

The staff was quick to put together impromptu celebrations for the arrival or departure of a group of psychology interns, or Halloween, or a baby shower or retirement. But there didn't have to be a particular occasion. All of them involved food, and potlucks reflecting the staff's many backgrounds might include lox and bagels, curry, and a flan.

A telling incident: On the evening of December 14, 2012, we'd scheduled a holiday party at a local restaurant. It turned out to be the day of an unspeakable event, the day of the Sandy Hook shootings, the day Barack Obama called the worst one of his presidency. Twenty-six dead, twenty of them children. When Obama came to the state a few days later to express condolences, some Secret Service agents were seen to have tears in their eyes.

Discussion ensued; should we cancel the party? More than a few members of the staff had children or grandchildren close in age to the casualties, and no one felt like partying anyway. In the end, though, we went ahead with it. The mood was somber, but somehow it seemed appropriate to be there. Those present sought out each other's company as they tried to process the horrific, to comprehend the incomprehensible. We comforted each other. We were, in fact, pretty close to family.

WHEN UCONN OPENED ITS doors in 1881, it started out as an agricultural school. This tradition lives on in things like the Animal Sciences major, still popular, and a Dairy Bar that may serve Connecticut's best ice cream. Beyond that, the university now offers 110 majors, from Arabic and Islamic Studies to Accounting, from Physiology and Neurobiology to Puppetry. You can also put together a major of your own, and students often do.

I've been impressed and intrigued by their academic pursuits. I met with a young man who double-majored in Civil Engineering and German. He didn't have a German background and had never visited a German-speaking country; he simply liked the language. I've met with students who studied abroad—fine arts in Florence, and wildlife preservation in South Africa, and Irish history in Dublin. I've met with those doing cutting-edge research in genetics and laser physics. Once, during a session with a young woman pursuing a PhD in Medieval Studies, the discussion turned to Old English. I asked if they could determine how a language sounded when it hasn't been spoken for a millennium. "Oh, we can do that," she told me. And then she started to speak it fluently.

Apart from their academic pursuits, they do useful and important things. A young man spent spring break in Oklahoma a few years ago with his church group, helping to rebuild houses after a spate of tornados. Another student spent her spring break in Florida assisting migrant farm workers. Another woman, an African American majoring in math, spent a summer trying to interest disadvantaged minority high school girls in STEM.

I liked working with this age group. Because they're young, they haven't as many difficult experiences to overcome, and they also have the wonderful, amazing resilience of youth. More than a few had lived through nightmares, and they'd managed to keep their sanity and motivation intact. But I had no illusions that all my student-patients were paragons of virtue. While some of them performed good works in Oklahoma and Florida, others spent spring break drunk and stoned in the Caribbean. While the majority took academic work seriously, others viewed classes as annoying distractions from online porn and gambling. As noted, a few have been as sociopathic as inmates I've known in Corrections. Nonetheless, working at UConn has made me more optimistic about the future than I used to be. Perhaps my generally high regard for them skews my vision, but I feel the world might become a better place because of them.

The UConn job wasn't perfect. Practicing psychiatry there, like practicing it anywhere, could be a slow and tedious business with frequent setbacks and recurrences. Some students had deeply ingrained symptoms and character flaws that made trying to treat them a constant battle, often lost. I've had to deal with parents who were frightened, irate, and frustrated, who sought information I couldn't give them; the HIPAA privacy laws kick in when you're eighteen. Despite the tendency of most colleagues to stay for years or decades, several to whom I felt the closest left for greener pastures. And the frustrations that beleaguer all medical specialties—dealing with insurance companies, trying to get through to gatekeepers, seeking approval for meds not on their formularies—could be crazy-making. The pandemic meant conducting sessions online and by phone, which could be exercises in frustration. Some student health administrators who came to UConn subsequent to my arrival, obsessed with the bottom line and cutting costs, were unsympathetic if not frankly antagonistic toward clinicians.

It wasn't perfect, but what job is? Perfect jobs are roughly as common as unicorns. But it was right for me. The overwhelming majority of workdays were interesting and left me feeling useful. I grew to love the campus with its tranquil grounds, its trees and ponds (even in January with its biting winds and thigh-high snow drifts). I remain indebted to Dr. H. for setting in motion the chain of events that brought me there. Now, three years after my retirement, I still dream about it. Of the twenty to thirty places I've done psychiatric work, from assisted living facilities to homeless shelters, from my private offices to death row, UConn remains far and away my personal favorite.

CHAPTER XIII

EXPIRED PASSPORTS

AS NOTED ELSEWHERE IN THIS RECOUNTING, I've been slow to throw out things. The result has been the accumulation of papers, memorabilia, and assorted junk, most of which I could discard without ever missing. Sometimes, though, I find items I greatly prize. So it is with my expired passports. They bring me recollections of people, places, and events that have enhanced my life. A sampling of such recollections follows.

U.S. PASSPORT F170XXXX, *issued March 1965, valid through March 1968. Within this time: Martin Luther King marches in Selma, Charles Whitman kills fourteen from a Texas tower, Nixon plots a comeback. Cultural contrasts:* Cat Ballou *and* The Graduate, *Liberace and* The Beatles. *A South African surgeon, Christiaan Barnard, performs the first heart transplant. Among those born: Julia Roberts, Mike Tyson, and Justices Brett Kavanaugh and Neil Gorsuch. Among those who died: Sharon Tate and five other victims of the Manson Family, Edward R. Murrow, and Mohamed Bin Laden (multimillionaire and father of ten-year-old Osama, when his private jet crashed). At the airport you went to a counter, presented a ticket, boarded, and that was it.*

STUDYING THE PASSPORT PHOTO, I see a youth of twenty-two with a baby-smooth forehead and a hint of a smile. Short hair, no beard or mustache, no sideburns. His eyes convey trust and perhaps ingenuousness. I try to process the obvious but impossible fact that I used to be this person.

I look untested, which I was. No firsthand experience with war, economic deprivation, or natural disaster. No illnesses more serious than tonsillitis and middle ear infections. No dealings with domestic violence or predatory priests.

This was my first passport. I didn't need one when my parents took me to the Caribbean at age twelve. As mentioned earlier, the trip included Cuba before Castro and Haiti before Duvalier. Haiti provided my first glimpses of real poverty. I saw skeletal children begging and men diving under a block-long cruise ship to fetch coins tossed overboard. I saw fog-tipped purplish mountains, I heard drummers in the streets with straw hats and the whitest teeth I'd ever seen. They played with a tempo too fast to see their hands as more than a blur.

I obtained the passport as a matter of necessity. That fall, I'd start medical school in Ireland.

The passport's stamps consisted solely of Shannon, Dublin and JFK. Every September Alice and I flew to Ireland to start the academic year, and every June we returned to the U.S. Our summer earnings could defray most of our year-around expenses. I've known doctors who spent a decade or more paying off their educational debts, whereas my tuition for all of medical school came to under $7000.

September 1965, the first crossing. Stopping at Shannon, once a refueling point for prop flights to Europe, now largely bypassed by jets. The short trip to Dublin—we flew low over the countryside with its fifty shades of green.

Getting used to the lovely lilting speech. Learning the currency. Learning the rudiments of Dublin's impossible geography; it seemed that no adjacent streets were parallel or perpendicular to each other. Getting used to the double-deck buses that careened around rain-slickened corners, defying gravity by remaining upright.

As noted, Ireland kept all its medical colleges open despite a population drastically reduced by famine, civil war, and the Irish diaspora. So the country took in students from across the globe, from every continent except Antarctica. Apart from what I learned of medicine, I would learn that Irish Catholics and Protestants, Indians and Pakistanis, Jews and Arabs, and South Africans of all races could become friends, sometimes lovers, and sometimes husband and wife.

From summer to summer, we returned to an America growing ever stranger to us. So many divisions: by gender and politics, by race and sexual orientation, by culture and counterculture. Us versus them. Despite my on-and-off attempts to write it, I've never been drawn much to poetry. But the words of William Butler Yeats struck me as appropriate when I thought about my homeland in that era:

Things fall apart, the center will not hold

The best lack all conviction, while the worst are filled with passionate intensity.

U.S. PASSPORT F170XXXX, *renewed at the American Embassy in Dublin in March 1968, valid until March 1970. Among those born:*

Jennifer Lopez, Senator Cory Booker, Steffi Graf, and Jay-Z. Among those who died: Ho Chi Minh, Judy Garland, and President Eisenhower. Within this time: chants outside the White House—Hey, hey, LBJ, how many kids did you kill today? The shootings of MLK and RFK, the Tet offensive, teargas at the Democratic Convention in Chicago. The Jesus-it-really-happened election of Richard Nixon. Five hundred thousand troops in Vietnam now. Woodstock. Old Hollywood gives way to the likes of Easy Rider *and* Midnight Cowboy. *What novel could do justice to those years?*

The passport photo bears little similarity to my earlier one. The long hair and sideburns verge on unkempt, and my face has broadened. No IBM-worthy outfit of three years ago—my wardrobe now includes flowered shirts, bellbottoms, and a red Nehru jacket.

My eyes beheld the world with less naïveté. Many Irish in the 1960s were desperately poor. Not as poor as the skeletal Haitians I'd seen a decade earlier in the Caribbean with my parents, but close enough. Intrigued by pathology, I observed and assisted at a number of autopsies that drove home the tenuousness of life. The first autopsy I observed was on a laborer of twenty-nine, only a few years older than myself, a muscular type with no known history of ill health. He came home from work, ate, and told his wife he had a headache. After dinner, while reading the paper, he keeled over without regaining consciousness. An autopsy revealed a ruptured aneurysm at the base of his brain.

My passport now bore stamps of France and England. The trip to France was especially memorable. We traveled in a twin-engine prop of Skyways, a long-defunct airline that flew between Lympne and Beauvais, small airports on either side of the English Channel.

Above the seats, along luggage bins, were bus-style advertisements for tea, sweets, and beer.

We left for France in December 1968. Staying in the Parisian apartment of an Irish friend who came home for Christmas, we made do with an electric plate, a miniscule communal bathroom, and a sink without an outflow pipe. At first we didn't understand what a neighbor tried to tell us. *"L'eau arrive mais il ne départe pas"* —the water arrives but does not depart? Carrying out the water that collected beneath the sink in a plastic garbage can, we were stunned to learn how much of it two people used.

We followed in the footsteps of Americans who succumbed to the Parisian spell for centuries, from Ben Franklin to Jim Morrison. Paid homage to the Louvre and the Rodin Museum. Listened to jazz at Left Bank *boites,* had red wine and bowls of onion soup topped with melted gruyere at *Les Halles.* But my sharpest image was of walking along the Seine one frigid night in January. There, before us, we saw Notre Dame, ablaze in floodlights as a light snow fell. High on the list of my favorite memories.

U.S. PASSPORT Z113XXXX, *issued March 1970, valid until March 1975. Among those born: Justin Trudeau, Winona Ryder, Elon Musk, and Cameron Diaz. Among those who died: Louis Armstrong, Nikita Khrushchev, Jackie Robinson, and J. Edgar Hoover. Within this time: Kent State, Attica, and Wounded Knee. In Washington, half a million demonstrators protest the War. Roe v. Wade, death penalty held unconstitutional. Nixon in China. Kissinger and Le Duc Tho (Vietnamese general and diplomat) share the Nobel Peace Prize, a gift to lovers of irony everywhere. Republicans dismiss Watergate as a third-rate burglary. The Vietnam War ends with helicopters on the embassy roof, less with a bang than a whimper. Hot pants and leisure suits, mood rings, Claes Oldenburg's big lipstick and Andy Warhol's soup cans. People seemed drawn to the silly and inconsequential. Given the sixties, who could blame them?*

The passport photo shows me with longish well-trimmed hair and sideburns. My eyes regard the world more warily than before, and my cheeks look rounder; I've gained ten pounds these last five years. No fitness club or jogging, although I did flirt briefly with rugby. My interest in it died when I lay prone in a patch of sheep manure—animals often grazed on the playing field—with two large Irishmen on top of me.

Few stamps adorned the passport. In 1971 I graduated, returning to a divided homeland for an internship and psychiatric residency. I lacked time and money for travel abroad.

Leaving Ireland, among the hardest things I've ever done. Ireland, and its people with their wit and verbal acrobatics, their resilience in the face of a beleaguered history. Ireland, where I won my bones as a doctor and drank hundreds of pints of Guinness with classmates from two dozen countries. Ireland, where our son, our only child, was born. Even before the plane took off, I found myself yearning for the pubs . . . for the theaters and riverside book stalls . . . for strolls through St. Stephen's Green with its ponds and gardens . . . for the sense that time wasn't always at a premium.

Despite limited use, the passport bears one stamp besides those of JFK and Ireland. The Bahamas, in September of 1974, the last year of my psychiatric residency. Alice and I had separated. I drank too much, used marijuana. Took pills to sleep and other pills to stay awake. I'm still grateful that I never tried cocaine; I'd have gotten hooked on it in a heartbeat. This was someone learning how to bring good mental health to others.

Yearning to get away, I saw an ad in the travel section of the *Hartford Courant* for a week in Nassau off-season. It cost under $500, airfare included. I called Hite, my former Yale roommate, and we arranged to meet there.

As trips go, this one proved unspectacular. No notable restaurants or fancy shops, no plays or museums, no fabulous scenery. We swam, walked along the beach, and explored the island on a rented motorcycle. We drank rum swizzles at Ronnie's Rumba Room across from our hotel. But mainly we talked, often till close to dawn. Hite, among his other virtues, was a first-rate listener.

The trip fixed nothing (geographic cures rarely do), but it did provide a respite. It imparted the unique comfort that talking with an old friend can *provide*. I'd known Hite since Eisenhower was in the White House. It helped me deal with the disarray of my life, much of it self-wrought.

U.S. Passport F175XXXX, issued August 1975, valid until August 1980. Among those born: Kerry Washington, Tom Brady, Reese Witherspoon, and Ron DeSantis. Among those who died: Werner Von Braun (father of the V-2), Vladimir Nabokov (father of Lolita*), and Elvis Presley (father of pelvic gyration). Within this time: a calming Gerald Ford, a star-crossed Jimmy Carter.* Saturday Night Live *changes TV forever. America takes a deep breath and enjoys its Bicentennial. The eruption of Mount St. Helens, 500 times more powerful than the Hiroshima bomb. The Supreme Court approves capital punishment after all. Teenage girls in leading roles: Mariel Hemingway in* Manhattan, *Jodie Foster in* Taxi Driver. *Golda Meir, Indira Gandhi, and Margaret*

Thatcher manage leading roles in the real world. Popes John Paul I and II. The Camp David Accords. Sadat comes to Israel, and for a moment it looks as if there might be peace in the Middle East. The Ayatollah Khomeini thinks otherwise.

The passport photo shows a rumpled man with still-long hair, slumping shoulders, and heavy-lidded eyes. He wears an open-collar shirt, no tie or jacket, and his appearance brings to mind sleep-deprivation and a hangover. Only five years passed between photos, but he looks ten years older.

This passport, like its predecessor, got little use. It had only one foreign stamp, for Aruba. In August, 1976, Judy and I went there on our honeymoon.

I remember the trip as I remember much of the 1970s, a foggy time with moments of extraordinary clarity. Aruba's beaches, the sand too hot to walk barefooted in the Caribbean summer. The divi-divi trees, their branches bent perpendicular to the trunks by trade winds. Windmills, pastel cottages, and oil refineries. *Rijsttafel* ("Rice-Table"), a unique buffet with caramelized beef braised in coconut milk, seafood satay, plantain fritters, and twenty or thirty other items. Casinos with high rollers who carried inch-thick wads of bills in their pockets. The beat of steel bands, and the beat of waves breaking against the shore.

I was thirty-three. Compared to the man-child of twenty-two who wed the first time, I felt worlds apart in outlook and experience. The first time I hadn't started medical school, and now I'd completed a residency. The first time I hadn't left the country without my parents, and now I'd spent six years abroad. Untested then, I now felt tested to the hilt.

U.S. PASSPORT B181XXXX, *issued July 1981, valid until July 1986. Within this time: Ronald Reagan and John Paul II survive assassination attempts. Di and Charles pledge eternal love. New acronyms: VCR, AIDS, HMOs. Among those born: Roger Federer, Scarlett Johansson, J.D. Vance, and Princes William and Harry. Among those who died: Joe Louis, Georgia O'Keeffe, Tennessee Williams, and 237 aboard a Korean 747 shot down by the Soviets. Lech Walesa, electrician and Nobel Prize winner, becomes the world's second best-known Pole, after Pope John Paul II. Star Wars. Millions watch Challenger disintegrate. Breakthrough women: Sally Ride, Sandra Day O'Connor and Geraldine Ferraro. Magic Johnson, Larry Bird, and Michael Jordan light up the NBA. A different kind of Soviet leader appears in the person of Mikhail Gorbachev and the cold war shows signs of thawing, maybe.*

The passport photo reveals the bearer's eyes as brighter and more rested now, the hair and sideburns shorter and neater, the eyebrows assuming a quizzical arch. The open collar shirt has given way to a tie and jacket. He looks less disheveled, more doctor-like.

The passport contains a stamp of my first trip back to Ireland since my graduation. A rushed affair, too ambitious. I wanted to show Judy as much as possible of the country I loved (also her ancestral homeland), the country that has played such a crucial role in my life.

We deplaned at Shannon, met Herbert and Anne Kupers, rented a car, and made our way around the island. In ten days we went up the Clare and Galway coasts to Mayo and Sligo in the far Northwest, then across the country to Dublin. Maintaining a clockwise route, we returned to Shannon via Cork and Kerry.

Despite six years there, we saw things new to me. Achill Island, off the Galway coast, its boulder-strewn beaches and gray hills almost lost in mist. The bleak beauty of the Burren in County Clare, a green-tinted desert, Ireland's equivalent of the Badlands. Yeats's grave in a Sligo churchyard with its haunting epitaph: *Cast a cold eye /On life, on death /Horseman, pass by!*

We paid respects to Dublin's pubs and parks, we saw *Hamlet* at the Abbey. I showed Judy around RCSI, stately but scarred, its columns pockmarked by machine guns in the Irish civil war. We wandered through Moore Street with women hawking produce from open carts as they've done for centuries, and through used bookstores near Trinity College, and through fine shops with Waterford glass and hand-knit woolens. And it occurred to me that I might return to Ireland again and again, discovering new vistas and rediscovering old ones, uncovering different facets of its history and culture, and I would never grow tired of it, never.

THIS PASSPORT ALSO INCLUDES the stamp of an unplanned trip to London. My parents had flown to Heathrow, embarking on a trip through England and Scotland. The next day my mother called to tell me that my father had had a massive coronary.

I drove to JFK and bought a ticket for the first available flight to London. A bare-bones trip, no cultural diversions. I mostly stayed at the hospital, sitting with my mother at my father's bedside. Her phone call hadn't prepared me for his transformation from the ruddy seventy-year-old who looked sixty to a gray-faced man with sunken eyes, a man who found the smallest act exhausting. He'd aged a decade in less than a week.

Hard to imagine more competent and attentive care. The nurses, from Trinidad and Bombay, from throughout the old British Empire, took a liking to this frail American gentleman. They cajoled and bullied him into eating, they joked with him. They chipped in and bought him a bathrobe because he always felt cold, and they refused to take payment for it. He was certain that he'd die, and they forbade it. In fact, he would live for five more years. That he survived at all was due, I believe, to the care he received in London, especially the nursing care.

U.S. PASSPORT H042XXXX, *issued January 1987, valid until January 1997. Among those born: Taylor Swift, Brittney Griner, Dakota Johnson. Among those who died: Lucille Ball, Gert Frobe (Goldfinger), Divine (star of* Pink Flamingos *and* Hairspray; People Magazine's *Drag Queen of the Century).Within this time: the twilight of Reagan, the interregnum of Bush I, the ascendancy of Bill Clinton. Nixon, dead now, on a postage stamp. Gorbachev, Yeltsin, and Putin (Stalin Light). New acronyms: AOL, MSNBC, SUV. Intifada, ethnic cleansing. Camilo Cela, Wislawa Szymborska, and Dario Fo win Nobel Prizes for literature, awards that eluded Anton Chekhov, Marcel Proust, and James Joyce. Two states, Texas and Florida, carry out 109 executions between them. One of those executed catches fire before dying in Florida's electric chair.* Time Magazine's *Persons of the Year include George H.W. Bush, Nelson Mandela, and Yasser Arafat ("Peacemaker.")*

The passport photo shows a serious sort, his eyes fixed on the far horizon, sporting a grayish beard in a photo taken during a brief experiment with facial hair. Black tie, white shirt, dark gray jacket. A man of uncertain age, maybe thirty-five or maybe fifty.

The passport has stamps of eight countries, from Barbados to Finland. I used it for psychiatric meetings in Toronto and Montreal, for respites on Caribbean beaches, and for the museums and scenery and cuisines of Spain and Italy. Spain provided my first look at the Mediterranean as we woke up on an overnight train from Madrid to Barcelona. We looked out the window and saw a sparkling sea in the morning light below us.

But the most memorable trip was to Eastern Europe. Extraordinary timing; I went with my mother to Poland, Czechoslovakia, and Hungary in October 1989. Her first ambitious trip since my father's death. It occurred just as the Soviet bloc was disintegrating, and Eastern Europe was now a never-never land suspended between totalitarianism and freedom.

A trip of dramatic contrasts. Stark poverty in Poland and the relative prosperity of Hungary, ill-stocked grocery stores and breakfast buffets with cheeses and pâté. The newness of Warsaw, eighty-five percent destroyed in World War II with heaps of rubble still prominent. Rebuilt replicas of graceful, nineteenth century Polish townhouses and Stalinist-gothic governmental buildings. Hungarian bookstores selling Michael Jackson's *Moonwalk* as well as a lot of pornography and cautions from our guide in Prague about the secret police, still active and feared.

Warsaw's Old Town, reconstructed with infinite patience, stone by stone. A striking street-level statue of a Polish Resistance fighter from only the waist up as he's about to descend below ground. Resistance groups used sewers to communicate. A white-knuckle flight from Warsaw to Budapest in a Tupelov 154, a clone of a 727 that shook and rattled like a wooden rollercoaster. Sandwiches, cappuccino, and world-class chocolate pastries at Café Hungaria, with its fin-de-siècle elegance, marble staircases and cantaloupe-sized light bulbs. Uniformed schoolgirls, no makeup or jewelry, praying in the Czestochowa cathedral. Auschwitz, looking too benign in the soft October light; rows of candles outside the crematoria; *Arbeit Macht Frei* on the main gate. An ersatz Gypsy ensemble playing non-Gypsy standbys like *I Lost My Heart in San Francisco*. The timeless beauty of Prague's Old Town Square, and the Town Hall with its Astronomer's Clock built half a millennium ago. German tourists, arms linked, swaying to an *umpah* number, looking ready to pay homage to another fuhrer.

Among the stranger side trips, an excursion to Konopiste, a castle near Prague. One of the homes of Archduke Ferdinand, whose assassination sparked World War I. Ferdinand was an insatiable and fanatic hunter. In his lifetime he reputedly killed tens of thousands of animals. Every wall of his castle drips with mounted heads and antlers, each labeled with the date and place of kill. The trophies give the place a pervading grimness, the perfect setting for an Alfred Hitchcock movie. Irreverent note: the man was crazy. How else to describe someone with such an obsession to take life? Perhaps there's an appropriateness in this. The insane killing of World War I was prompted by the killing of an insane man obsessed with killing.

We encountered all kinds of people on the trip. Fellow tourists, guides, and black marketers. A flight attendant on Malev, the Hungarian airline, hard-pressed to contain her joy when she talked about how she could vote now. An American on our tour who'd been in Europe during World War II, part of a unit that liberated one of the death camps, and his descriptions of the barely living apparitions who greeted them. But the one who best epitomized the trip for me was Edina, our guide in Budapest, and the look on her serious, pretty face as she talked about her country's long-awaited love affair with freedom. The look of someone with a strong if cautious optimism, ready for anything.

U.S. Passport 15523XXXX, issued *November 1996, valid until November 2006. Within this time: Bill Clinton survives Newt Gingrich, Ken Starr, and his own formidable demons. Among those who died: Princess Di, Ronald Reagan, John Paul II, and multitudes in unmarked graves in the Balkans, Rwanda, and Iraq. Also among the dead, the 2,977 casualties on 9/11. The Red Sox and White Sox win the World Series after droughts of eighty-six and eighty-eight years respectively. Quality cable:* The Sopranos, Deadwood, Six Feet Under. *Glamorous women in plain-Jane roles, Charlize Theron in* Monster, *Hallie Berry in* Monsters Ball. *The president reads* My Pet Goat *to second-graders while America is under siege. Iraq invaded, Mission Accomplished, Saddam extracted from a spider hole. Katrina—Heckuva job, Brownie. Al Gore loses the election but wins a Nobel Prize and an Oscar for presenting inconvenient truths.*

The passport photo shows a man with deeper furrows in his forehead, thicker eyebrows, and modest jowls. Despite racquetball, swimming year-round, and watching his diet, he has to work to keep his weight in check. His salt-and-pepper hair remains abundant, but the photo doesn't show his bald spot. He wears a gray sports coat offset by a flowered tie suggestive of the 1960s.

Like its predecessor, this passport received considerable use. Stamps of ten countries, mostly in Europe and the Caribbean, embellish it. I recall three trips as particularly noteworthy. One was to Spain, a father-son venture. From Madrid we went north to the Basque region. Both of us were duly impressed by Frank Gehry's masterpiece, the Bilbao Guggenheim, a multi-angled arc of a museum shimmering in its titanium skin. The word *genius* has been devalued by overuse, but in Gehry's case it's appropriate. Another noteworthy trip was to the Canadian Rockies, where Judy and I heli-hiked at 9000 feet, where our group had a snowball fight at Lake Louise on the Fourth of July. Another, to Costa Rica with its fascinating biodiversity. Its sloths and spider monkeys, its orchids and banana plants, its poisonous red frogs the size of thumbnails. Besides the flora and fauna, you have to like a country with one hundred percent literacy and no standing army.

But our most memorable trip required no passport. For our twenty-fifth anniversary we went to Hawaii.

We split most of our time between Maui and the Big Island. Our hotel in Maui, rows of villas amidst Eden-lush gardens, minutes from the ocean. We upgraded the car rental and traversed the seaside and mountain roads in a red Mustang convertible. On the Big Island we circled Crater Rim Drive, we saw the lava-strewn moonscapes of Hawaii Volcanoes National Park. Taking an aerial tour, we saw the unforgettable spectacle of new land forming as lava poured into the ocean, producing clouds of steaming hydrochloric acid. Come back in a few million years and you might conceivably drive between Hawaii and California.

A near-perfect vacation—restful and restorative with stunning sights, geological wonders, obliging people, and ideal weather. Then we left for home, on an overnight flight from Honolulu to St. Louis, arriving the morning of September 11, 2001.

We waited for the connecting flight to Hartford when it happened. No overhead announcement. An anxious TWA employee, looking like the bearer of dark secrets, made rounds from gate to gate. He conferred with agents at each Jetway. Boarding stopped, and word spread that all flights were grounded. First interpretation: *There's a problem in the tower. A computer must be down.* Then word spread that flights were grounded everywhere.

Later, we learned about the World Trade Center. It was one of a number of combined facts and rumors, all preposterous. Other planes had crashed into the Pentagon, and a car bomb exploded in front of the State Department, and an unknown number of airborne flights hadn't been heard from, and LAX may have been a target, and they'd evacuated the White House.

TVs hung suspended every hundred feet or so, and instantly they went dark, but people crowded into bars and restaurants where they stayed on. And there it was: a plane crashing into a tower, and then another, and apocalyptic clouds of flame and smoke, and people running. News drifted in from Washington and rural Pennsylvania. The events turned into facts, no longer rumors, but still impossible to grasp. You lack a frame of reference for such things.

People stayed mostly calm despite the palpable tension. Cell phone conversations, quieter than usual. *I love you* came up a lot.

The airport became a lobster trap. Planes arrived, not just flights to St. Louis but all planes in the vicinity, and they weren't taking off. Crowds grew particularly dense at the baggage claim, where mobs of stranded travelers intermingled with cops, airport employees, and sniffer dogs. Baggage came randomly off the carousels, mounds of it lined against walls. A given mound might have bags from Seattle and Sarasota and four or five other places.

More news trickled in. They'd evacuated the John Hancock in Boston and the Sears Tower in Chicago. No one could estimate the number of terrorists yet, but their power to destroy was formidable, their power to disrupt even greater. Apart from the terrorists themselves, a few psychopaths called in bomb threats.

By coincidence, Judy and I had spent our last day in Hawaii at Pearl Harbor with its somber dignity and beauty, where oil still leaked from the U.S.S. Arizona. We wondered how Japan could have executed a surprise attack of such enormity. Surely nothing similar could happen now. Surely our satellites and electronic wizardry, our worldwide intelligence networks, left us more or less secure. Of course they would.

That had been less than a day ago.

It took three hours to collect our baggage, another three to leave the airport. We were luckier than many; we had relatives across the Mississippi, in Illinois. Every hotel filled within hours of the attacks, every rental car was either gone or available at ten times the normal rate.

As we finally drove off (my brother, who lived in Southern Illinois at the time, picked us up), I stole a glance at the airport behind us, the runways and tarmacs motionless and silent, planes jammed wing-tip to wing-tip, as on the flight deck of an aircraft carrier. Overhead, a cloudless sky. It would have been a perfect day for flying.

U.S. PASSPORT 42021XXXX, *issued December 2006, valid through December 2016. Within this time: first African-American President, first female Speaker of the House. Worst economic crisis since the Depression, endless entanglements in Iraq and Afghanistan. Steve Jobs presents the world with iPhones. Harry Potter, Iron Man, and Ninja Turtles provide escapist fare. "Who am I to judge?" asks Pope Francis, former nightclub bouncer, a man who laughed when a child snatched the Papal Beanie. Bashir Assad, Syrian eye doctor, gives up medicine and attacks his citizens with poison gas and cluster bombs. Among those born: Prince George and Princess Charlotte. Among those who died: Margaret Thatcher, Andrew Wyeth, Shirley Temple, Osama bin Laden, and 15,000 when Cyclone Sidr hit Bangladesh. Daniel Day-Lewis* (Lincoln) *and Meryl Streep* (The Iron Lady) *win their third Oscars. Stranger than fiction: despite losing the popular vote by 3.5 million, Trump wins the 2016 election.*

The passport picture captures a man in late middle age. A neutral facial expression, hard to read, rather stoic. His hair isn't much grayer than in the previous photo, but furrows of his forehead are deeper and wrinkles on his neck more prominent. He made numerous trips since receiving this passport, more of them domestic than foreign—family visits, professional meetings, school reunions.

Judy and I did make a trip, too hurried, to the Netherlands and Belgium. In Amsterdam we went to the Anne Frank House, the Rijksmuseum and the Van Gogh. Not to mention the KattenKabinet, possibly the world's only museum dedicated to felines. The Belgian highlight: a day in Bruges with its medieval guild halls and townhouses, its swans swimming lazily on a network of canals. A wondrous place, deservedly a UNESCO World Heritage Site.

More leisurely was a trip to London, our first trip there together. We visited the Tower, its ravens cawing timelessly, and the Tower Bridge, completed in 1894, still an impressive piece of engineering. We paid respects to the newly refurbished Globe Theatre, which gave a sense of what productions were really like in Shakespeare's day. Never easy, the theatrical life. Case in point, actors routinely used arsenic-based makeup. We went to the British Museum, ate

Cornish pasties, and saw *Spamalot,* a nice capturing of the British gift for self-parody.

We also made our first trip to Switzerland with the snow-capped grandeur of the Alps, its virgin forests and spotless cities. The sparkling lakes along the Italian border (Como, Lugano, and Maggiore), among the two or three most beautiful places we've ever seen. I know many Europeans regard the Swiss as arrogant and standoffish, but we found them friendly and obliging, quick to help with directions and recommendations, and tolerant of our mediocre French.

But our favorite trip was to Scotland, especially the Highlands. Flying to Edinburgh, we took a train to Inverness. From there we embarked on an inland cruise through mountain-rimmed lochs, bordered by battlefields and castles, as we drank in the land's harsh but beguiling scenery. For my second time, Judy's first, we ate haggis (she wasn't smitten). A serendipitous side trip: walking through the cemetery on Iona, an island off the northwest coast where Scottish royalty was buried, where the bones of Macbeth and Duncan lay beneath us. Lady Macbeth's were buried near the ruins of an adjacent convent.

U.S. PASSPORT 55776XXXX, *issued November 2016, valid through November 2026—not yet expired as of this writing. Within this time, so far: Civil wars drag on in Syria and Yemen, the U.K. atwitter over Brexit. Trump survives two impeachments and leaves Washington in a schoolboy sulk, first president since 1869 not to attend his successor's inauguration. Putin invades the Ukraine. Worst racial unrest since the 1960s. Derek Chauvin, not looking the least bit angry, knees George Floyd in the neck for nine minutes. Among those who died: Kobe Bryant, Mary Tyler Moore, Fidel Castro, Toni Morrison, and*

Queen Elizabeth. Also Li Wenliang, a Chinese doctor who gave the first warnings (unheeded) about COVID. Joe Biden rebounds on Super Tuesday, but Michael Bloomberg wins Samoa. The pandemic wreaks havoc; people wait for hours at foodbanks; others fight in stores over toilet paper. Patriots fans sit Shiva when Tom Brady signs with Tampa Bay. Scientists discover the fossil of an ancient anchovy, a yard long, with fangs and a saber tooth— "You think you're gonna put me in a Caesar salad? Fuggedaboutit!" By February 2021, the number of Americans killed by COVID exceeds U.S. deaths in World Wars I and II and Vietnam.

The picture on my current passport shows a man who has faced the years advancing without mercy. His hair is undeniably grayer and thinner, his eyes bemused, as if he's wondering, *Dear God, how did I get to be this old?* His first passport photo captures someone more a boy than a man, and this one captures someone in his seventies.

More travels have been domestic than foreign as I visited members of my small but far-flung family. Trips to Virginia, where my son lives, where my only granddaughter was born. Trips to New Mexico where, on one memorable occasion, Lolly took me to the Albuquerque Balloon Festival, a cavalcade of color against a crystalline blue sky. Trips to Maine, where Judy and I unwound in Sloane's idyllic lakeside retreat—where I swam, canoed with Sloane's husband, and threw my mind out of gear.

Several trips to California, where I watched helplessly as time took its toll on Eileen. Frail, slow, and often losing words, she nonetheless enjoyed a good meal and a good book and visits with her children and grandchildren. She could still be good company. She spoke well; her wit could still be quick. And you have to like a woman of ninety-nine who saw Trump on TV and erupted, "I can't believe that fuckhead is my president!"

On an April Saturday in 2019 she spent the afternoon at the ocean with a friend, had dinner with Lisa, went to bed and never woke up. One could ask for no better ending for a much-loved parent or anyone else one cared about. All four of her children made it to her bedside before she died, as she lay unconscious. Hoping she sensed our presence, even if she couldn't see us . . . hoping she felt our hands on hers . . . hoping she heard our voices, maybe recognizing them, even if she couldn't make out the words.

To date I've used the passport for five trips. Two to Canada, Montreal and Quebec. One to the gently rolling Cornish countryside in the U.K.'s southwestern shores. Doc Martin's turf, perhaps Great Britain's loveliest scenery. I also went solo to Germany, where the Donaldsons and I saw Herbert for a last time. Herbert was diagnosed with Lewy Body Dementia in 2018. He could still recognize his visitors, and most of the time he spoke coherently, often about our Dublin days together. The Kupers lived in Karlsruhe, close to France. We crossed the border and took in the canals and cathedral of Strasbourg, surely among the world's most photogenic cities.

The most recent trip was to Berlin. I joined my sister Lolly there, when she attended a gathering of glassblowers from all over the world. Berlin, one of the three or four most interesting cities I've seen so far. Among the highlights, remaining parts of the Wall, now turned into a de facto outdoor art gallery with paintings, drawings, and all kinds of graffiti. Another highlight, the Memorial to the Murdered

Jews of Europe, almost five acres, with its grid of 2,711 concrete slabs ("stelae"), a metaphor for a graveyard? A subterranean museum beneath them features photos of the Holocaust and clips of interviews with survivors. None of which does justice to what happened.

On a much happier note, the trip included a stopover in Dublin and quite possibly my last visit to RCSI. Krasna, a young Canadian woman living in Ireland and working for the school now, showed me around. The unchanged battle-scarred exterior is still marred by evidence of the Irish Civil War, but most of the interior is unrecognizably new. They now use rubberized smart mannequins that can be programmed to replicate cardiopulmonary symptoms and even to teach students about obstetrical problems—a breech presentation, for instance. They can also give students a chance to learn to do procedures like lumbar punctures before taking on living, breathing patients.

Among the many differences between contemporary Dublin and the city as I first remembered it: The airport's about three times bigger and ten times busier. Flights to Helsinki, Cairo, and Qatar as well as New York, Boston, and the major European capitals. Several Aer Lingus gate agents were women with Islamic head coverings. Local elections were coming up, and signs promoted candidates with names like Diaz, Napolitano, and Al-Ramahi. Coffee bars on almost every block. Indian, Thai, and Halal restaurants, as well as French and Italian ones. Kum Tong, with cauliflower in the chow mein, is long gone, alas.

Still, so much is the same. The double-deck buses, defying gravity by remaining upright. Irish soul food—sure, there are restaurants where you can get your boeuf bourguignon and pad thai, but you can still get your bangers and mash and colcannon. The pub scene,

St. Stephen's Green with its well-fed ducks. The General Post Office on O'Connell Street, where the Irish Uprising began. The lousy weather. The people, the accent, the Irish way with words. The people, especially the people.

MY PASSPORT EXPIRES IN 2026. If alive, I'll be eighty-four. Will I be able to travel? Will I want to? Will anyone? Who'd have dreamed of block-long lines to get through security? Of worse service on fewer flights, always packed? Of paying extra for baggage and pillows? And how will Americans be received abroad? Will we be welcomed? Shunned? Spat upon?

Still, I'm guessing I'll travel as long as possible, assuming COVID-19 and other pandemics don't preclude anyone from going anywhere. Looking at my passports, I can't imagine my life without them. They've allowed me to see London's Westminster Abbey and Venice's canals, the Bilbao Guggenheim and the Rijksmuseum with its Rembrandts and Vermeers, and Costa Rican rainforests and the Alps. They've allowed me to meet Dr. R., a Belfast-trained surgeon who became a reluctant expert in treating bomb injuries when The Troubles heated up again, and Edina, the Hungarian guide who awaited life after communism with her bright but wary eyes, and the interestingly-named Pringles, a reptile expert from whose boat we snorkeled in the Turks and Cacaos—to meet hundreds more who've enhanced my life.

I'll use this passport because, among other things, there's a family tradition to maintain. My mother went to Australia and my grandfather to Mainland China when both were in their nineties. I'll use this passport because I've yet to see the Acropolis and the

Pyramids, Mount Aetna and Mount Fuji, and a score of other places on my bucket list. Because travel is first and foremost a matter of people, of discovering a common humanity with strangers (or so we might hope). Because the world, for all its flaws and cruelties, is too interesting for one to stay at home.

CHAPTER XIV

THE WRITTEN WORD

I CAN'T RECALL WHEN IT FIRST OCCURRED TO ME that I liked to write. It probably was in the third or fourth grade, around the time they start assigning book reports. Like all good passive-aggressive preteens, I joined my classmates in grousing about them, but in fact I quite enjoyed them. I enjoyed the process of condensing the gist of a book into a few pages and throwing in my own comments and opinions. I enjoyed working with words and sentences, the bricks and mortar of the writing process.

I especially enjoyed it when I got older, and teachers—as a rule, the better ones—let students pick their own books to report on. I still remember one of them, written for a history class, *The Young Hitler I Knew*. The author, an elderly Austrian named August Kubizek, had been Hitler's friend and sometime roommate in Vienna before World War I. The book made no attempt either to glamorize or demonize the future Fuhrer who, during the period Kubizek wrote about, was scarcely older than I was when I read it. While hardly a sympathetic figure, already filled with prejudice and anger, unable to tolerate opinions other than his own, Hitler was still less fiend than human. He enjoyed opera, aimed for a career in art and architecture, and was even a pretty good friend to the young Kubizek. Despite my youth, I found myself caught up in the tantalizing and ultimately unanswerable question of how terrible people got that way.

At Culver and Yale, I wrote the requisite papers. Subjects ranged from Martin Buber's *I and Thou* to the life and work of Philippe Pinel, 1745–1826, the French psychiatrist who espoused the radical notion that the insane should be treated humanely and not chained up. One of the figures I wrote about with less reverence was William Wordsworth, the English poet, who debated at length about which tree he should sit beneath while he waxed poetic. I likened him to a dog agonizing over fire hydrant selection. The graduate student who graded the essay, a humorless sort, didn't care for the analogy.

Although I'd excelled in it at Culver, I took few English courses in college. But I did sign up for Yale's well-known course, officially called Daily Themes, sometimes referred to as the DTs. As its name suggests, a straightforward format: Students wrote brief papers, on a daily or near-daily basis, on subjects of their choosing. Book reviews or snippets of personal experience, fiction or nonfiction. Practically anything was grist for the mill. Students took turns reading them out loud.

The course proved disastrous for me. Part of that stemmed from the freedom I'd had at Yale—as noted, a freedom for which I was ill-prepared. I'd flourished at Culver not just because of its first-rate teachers but also because of the structure there. Culver was a military school, after all. Things were done in certain ways and at certain times. You got up and went to bed when they told you to, and you cut no classes, and you turned in assignments on due dates. Drinking alcohol was grounds for dismissal, and marijuana was unheard of. At Yale, on the other hand, you could routinely go to bed at 5AM and sleep till noon, and you could skip classes for weeks or months, and you could spend your days drunk or stoned if you felt like it. You didn't even need a fake ID to get hold of liquor. You could simply go to New York State, where the drinking age was eighteen.

To write essays on demand required a degree of self-discipline I couldn't summon at the time. I dropped the course before I failed it.

The course did teach me a few things though. First, the experience of reading my stuff out loud was valuable. When I write now, I try to imagine how it would sound to a critical and not innately benevolent audience. It also taught me to edit and criticize my own material unsparingly before others have a chance to do it for me.

I WROTE LITTLE WHILE in Ireland, apart from detailed letters to family and friends. But I did write something modestly ambitious about George Orwell.

Orwell has been near the top of the list of my favorite writers since I first discovered him as a teenager. I admired his unwillingness to use twelve words when he could get away with ten. His rich but succinct descriptions. (A glimpse of the protagonist's wife in *Coming up for Air*— "When she's more upset than usual, she's got a trick of humping her shoulders . . . like an old gypsy woman over her fire.") His inclination to take on some of the biggest and most daunting topics. The sins of colonialism in *Burmese Days*. The fragility of idealism, and how readily it can be corrupted, in *Animal Farm*. The vision of a dystopia lacking all hope in *1984*. Who could forget Orwell's vision of days to come as enunciated by O'Brien, the novel's antihero. "If you want a picture of the future, imagine a boot stomping on a human face, forever."

Since a number of European medical students began to study medicine as soon as they graduated from secondary school—that is, without an undergraduate degree—they often sought to broaden their education themselves on nonmedical matters. At RCSI we occasionally met in informal groups in which students picked a subject of interest to them and then talked about it for an hour or two. The subject might be King Louis XIV and his reign, or the plays of John Millington Synge, or something pertaining to contemporary politics.

I picked Orwell. About his growing up in Burma, the son of a minor British bureaucrat, and how that led to his disenchantment with colonialism. About making his way through the underbellies of two great cities *(Down and Out in Paris and London)*—working as a dishwasher; living in an attic cubbyhole where "[an] S-shaped chain of bugs marched slowly across the wall above the bed." About his taking a bullet in the neck while fighting in the Spanish Civil War *(Homage to Catalonia),* and reporting for the BBC during World War II. And finally, the writing of his two dark masterpieces, *Animal Farm* and *1984,* before he died at forty-six.

The presentation gave me an excuse to reread several of Orwell's classics. It proved to be of interest to my classmates, and it renewed my appreciation for one of the twentieth century's most important authors. It also reignited my efforts to write as concisely as possible.

I WROTE NOTHING DURING internship and residency. Given the workload, moonlighting, and the brouhaha of my personal life, I'd have been hard-pressed to write a postcard.

That began to change in the late 1970s. I started with nonfiction. At the time, the *Hartford Courant* had a Sunday magazine called *Northeast*. The editors welcomed submissions by local authors. Through the years, I sent them pieces on a variety of topics. Two of these dealt with practicing psychiatry in correctional settings. Another dealt with blended families, a subject I learned about the hard way in the years following my divorce and remarriage. Another dealt with managed care, which was just beginning to befoul the medical landscape—a rant, of sorts, but therapeutic in the writing. Another, definitely a rant, concerned the Red Sox fiasco of 1986, when they were *one out away* from their first World Series championship in sixty-eight years. Judy, a Massachusetts native, a veteran of Red Sox fadeouts since grade school, tried to warn me. Would I listen to her? *No-ooo* . . .

I started to try my hand at short stories. Quite a few were forgettable but others were okay, and some of them actually made it to the printed page. I also wrote a novel I try not to think about. A warmup exercise (a generous assessment), deservedly unpublished.

ONE OF MY MORE memorable literary endeavors concerns a novel never written.

In the 1980s I read an article in *Newsweek* about the death penalty as applied to criminals convicted for crimes committed as minors. The article mentioned, in passing, the case of George Stinney Jr., a Black youth who lived in South Carolina. In 1944 he was convicted of the murder of two white girls, eleven and seven. Stinney himself was fourteen. The evidence against him was questionable at best. In a trial that lasted two hours, an all-white jury found him guilty after deliberations that took less than ten minutes. He was sentenced to death.

Eighty-three days after the girls' deaths and fifty-three days after his conviction, the boy died in South Carolina's electric chair. The date of his execution, June 16, is significant. There might have been an outcry against doing away with one so young, even a Black youth in the Deep South convicted of killing white girls. He might have been given a reprieve, or his case might have been appealed. But his death occurred less than two weeks after the Normandy invasion, and the nation's attention was focused elsewhere.

Given his size—five feet one, weighing ninety pounds—it proved challenging to execute him. He was literally too small for the chair, so they had him sit on a phone book. The hood was too big for him too. In the course of his execution, it slipped off his face and revealed a weeping child.

My reaction to the article was immediate, visceral, and unarguable: *I have to write a historical novel about this.* The idea took hold of me like no other literary project, before or since.

I found out whatever I could about the case. By chance, the annual meeting of the American Psychiatric Association was in Washington that spring, and I spent most of a day at the Library of Congress. I read microfilmed accounts of Stinney's arrest and trial as covered in contemporary newspapers. I wrote letters to defense attorneys throughout the country who'd been active in death penalty cases involving underage defendants. Within a few months I'd put together an outline for the novel. I even had a tentative title for it, *The Boy in the Black Hood.*

The book became close to a full-blown obsession. At least twice a week, often more, I dreamt about the electric chair. Sometimes I witnessed an execution and sometimes I was in the chair myself.

One day I telephoned a lawyer in Ohio who listened patiently while I spoke about the book as I'd envisioned it. When I finished, the lawyer paused before replying. When he did, his tone suggested a surgeon about to tell a patient the pathology had come back ominous. "I don't know if you're aware of this," he said, "but there's a reporter for the *New York Times* who just finished a novel about the Stinney case."

I always thought it was a figure of speech when someone said his heart sank, but I distinctly felt a large mass shift downward in my chest.

The lawyer went on to tell me that the reporter's name was David Stout, and I contacted him straightaway. Hoping against hope that Mr. Stout's book might turn out to be sufficiently different from what I had in mind, I asked him to meet with me.

A couple of weeks later, I went into New York City. David Stout had, indeed, just finished a novel about the Stinney case. *Carolina Skeletons,* he'd titled it. The novel was not identical to what I had in mind, but the similarities were way too close for comfort. Published in 1988, it was subsequently made into a well-reviewed TV movie of the same name, and I abandoned my own project.

This episode brings up an interesting point. Among the potential problems writers face, it's unlikely they'll consider that someone, somewhere in the world, is busily at work on essentially the same thing. Or worse yet, has just finished it.

THROUGHOUT THE LATE 1980s and early 1990s, my writing became cleaner and tighter, less self-referential and self-indulgent. I went to conferences and workshops, although not as many as I should have. Slowly and painstakingly, I learned the prevalent conventions. Show, don't tell. Begin as close to the end as possible, a piece of advice from Kurt Vonnegut. Don't be afraid to beat up your protagonist. I also read books by writers about writing, books by authors as diverse as Annie Dillard, Stephen King, and Joyce Carol Oates.

In November 2001, on Cape Cod, I attended a memorable conference. The attendees were doctors interested in writing fiction. We came from throughout the U.S. and Canada. The one who'd traveled farthest was a pediatrician from Winnipeg, a long and arduous trip in the wake of 9/11. We represented a dozen different specialties. Some of us hadn't finished residencies and others had retired. Some of us had already published articles, poems, and stories, and others were just starting out.

The main presenters were two doctors whose books had made it to the bestseller lists. The late Michael Palmer, an internist, wrote over twenty works of crime fiction with a medical slant, translated into thirty-five languages. Not a natural writer. As an undergrad, he wrote an English paper so bad he not only received a failing grade, but the professor refused to read the second half of it. Palmer exacted a nice revenge; he named the villain in his first novel after him.

Palmer's co-presenter was Tess Gerritsen, who mostly wrote medical thrillers. Among her claims to fame: her books led to the *Rizzoli and Isles* TV series. An odd couple, Palmer and Gerritsen. He was a large, pleasantly tousled man (he reminded me of an unmade bed) who liked to go off script. She was a trim, petite, well-organized woman who spoke concisely and to the point. Like Palmer, though, her presentations included interesting tangents. In researching NASA for one of her books, for instance, she found out there are pre-written obituaries for every astronaut on a given mission. She also found out that people in NASA and the military tend to hate each other.

Notwithstanding their differences, Palmer and Gerritsen worked well together. They had a good chemistry between them.

What ensued were two solid days of seminars that touched on all the bases. The mechanics of plot and subplot, the creation of three-dimensional characters. The pros and cons of using first and third person. The avoidance of wooden dialog, a frequent shortcoming of physicians who lapse into overly technical jargon— "As you know, Doctor Fubar, the half-life of mirtazapine is thirty hours." A reiteration of the importance of showing versus telling. Palmer gave an example. *My father was an abusive alcoholic.* (telling). *"Yurr late," my father slurred, as he threw an empty beer bottle at me.* (showing).

The more daring ones took turns reading excerpts of their work out loud, receiving the candid but generally kind feedback from Palmer and Gerritsen as well as from fellow attendees. The most daring—or grandiose, take your pick—read excerpts about intimate encounters, myself not among them. I admit to finding it hard to write graphically about sex. There are, for instance, the dual dangers of becoming overly romantic *(Doug and Daphne coalesced into a pool of liquid silk)* and the overly macho *(She writhed and moaned as I drove the old rapscallion home)*.

The conference was a useful, stressful, invigorating, exhausting, and ultimately heartening couple of days. Perhaps its main usefulness was to learn (relearn) the not-so-obvious truth that I had company. That countless others—not merely from medicine but from every walk of life, no doubt—shared the dream of writing with its attendant loneliness and frustrations as well as its near-addictive lure.

IN THE EARLY 1990s I wrote a novel about psychiatric testimony and the death penalty, never published, but this one I could reread with a measure of pride. I wrote another novel, and another. Then, at an age that made me eligible for Medicare, I got one published, called *Model Child*. Its main plot: a middle-aged man with no criminal or mental health history, an ordinary sort, commits a heinous and apparently senseless crime. There's no mystery about who did it, but the question is *why?* By this time, I'd also self-published a prison-centric collection of six short stories and a novella, *The Stephen Hawking Death Row Fan Club*. While the primary focus was on the prisoners, the book also concerned those who worked in correctional settings. The correctional officers, administrators, and health care professionals. It also concerned those victimized by violent crimes. Writing it brought to me the recognition that my stint with Corrections had had a much more profound effect on me than I'd imagined.

In addition to fiction, I wrote a screenplay about Lady Macbeth, my candidate for the most fascinating woman in Western literature. Sad to say, neither Martin Scorsese nor Francis Ford Coppola optioned it.

The summer before my last year in Dublin, I did an externship at a hospital in Washington. Among the attendings was Xavier Rios, a Spanish cardiologist. One day, making rounds, we came to the bedside of a woman with serious heart problems. When the group left the patient and reconvened in the corridor, Dr. Rios addressed the others. "As we can see, she has an abnormal and most unusual EKG. I have discussed that abnormality at length in my book on EKG interpretation." The book, he went on to say with mock-grandiosity, was a masterpiece. He paused. "*All* books are masterpieces. If any of you ever write one, you will understand this."

When I began to write my own books, I understood what Dr. Rios was talking about.

As I mull over my attempts to write, I consider what I've learned along the way. I especially consider things I wish I'd learned at the onset, things I'd try to impart to others as they're starting out. Things I'd tell my students in the unlikely event I ever taught a creative writing course. They include, in no particular order, the following:

IF WHAT YOU WRITE DOESN'T STRIKE YOU AS ALTOGETHER RIGHT, IT'S WRONG.

This is not as obvious as it may seem. It's late, and you're tired. You write something that looks okay, or at least sort of okay, or in any case it's not bad. You've already rewritten it nine times, and you don't feel like pushing for ten. You go to bed, having tried to persuade yourself that it's better than it is. The next morning you reread it, delete it, and start over, which is altogether appropriate. Every writer goes through something like that, repeatedly, *ad nauseum.*

WRITE ABOUT YOURSELF IF YOU MUST, BUT DO SO GINGERLY.

Try to remember you're not the first person who fell in or out of love, had sex, had your heart broken or broke someone else's heart, became a parent, lost a parent, contemplated suicide, or contemplated your own mortality.

I've written about all these things with varying degrees of success. There's a fine line between appropriate self-exposure and a masturbatory narcissism. Finding such a line can prove difficult.

READ CRITICALLY.

Again, not as obvious as it may seem. It's not merely a question of whether or not you find a book well-written or absorbing or useful. You need to figure out why you like or dislike it. The writer who made you laugh or cry or made you want to hit him. How did he do it? What makes her a good writer? Why would you go out of the way to read more of her? Why did you forget about his novel as soon as you finished it, and why does hers stay with you indefinitely?

Haruki Murakami, perhaps Japan's best known novelist, puts it more succinctly. He advises aspiring novelists "to read everything you can get your hands on—great novels, not-so-great novels, crappy novels, it doesn't matter (at all!) as long as you keep reading."

YOU DON'T HAVE TO BE AN EXPERT TO WRITE ABOUT SOMETHING AS LONG AS YOU'RE WILLING TO DO THE HOMEWORK.

You're only supposed to write about what you know or what you've experienced, or so goes the conventional wisdom. A dubious assumption, in my opinion. If this were altogether true, there'd be no such thing as good historical fiction since no writer has lived in other than his or her own lifetime. Few, though, would dispute the excellence of the likes of Hilary Mantel and E.L. Doctorow.

You can look things up, and such research can be one of the most interesting and serendipitous parts of the writing process. I've delved into Nevada atomic bomb tests in the 1950s, cross-cultural concepts of the devil, the history of the death penalty in America, and eye injuries, among other things. My *a priori* knowledge of these subjects ranged from limited to close to nil, but I was willing to find out about them.

I've also consulted experts. They've included a prison psychologist at Somers, pharmaceutical reps, a Congregational minister, two public defenders, a state cop, and my glassblowing sister. They've included nurses and social workers with whom I worked. Most have been happy to share their expertise.

TAKING A STEP AWAY FROM WHAT YOU WRITE CAN BE INVALUABLE.

Let's say you've written something, and you've gone through a bunch of rewrites, and you're reasonably happy with it. You really believe it's the best you can do. You put it away and come back to it in three or six months, and you're stunned by all the possible improvements that jump out at you. A change in punctuation here, an added or subtracted paragraph there, a new descriptive detail, the substitution of a better word or phrase. Tightening a segment of dialog that's awkward or redundant. These changes may seem extremely obvious to you once you've taken a hiatus from what you've written.

I've never revisited something I wrote without noting how I might improve it.

YOU CAN BREAK ALL THE RULES IF YOU'RE GOOD ENOUGH, BUT YOU PROBABLY AREN'T.

Hemingway's sentences were famously clipped and short. Curt. Unadorned. Maybe to a fault. You're not supposed to write like that. But it worked for him. He was Hemingway. Dickens, on the other hand, wrote sentences that were twice, nay thrice as long as they should have been, and they could be as ornate as Miss Havisham's crumbling wedding cake, and he rarely met an adjective or adverb he didn't like, all of which he used with an overabundance of generosity, but he was Dickens, after all, so we shall not quibble with him.

A number of Shakespeare's plots were preposterous, relying as they did on coincidence, outlandish misrepresentations of persons, and *deus ex machina*. He could even get his history wrong. The historical Macbeth was a virtuous man, in fact, and Duncan was a villain. But he was Shakespeare, so who gives a flying one?

ACCEPT THE FACT THAT YOU'LL HAVE TO MARKET YOURSELF.

When I became serious about writing, and as I gradually grew better at it, I believed the marketing would take care of itself. I would write a few letters to a few prospective agents, or so went the happy fantasy, and one of them would sign me up forthwith. A publisher would fall in love with the book at first glance, and best seller lists awaited me. This is akin to believing in the tooth fairy, and I marvel at the extent of my innocence and undue optimism. It must have made God laugh heartily.

I still regret my unwillingness to promote myself earlier and more vigorously and to network. My unwillingness to attend more conferences and workshops.

Self-promotion goes strongly against my nature. Moreover, I hate rejection. As I said to a fellow writer once, I'd make a terrible stalker. One summer, in a moment of ill-conceived folly, I tried selling brushes door to door. I lasted all of two hours. But I've come to acknowledge self-promotion as a necessary evil. If my letters of rejection could paper a ballroom, so be it. Goes with the badge.

THE ULTIMATE TRICK IS NO TRICK.
Tricks are fun, and I've used a fair number of them. Writing in the second person, which I stole from Jay McInerney in *Bright Lights, Big City*. Burying key dramatic details in the middle of an otherwise innocuous paragraph. Anne Tyler, among others, does this beautifully. I tried but failed to write a piece of fiction in which a major subplot remained unsettled *until the very last word*. Max Byrd did so in *Jackson*, a masterful historical novel based on the life and times of the seventh president. A hard trick to pull off, but Byrd managed it.

But the most basic trick may be the hardest, to create a clean straightforward piece of writing, neither too spare nor overly detailed. A piece that's well-paced, honest, and believable. Something that may inform readers, or make them laugh or cry, or enrage them, but doesn't condescend to them. Something that grabs their attention right away and keeps it.

YOUR OPENING LINES ARE ABSOLUTELY CRUCIAL.
If there's one thing agents, editors, and writers can agree upon, it's that you have a very brief opportunity to hook a prospective reader. Consider three openers. "There were hateful presences in me." (E.L. Doctorow, *Loon Lake*). "It was a queer, sultry summer, the summer they executed the Rosenbergs, and I didn't know what I was doing in New York." (Sylvia Plath, *The Bell Jar*). And there's Orwell. During World War II, during the worst of the Blitz, he wrote a book called *The Lion and the Unicorn*. In it he strived to elucidate why England was worth fighting for. "As I write," he began, "highly civilized

human beings are flying overhead, trying to kill me." Could anyone have done it better, or more simply?

My list of memorable opening lines should include Roy Blount's beginning sentences of his enjoyable *First Hubby*, about the spouse of the first woman president. The protagonist introduces her thus— "The first time I saw her she was naked, except for pearls and the look in her eyes. My thoughts, as best I can reconstruct them, were 'What? Hm? *Well*.'"

Apropos, writers often try to tell too much too soon when they're starting out. To wit, *Bridget Boysenberry, a thirty-three-year-old anesthesiologist with curly red hair, dazzling blue eyes, and an omigod body, the daughter of an architect and an ex-nun turned cocktail waitress who divorced when she turned twelve, was born in Reno but grew up in Boston, where she lost her virginity at seventeen.*

This opinion, we should note, is not universally acknowledged. Kurt Vonnegut took the opposite view. "Give your readers as much information as possible as soon as possible."

YOU CAN ALWAYS FIND REASONS NOT TO WRITE. LEARN TO IGNORE THEM.

It's been raining for three days straight, and you're too depressed to write a restaurant review for Tripadvisor, much less an article or short story. Or it's a perfect early summer day, and every cell in your body pleads with you to go outside. Or the French Open is on TV, or the World Series, or the Discovery Channel has a must-see documentary on aardvarks. Or you're worried about the meeting you have with your accountant next week, or the colonoscopy scheduled for the week after that.

The intended plot of your screenplay has gotten hopelessly

muddled. Or the characters in your short story won't do what you think they should; they're like recalcitrant children who won't listen to you. Or your novel has a courtroom scene, and one of the lawyers has to give a summation, but you're not a lawyer. This happened me when I wrote about a murder trial in a capital case.

There's only one answer to these dilemmas. Think Nike; Just do it.

CHAPTER XV

A TERRIBLE THING TO HAPPEN TO A LITTLE BOY

In 1951, at the age of seventy-six, Winston Churchill became prime minister for the second time. A year later he suffered a catastrophic stroke. His illness remained a closely guarded state secret. Those who divulged it, including medical personnel, might have been found guilty of treason as defined by the Official Secrets Act. They could conceivably have been hanged.

Masterpiece Theatre made an engrossing movie, *Churchill's Secret*, based on his illness and recovery. The move goes back and forth in time, portraying him as both a carefree child and a failing septuagenarian. "Old age . . ." the prime minister tells a nurse who became his friend and confidante, "what a terrible thing to happen to a little boy!"

As they say in Parliament, *Hear, Hear.*

My attitude toward my own advancing years has swerved between halfhearted denial and glum acceptance. Denial, I believe, can be useful in spite of its bad reputation. Yes, it can refer to an alcoholic's refusal to accept his alcoholism, or a sociopath's refusal to accept responsibility for anything, but it can also refer to someone's belief that he'll survive a near-fatal heart attack. Someone else with a less serious heart attack who believes he'll die is more likely to do so. Attitude counts.

Denial, in my own case, consists mainly of trying to hold on to the level of activity and degree of vigor I had a decade or two ago. I know that's a losing proposition, but I try, dear God, I try. One positive result: I maintain a fairly healthy lifestyle. Exercise, a decent diet, modest drinking, no smoking—I quit during Reagan's first term. Keeping my weight and blood pressure in check. I make plans for the future, not just for the immediate future but for ten or fifteen years from now. I look forward to attending my grandchildren's weddings, the oldest of whom is twenty.

Working at a university made this denial a bit easier. To be around college students won't make you younger, but it may promote a more youthful worldview. Of course that can backfire. "I broke up with him," a co-ed of nineteen told me. "He was *way* too old for me! He was *twenty-five!*"

But denial takes me just so far. People occasionally tell me I look younger than my age, but the birthdate on my driver's license doesn't lie. The cold realities of diminished strength and stamina, word-searching, and difficulties in assimilating new information aren't lost on me. Twenty years ago I might scan a psychiatric article and recall its contents indefinitely. A comparable article might now take two or three readings, and even then my retention of it might be spotty. When I read a novel, I can tell you about the plot and setting a year later, and I can probably tell you about the main characters' foibles, but I often can't tell you their names. Paradoxically, I might recall the names of major and even minor characters in a novel I read at Culver.

A variety of aches and pains aren't lost on me either. When I get out of bed, I take ibuprofen and a long hot shower before I feel as if I haven't been stomped on. To paraphrase John Updike, there comes a point in life when getting out of bed becomes an unnatural act. The hardest part of my day, vis-à-vis my physical condition, is often bending down in the morning to feed Penelope.

Ageing has affected my life in a number of ways, obvious and otherwise. Everything seems to take twice as long as it did, from making my way through the paper to making myself a cup of tea and an English muffin. Using a computer also takes longer than it did since my fingers have a way of slipping off the proper keys. Lest I start the day with a treasure hunt, I try to leave my wallet, phone, and briefcase in one place. I lose and misplace things so frequently that I've learned to factor in an extra fifteen or twenty minutes a day to look for them. (I felt better when I told Terry Holcombe this. Terry's reply, "Is that all?") Of necessity, I jot down lists of everything, even when going to ShopRite for bread, eggs, milk, and orange juice. As a rule, I can remember three items, but four of them is a stretch. In a museum, I find myself taking note of how long an artist lived. *Marvin Gardens, born 1887, died 1971. Hmm, eighty-four. I'm getting pretty close to that.*

Among the strangest phenomena is what might be called hiding in plain sight. I'm about to brush my teeth, but where's the toothpaste? I look through bathroom shelves and cabinets and repeatedly around the sink. Five minutes later I see it, on the counter where it has been all along. For no obvious reason my brain didn't recognize or conceptualize it as *toothpaste*. That scenario is only mildly annoying, but the phenomenon could be serious or fatal. Suppose I'm driving, and I don't register a stop sign or an oncoming car as such.

I suspect there's a point when fatigue becomes the default setting. Fortunate in energy and stamina I've had throughout my life, I find it yet another narcissistic blow to note their ebbing. I can't recall where I read this (maybe in Updike?), but the gist of it is that most people die because they're too tired to go on living. Sure, the heart disease or cancer might precipitate and accelerate their tiredness, but the tiredness per se is what does them in.

As I contemplate the overall increase of my fatigue, I remember a visit my parents made to Ireland a few years before I finished at RCSI. The three of us were driving around Wicklow, the postcard-perfect county just south of Dublin. We came to a graveyard nestled against the base of the Wicklow Mountains. A venerable site, the tombstones pushed into skewed angles through the centuries, many epitaphs too worn away to be read. As good a place as anywhere to spend the hereafter.

My father, an excellent photographer, took out his Leica and went to work. One shot in particular was to his liking. Perfect composition; gray cloudbanks with patches of blue sky and speckles of sunlight; mountain shadows falling just right across the cemetery. "I might have that one framed," he said, more to himself than to my mother and me. "If I do, I know what I'll call it. '*So Tired*.'"

A perfect title, I thought half a century later. *Not just for the photo, but for the winding down of life in general.*

I'VE TOYED WITH THE idea that a mild attention deficit disorder might be, in fact, a normal part of ageing. I note my own loss of focus, my distractibility, my going from kitchen to living room and then forgetting why I embarked upon the trip. How I frequently struggle to hold on to the thread of a conversation and how I find myself interrupting, a habit I abhor. It's not that I believe older people are inherently rude; I wonder if they interrupt because they fear they'll forget what they want to say if they don't. I usually finish what I set out to do but increasingly find it hard to stay on task, even when the task is interesting.

All these things are symptoms of attention deficit disorder.

There's this to be said for ageing, at least it's more or less gradual. One day, emerging from a shower, and you glance down and notice that your bunions are big enough to have their own zip codes. Four months later, halfway to your office, you have to double back because you left your glasses on the kitchen table—or your wallet, or your ear trumpet. Five months after that, you realize you haven't had sex since New Year's Day and it's already January 28. Worse, it dawns on you that you've barely missed it.

You glance through your address book (you still keep addresses in an address book and not in your phone, another manifestation of your age), and you find the name of at least one person who died on nearly every page. It jars you to note that virtually all your contemporaries have had life-threatening illnesses or injuries. You outlive relatives, you outlive a lot of friends, you outlive pets. You don't pray often, but you do pray you won't outlive your children or grandchildren.

You make room in your schedule for doctors' visits, and cataract surgery, and colonoscopies: commonplace but not insignificant procedures. You have a slew of routine tests—blood work, urinalyses, EKGs et al—and you wonder when they'll turn up something not routine.

My denial took its biggest hit on October 11, 2015. A Sunday morning, nothing extraordinary going on. No new health concerns or symptoms. No alcohol or other drugs the night before, not even a sleeping pill. No unusual sources of anxiety. If anything, I felt uncommonly relaxed.

I was in the living room with Penelope, drinking coffee, when Judy came in and sat next to me. She scrutinized me. "You look weird," she said finally. "You look like a gargoyle."

"I can't remember who the president is," I answered.

"Come, now."

"No, I really can't. Ask me some questions." I didn't know the kind of questions I had in mind.

"All right," she played along. "What major purchase did we just make?" We'd bought a Toyota Camry the week before.

I thought about it for maybe fifteen seconds before giving up. "I don't know, what?" When she told me, it was news.

I was getting her attention. "Who died recently?" she asked. Ten days earlier, Erik Linnolt, my mentor and friend for over forty years, had passed away at ninety-five."

I had no idea.

"Erik," she told me. "Erik Linnolt, your first supervisor."

"Erik died? *Erik*?" I felt my eyes well up.

Now I *really* had her attention. "What's the date?" she asked next.

I looked outside and saw the leaves in their multi-colored glory. "October," I reasoned. "I don't know the day."

She asked how long it was until my birthday (four days hence). I didn't know that either.

By the time we got to the hospital, I felt like myself, more or less. I knew the date and where I was. I could even think clinically—no numbness or paralysis, no gait impairment or facial droop, no slurred speech. Still, they admitted me. Just for a night, just to be sure.

I had the works. Lab tests, an EKG, MRI, a Doppler ultrasound of my carotids, whatever else they could think of. They checked me around the clock for neuro signs and vital signs. No evidence of anything out of the ordinary.

What happened to me is called transient global amnesia, or TGA. Per the Mayo Clinic website: *a sudden temporary episode of memory loss that can't be attributed to a more common neurological condition, such as epilepsy or stroke*. It's more common in the middle-aged or elderly, more common in men than women. As a rule, it impairs recent memory. If Judy had asked me where I learned JFK had been shot, most likely I could have told her. But if she'd asked me about the movie we'd seen the night before, most likely I would have drawn a blank.

It doesn't last long, typically two to eight hours. There's no known cause, although use of certain drugs, including digitalis and statins, have been associated with it. Despite the loss of memory, other cognitive functions remain mostly intact. You might conceivably play Scrabble when you had an episode of TGA, but you might not recall names of people you were playing with. I couldn't remember the date when Judy asked me, but I could determine that the month was October because of the foliage. It's benign. No residual problem with memory, no increased likelihood of serious problems later. But it still gets your attention.

My case was mild, but it reiterated what I already knew, that anything can happen to any of us at any time. It also fed into my fear of a debilitating neurological event, of cognitive impairment. In large part, the aftermath of hundreds of hours spent in nursing homes.

On some deep irrational level, I never quite believed that old age would happen to *me*. No doubt this made God shake His head and laugh quietly.

~

IN MY MORE DOUR moments, I think of ageing mainly in terms of loss. Loss of family members and friends, loss of strength and stamina. Loss of memory and an ability to assimilate new information. I often think about a quote (but can't remember who said it or where I heard it, an increasingly common phenomenon): *Life, among other things, is an exercise in tolerating losses.*

And then, of course, there comes grand finale, loss of life. Not that I want to live forever, but I'd prefer to live long enough to do and see more, and learn more. Maybe to add to my stores of wisdom, such as they are. *Had I but world enough, and time . . .* so went the lament of Andrew Marvell over three hundred years ago. The lament is still valid. The world is still too big, and there's never time enough for it. The way it always was, the way it always will be.

Those aspects of ageing are obvious enough, but there's a slew of subtler ones. Loss of gusto, for example. I still enjoy things, but not the way I did twenty or even ten years ago. Loss of possibilities. Loss of an ability to rectify mistakes, to do things better or at least differently. It occurs to me that the number of things I'll do for the first time, already small, will diminish to the vanishing point. I'll miss the marvelous, exhilarating *newness* that goes with first experiences. The first time I rode a Ferris wheel at the Illinois State Fair. The first time I hit a baseball out of the infield, or waterskied, or won a racquetball tournament (the only sport I was good at). The first time I drank Guinness in a Dublin pub. The first time I had sex.

It wasn't as dramatic as the transient global anemia, but something happened in 2017 that further drove home an awareness of my advancing years. That August, Hurricane Harvey hit the Gulf Coast. It wreaked havoc on Texas, Louisiana, and much of the West Indies. Houston, especially, was devastated.

As I drove to UConn one morning, I listened to NPR's account of the storm. One particular item caught my interest. People, including rescuers and first responders, were in a bad way emotionally. Traumatized, depressed, and exhausted, they found it harder and harder to function. Houston had put out a call for psychiatrists, psychologists, and social workers to come down and help. Any mental health professional with licensure from any state would be welcomed.

I considered going. The need was obvious, the suffering profound. I could help, I could do the work I'd done for decades. Betsy, my boss at UConn who'd become a close friend, would allow me the time off without objecting. If anything, she'd encourage me to go.

For a day or two I thought about it. And then the revelation came to me, as unequivocal as it was unwelcome. *No. I don't have the energy or stamina to go there, to do such grueling work. I couldn't keep up, I'd get in the way, I'd probably make everyone else's job harder. I could have done it ten years ago or maybe even five, but not now. I'm too goddamn old.*

I'D ALSO BEGUN TO deal with the retirement conundrum. The notion of giving up private practice had appealed to me powerfully, even though it was always tainted with ambivalence. I still liked the work per se, but I'd grown exceedingly tired of the baggage that went along with it. The telephone menus and canned recordings *("Your call is very important to us . . .")* when I tried to get through to an HMO or insurance company. The need to get prior authorizations for safe, effective medications a patient may have taken for twenty years, including those available as generics and were therefore fairly cheap. Such authorizations were often made by mindless dweebs who may know less about medicine than the receptionist in your internist's office. One of them once asked me how to spell *lithium*. These oafs are often called upon to make life and death decisions.

What else disenchanted me? Paperwork, of course. The notes kept on every patient's visit, more detailed and thorough as my memory grew less reliable. The letters to social service agencies, lawyers, and those who determined disability. The inevitable backlog of phone calls. And let's be honest here, I got tired of some of the patients. The whiners and help-rejecting complainers and professional victims. The ones who came with a lifetime of unmet needs and expected, *demanded,* that I find a way to meet them.

The one who put in a call for me late at night on a December 23. "I just threw my Christmas tree into a dumpster!" she informed me.

"Why are you telling me this?" I asked. "Did you want me to come over and take it out for you?"

I should add that such patients were exceptions, not the rule. At the other extreme were those like Liam, the career Marine who left the Corps after three tours in the Middle East, with one of a half dozen worse cases of PTSD I've ever seen. Liam used alcohol, cocaine, and every other drug he got his hands on. He wrecked his two marriages, he estranged himself from most of his family. At least once, he almost ate his gun.

Liam, a gruff man not particularly comfortable with displays of emotion, was leaving my office after a session when he stopped himself, put a hand in his pocket, and took out something. "I want you to have this, Doc. It's my AA medallion, been sober for eleven years now. I, uhm, couldn't have done it without you."

I keep it in my wallet.

Let's be honest about something else. No small part of my self-worth related to my profession. Sometimes it felt like I'd been doing it forever. When I graduated from medical school, Richard Nixon was still president, for God's sake. Of course you don't need an advanced degree to become overinvested in your career. A former patient was a skilled machinist who took great pride in his work. His marriage had grown tedious at best, and his children lived thousands of miles away. In the most telling Freudian slip I've ever heard, he said, "After I died . . . I mean, after I retired . . ."

In fact, I thought I should be in pretty decent shape when I retired. I had other interests and pastimes, from writing to photography to ambling along New England's hiking trails. As noted, there was much of the world I hadn't seen. Unless the stock market collapsed and the economy tanked completely, I should be able to live in reasonable comfort. I had a small but supportive family, and a number of my friends had had the kindness not to die yet. But this knowledge provided limited consolation.

I also wondered how my marriage would fare in the course of my retirement and the near-nonstop togetherness that would ensue. I had little doubt Judy and I loved each other, but I wondered how much we'd *like* each other after ten or twenty years of such togetherness. I've often contemplated the fact that marriage evolved when life expectancy was scarcely more than your late teens. In which case, marital burnout didn't matter very much. You married at twelve and you died eight or nine years later when you were practically still honeymooners.

Romeo and Juliet may be the greatest love story ever written. But Shakespeare, with his typical brilliance, killed off the lovers when they were little more than children. In a mordant flight of fancy, I speculated about what might have happened if the principals had made it to their seventies.

Romeo: *Thy nagging likens to a boil that burns upon my nose and ne'er does heal. Brusque of speech and grim of face thou art, with smiles less frequent than the sun's eclipse!*

Juliet: *And thou, my lord? Surely thou must know thou art no romp upon the beach! Go, ye daylong grumbler, hie thee from thy sofa and find thyself a volunteer job!*

In the end I overcame my ambivalence and closed shop on January 1, 2019. I resigned from UConn two and a half years later.

After deciding to do so the previous spring, I sat down and wrote a rough schedule for terminating my practice. When I'd stop accepting new patients and when I'd start telling current ones. When I'd send out letters notifying ex-patients, who had the right to their records if they wanted them. When to put together a list of other doctors and APRNs, to whom I might make arrangements for their transfers.

A surfeit of things to think about. How and when to notify referring colleagues, some of whom I'd known since the 1970s. How and when to notify Medicare. How and where to dispose of drawers of samples, most of them expired. How to find out the length of time I needed to keep patients' records.

So many things I'd miss. Patients, first and foremost. Contact with Denise, my secretary/office manager/factotum. Impossible to list everything she did, from billing to purchasing supplies and reordering stationery to making a quick run to McDonalds when I hadn't left myself enough time for lunch. She began to work with me in the early 1980s. Indispensable.

High on the list of what I'd miss was the office itself. A reflection of my taste, from the green and gray color scheme to the décor (a hodgepodge of original art, posters, and some of my better photos) to the knickknacks (I liked owls, had close to thirty carvings and miniaturized statues of them). I relished the chance to be able to sit and think there—to doodle—to jot down ideas for articles or short stories—to write reprehensible limericks. It was mine. Our home was mine and Judy's and that was fine, but the office was mine alone.

Contemplation of the loss of income didn't keep me awake at night, but I wasn't unmindful of it either. I *thought* we'd be okay without income from the practice, but would we be? We might find ourselves living in a world where a Big Mac cost thirty dollars and a gallon of gas cost a ten-spot. How long would our savings hold up in such a world? Moreover, my family has significant longevity. As noted, two grandparents made it to their nineties and my mother to a hundred. I'd never been obsessed with making money, but being old would be hard enough. I had no wish to be old and poor.

I began to clear out shelves and drawers, one at a time. For years I'd carted off a paper bag or two of stuff every few weeks to be discarded or shredded or recycled. In my office, unlike at home, I felt I'd done all right at getting rid of papers and whatnot . . . and I'd been wrong. Drawers contained tax documents no longer needed, obituaries of deceased colleagues, Belgian postage stamps from a trip taken ten years earlier, and clipped reviews of books I'd never get around to reading. They contained defunct hand-held tape recorders, ant traps, and enough paper clips to make a chain from Connecticut to the Canadian border. The forgotten treasures included a bottle of rum. An alcoholic patient had bought it. She really didn't want to start drinking again, but neither did she want to throw it out, so she asked me to keep it for her.

Spring turned into summer, and summer into fall. And it occurred to me, *this is really going to happen.*

Some patients took the news calmly, some with indifference. Some cried, and some were angry. Some of them made me feel like a shit. "I can count the number of people I've trusted in my life on the fingers of one hand," said a man I'd been treating for close to twenty years, "and you're one of them. And now you're leaving."

THE FIRST OF JANUARY arrived, and the world continued to spin on its axis, and my life went on. I wondered how long I'd feel the void left by the loss of my practice, how long I'd feel gut-punched.

In fact, 2019 proved to be a kind of turning point. A year like no other, when I not only knew I was old but began to feel it. Additional losses: my mother died—not a shock, since she was 100. But there'd still been a buffering generation between me and the endgame as long as she lived, and now that buffer had disappeared. And 2019 was the year my brother-in-law died as well. John Francis Carney III was almost exactly one year older than me. A warm and personable man whose life was a lockstep of successes: PhD in civil engineering in three years; the youngest tenured professor at the University of Connecticut who climbed the academic ladder to its highest rung.

Also a man who led the healthiest life imaginable, who worked out and drank in moderation, and most likely never smoked a cigarette. None of which protected him from a multiple myeloma.

Furthermore, 2019 was also the year I had prostate surgery and went to physical therapy three times weekly for my back, problematic on and off since my thirties. Also the year I had surgery for a ruptured Achilles tendon, incurred mindlessly when I tripped over Penelope's dish of cat food.

If 2019 had been the perfect storm, I believed 2020 would have to be better. Silly me. God probably guffawed.

THERE IS, HOWEVER, ONE blessing that almost makes the whole senescence package worth the trouble. On a wind-whipped February night in 2004, Elizabeth's son Jack, the first of our grandchildren, made his way into the world. Then came Jack's two brothers, Cole in 2006 and Nick in 2008. That same year, 2008, saw the birth of Amelia, joy of my heart, the daughter of my son and daughter-in-law. Amelia Therese Goodwin, the first girl born in the family in half a century.

The appeal and allure of grandchildren are universally well-known, and there's not much new you can say about them. The way they return love and affection a thousand fold, the full-hearted clamor of their laughter. The chance to watch them grow and learn—sometimes you can practically see the wheels turning in their heads as they process a new sight or experience. Their humor, intentional and otherwise. The accumulation of their quirks and likes and dislikes, of aptitudes and abilities as they develop personalities unduplicated in the whole of human history.

Among the hundreds of instances I cherish: Jack sitting in the cockpit of a Korean War era fighter jet at an air museum. Cole's joy upon scoring a soccer goal. Nick, trick-or-treating as Harry Potter, complete with glasses, wand, and cape. Amelia, already enamored of animals at age two, reaching over a fence in a zoo to pet the neck of a giraffe that soars over her like a skyscraper. All four of them singing *Happy Birthday* when I turned seventy.

Apart from the incalculable pleasure they give me in the here and now, I take joy and comfort in the unbounded promise of their futures, and the link they provide between me and unborn generations, perhaps stretching forward to the end of time.

CHAPTER XVI

INTERVIEW

Q: HOW DID THE IDEA FOR THIS BOOK COME ABOUT?

A: It evolved gradually; there was no eureka moment. Over the last few years I found myself reading more memoirs than I used to. I mentioned some of them in Chapter X, but there were others, from Ann Patchett's to Tobias Wolff's to Nora Ephron's. At some point I thought it might be interesting to have a go at one myself.

I'm also at an age when people tend to look backward more than forward. They tend to review their lives—to critique them, if you will—to try to make sense of them in a rather existential manner. This journey of mine, unremarkable but at the same time unique: What's been the point of it? How much has it mattered? What, if anything, will I leave behind? How will I be remembered? My patients have wrestled with such questions, and so do I.

Q: WHAT WAS THE HARDEST PART TO WRITE? WHAT WAS THE EASIEST?

A: The hardest part was to write about my divorce. An awful time. It may have been more than forty years ago, but the principals still bear scars of it. I know there are those who went through four or five or more of them, people like Larry King and Elizabeth Taylor, and I don't know how they did it. In my case, and certainly Judy's, one sufficed.

I allude to this in an earlier chapter, but it bears repeating. There've been potholes in my present marriage, some of them deep enough to swallow a VW Beetle. One of the most important things holding us together was not wanting to go through another divorce. Apart from whatever else you can say about a divorce, it's the most avoidable of life's traumas. Unless you lead a charmed life, which is as likely as encountering a woolly mammoth as you drive home from work tonight, you have to endure disappointments and losses. You have to grow old, assuming you don't die young, and you have to die in either case. But you don't have to go through a divorce.

Another part that made me pretty uncomfortable was writing about my protracted period of indecision as an undergraduate. The way I had no idea what I wanted to do with my life from one week to the next, and I had grave doubts I'd succeed in anything anyway. I touched on this point, but if I've helped one UConn student to make it through a similar period, I consider my time there to have been well-spent.

The easiest part was writing about a typical workday in the life of a psychiatrist. The main problem was deciding what to include, since there's such a wealth of material from which to choose. I could have done a hundred pages on that one chapter. Probably more.

Q: CONSIDERING THE BOOK AS A WHOLE, DO YOU THINK IT WAS AN HONEST RENDERING OF YOUR LIFE?

A: The short answer, as honest a rendering as I could tolerate. There were sins of omission, and I suppose they constitute a certain dishonesty. Of course if you carry that out to its logical conclusion, there could be no such thing as a completely honest memoir or autobiography. How could there be? Putting aside the facts of your life, how could there be anything like a complete rendering of everything that had a significant bearing on it? Such a book would be longer than the collected works of Tolstoy.

There's something else, and Gabriel García Márquez captured it beautifully in Love in the Time of Cholera: *". . . the heart's memory eliminates the bad and magnifies the good, and . . . thanks to this artifice we manage to endure the burden of the past." An example from my own life concerns my father. I loved him, but—as I think I've made clear—he could be a difficult, querulous, and infuriatingly mercurial man. When he died, I didn't erase the troubling memories of him, but I immediately and almost involuntarily put them in a safe, in a locked storage room where they no longer weighed upon me. I know they're there, but most of the time I leave them there. I have the key to the room and the combination of the safe, but I don't use them. Why would I want to? Does this constitute a manner of dishonesty? Perhaps.*

Q: YOU WROTE ABOUT THE PROCESS OF WRITING. HOW DOES WRITING FICTION COMPARE WITH WRITING NONFICTION?

A: *Writing fiction is much more difficult. For one thing, you have to devise a suitable plot, which is the hardest part of the process for me. There are simply not that many of them from which to choose since they're mostly variations on the major themes. I forget where I heard or read this, but someone said there are basically just two of them: a person goes on a journey or a stranger comes to town. You also have to devise subplots and then blend them all into a smooth, cohesive whole.*

While I find writing fiction much harder, it definitely has its own rewards. There's the pleasure of creativity, of making up nonexistent characters and places. You can also create the ending you want, a luxury you don't have in nonfiction, much less in real life. I should add that I find the process of writing per se fascinating. The way ideas can come to you when you least expect them. When you're in the shower or stuck in traffic, or how they can come to you in your sleep. The way characters do things you didn't expect them to, things that weren't in your plan for them. It's a cliché, but it's true that they develop a reality and even a personality of their own. You may have created them, but paradoxically they're somewhat independent of you.

Of course there are common denominators. Striving for the well-crafted phrase and the telling detail, the revealing show of character and the unexpected twist of narrative. In that respect, writing fiction and nonfiction are similar.

Q: HAVING AN IDEA COME TO YOU WHILE YOU SLEPT: DID THAT EVER HAPPEN TO YOU?

A: *Yes. A major character in my first published novel, a married man, becomes the friend and confidante of another woman. I couldn't decide whether or not they should have an affair. One morning I woke up, and the answer was there for me.*

The best example I know of a sleep-induced epiphany comes from chemistry, not literature. A nineteenth century German named Kekulé was trying to figure out the structure of the benzene ring, a basic building block in organic chemistry, and it stymied him. One night he dreamt of six snakes that formed a perfect hexagon, and that proved to be the answer, six carbon atoms arranged in a hexagon.

Q: BACK TO YOUR BOOK. HOW DID YOU DECIDE WHAT OR WHAT NOT TO INCLUDE?

A: *A large part of making those decisions was trying to figure out what might or might not be of interest to others. Something or someone* may have had a huge impact on me but be of little or no interest to most readers. Besides, small things can be as revealing as large ones, maybe more so. That makes sense when you think about it. The small things can be dead giveaways. Ask a cop or a good poker player; people have tells.

Another consideration, and this may be a reflection of my own personality: some major life experiences are too intimate or painful to write about. I greatly admire someone who has the wherewithal to take unspeakable events and write about them. How Elie Wiesel wrote about Auschwitz, for example, or how Aleksandr Solzhenitsyn wrote about the Gulag. I know that writing about your most nightmarish experiences can be cathartic. Even so, if I'd been unlucky enough to have had them, I don't know if I would have included them.

Q: ANY REGRETS ABOUT THINGS YOU'VE OMITTED?

A: Sort of. I let myself be talked out of writing more about my family, on the grounds that it would bore a lot of readers. Maybe so, but there are relatives who would have made for interesting cameos. My great uncle Arnold, for instance, who became a highly successful lawyer without going to law school. By all accounts, a brilliant man. He taught himself enough law to pass the bar exam without it. Or my great aunt Linda, a beauty with long red hair and azure eyes, who became a rich man's kept woman. Or my cousin Jim, who became very strange after flying too many missions over Germany with the Eighth Air Force during World War II, and whose brother Don had one of the family's more successful marriages with a Mormon woman twenty-three years his junior.

Q: YOU'VE OFTEN MAINTAINED THAT WRITING CAN BE THERAPEUTIC, AND YOU'VE ENCOURAGED YOUR PATIENTS

TO WRITE ABOUT THEMSELVES. TO WHAT EXTENT, IF ANY, HAS WRITING THIS BOOK BEEN THERAPEUTIC FOR YOU?

A: *Getting something off your chest is nearly always a useful exercise. Common parlance captures that. "It's been so good talking with you," we say to a friend. The spoken word, the written word, it doesn't matter. Communication always has the potential to be therapeutic. Of course it can also become an exercise in narcissism.*

Writing about my ageing was unabashedly therapeutic. To do so was to ventilate, to have a kind of mini-tantrum. Besides, when I tallied up the negatives—problems with health and memory and stamina and the rest of it—they didn't seem so bad. Writing about them underscored what I suppose I already knew, that I've had no grounds for serious complaints. So far, at least. Furthermore, I'm still here. To paraphrase the great philosopher and wordsmith, Casey Stengel, most people my age are dead at the present time, and you can look it up.

I acknowledge that Judy, who is better at acceptance than I am, has helped me come to terms with ageing. At times she used a dollop of tough love when she did it. A month before my sixtieth birthday, we went to a wake of the husband of one of my co-workers. He'd died of cancer of the colon while still in his forties. Two children, one in college, one in high school. I'd been grousing about The Big Six Zero endlessly. When we left the wake, Judy turned to me with a singular lack of sympathy— "I never want to hear you bitch again about turning sixty."

Q: YOU WROTE A FAIR BIT ABOUT GROWING OLD BUT NOT SO MUCH ABOUT DEATH AND DYING. WHAT'S YOUR THINKING ABOUT AN AFTERLIFE?

A: *I'll answer in a roundabout way. One of my all-time favorite films is a documentary,* The Wild Parrots of Telegraph Hill. *In it, a character describes a concept that goes something like this: There's a river at the top of a waterfall and another at the bottom. Neither has a beginning nor an end. We'll call the higher one the River of Before Life and the lower one the River of After Life. Our own lives are individual drops of water as they cascade down the waterfall. The concept resonates with me, and I love it. Something like that happens, I suspect, but I'm no clearer on the details than anyone else.*

My personal preference for the afterlife would be to spend it as a guardian angel, assuming they exist. I'd like to be on hand for people left behind who are important to me, the children and grandchildren in particular.

Q: GOOD LUCK WITH THAT. LET'S GO BACK TO YOUR BOOK. ANY MAJOR SURPRISES WHEN YOU WROTE IT?

A: *The biggest surprise was finding out certain people have had much more of an impact on me than I realized. Felix, for example, the gay friend who came out to me when we were both at Springfield High School. I hadn't consciously thought about him in thirty years. But I remembered him, and our conversations, with extraordinary clarity when I began to write about him. I wonder what happened to him. As a gay man, a young adult during the worst of AIDS, he would have been at tremendous risk for it.*

I found myself wondering about a lot of people who aren't included in this book. Where did they go, and what did they wind up doing? Why did we lose contact with each other, and what would have happened if we'd stayed in touch? And the women: What would have happened if I'd ended up with her, or her, or her? Life, among other things, is a great collection of loose ends, what ifs, and what might-have-beens.

Q: WHAT DO YOU HAVE IN MIND FOR FUTURE WRITING PROJECTS?

A: *I might try more short stories. Writing fiction (and much of nonfiction too, for that matter) is mainly a matter of telling stories. I like to read them, and I like to try to write them. I like the inherent challenge of them, which is different from the challenge of writing a novel. If you're writing a story of five or ten thousand words, there's not much of a margin for error. It has to be practically perfect. On the other hand, if you're writing another* War and Peace, *no one's going to crucify you for an awkward sentence on page 699.*

The New York Times Book Review often has interviews with writers. Among their favorite questions: Which three writers, living or dead, would you most want to have dinner with? My own choices would be Geoffrey Chaucer, Mark Twain, and Isaac Bashevis Singer. As different as they are—writing in different styles, the products of different cultures, living in different centuries—they have this in common, they're all masterful storytellers. Plus, in the case of Chaucer, there'd be the bonus of learning about life in the late Middle Ages.

Mark Twain, incidentally, came up with one of my favorite quotes. "Man is the only animal who blushes. Or needs to."

Q: THEY HAVE ANOTHER FAVORITE QUESTION IN *THE NEW YORK TIMES BOOK REVIEW*. IF YOU HAD TO PICK ONE BOOK YOU'D WANT A PRESIDENT TO READ, WHAT WOULD IT BE?

A: *John Hersey's* Hiroshima. *Hersey's descriptions of what it was like in the aftermath of an atomic bomb going off are unforgettable. If you're the president, you're automatically in charge of hundreds or thousands of nuclear weapons, and it would be nice if you knew what happened when you used one. There's also the sobering thought that* the Hiroshima bomb, for all the destruction and death it caused, was picayune compared to weapons we have now.

I'd also like a president to read Barbara Tuchman's The March of Folly. It's an excellent and superbly written account of our collective inability to learn from history and the enormous price we pay for that. Apart from what you could learn from her, the book would be an antidote for people who think they dislike history, who regard it as a mere laundry list of names and dates.

Q: NO MORE NOVELS?

A: Thing is, a novel is a two-year undertaking, or maybe two or three times that. At my age, I'm not sure I want to commit to such a long and arduous undertaking. How many years do I have left, after all? But I did come up with something that intrigues me. It's about Estella, the femme fatale in Charles Dickens's Great Expectations. Dickens leaves her fate hanging in the novel. I'd like to write something about her later years and what happens to her. Sometimes an idea will grab you and it won't let go. An idea like the Stinney book, let's say.

Q: SO, YOU'D BE PICKING UP WHERE DICKENS LEFT OFF. IMPROVING ON HIM, SO TO SPEAK. I SEE YOUR CHUTZPAH REMAINS INTACT.

A: Next question.

Q: I WANT TO ASK YOU ABOUT YOUR TITLE. I ASSUME YOU MEAN IT FIGURATIVELY. YOU DON'T REALLY BELIEVE GOD LAUGHS AT US WHEN WE MAKE OUR PLANS, OR DO YOU?

A: No. As I mention in Chapter I, however, I've toyed with the notion that God allowed us to evolve, at least in part, for His own amusement. Also to alleviate His loneliness. As a child, I actually felt sorry *for Him. Here He was, alone in His infinite universe. I thought He must be unbearably lonely, and it made me sad. I had a strange mind.*

At this point my concept of God is less concrete and personal, although I haven't ruled out His having an extremely dry, sardonic sense of humor. There's evidence for this, you know. Consider puffins, dachshunds, and ostriches.

My favorite quote about the nature of God comes from Isaac Bashevis Singer. "I believed that God is a novelist who writes what He pleases, and the whole world has to read Him, trying to figure out what He means."

A beautiful piece of writing, but I actually think of God in an amorphous kind of way, like the Sum Total of Possibilities. The Great Everything. I don't believe we're designed to understand Him, any more than a worm can understand quantum mechanics, but maybe that changes when we die. In which case, we might actually find out what His story is. Or maybe not, and that would be all right too.

ACKNOWLEDGMENTS

PARTS OF CHAPTER VI, *"Céad Míle Fáilte,"* were first published in the *JOURNAL OF THE IRISH COLLEGES OF PHYSICIANS and SURGEONS*, Vol. 13, No. 2.

Parts of Chapter I, *"Ground Rules,"* and Chapter XI, *"Psychiatry in the Rough,"* were first published in *NORTHEAST* (March 9, 1986; August 10, 1986, and December 12, 1993).

My first and most important acknowledgment is the debt of gratitude I owe to my patients. Through the years I've learned more from them than from all the books and articles I've read and all the lectures I've attended combined.

My heartfelt thanks: to Liz Delton, the best beta reader going; to Sam Silverman and the late and greatly missed Terry Holcombe for reading and critiquing several chapters. To Penny Goetjen and Judy Roth. Again, my thanks to Cynde Acanto for her ever-appreciated encouragement. And last but never least, to my wife, Judy Goodwin for her inevitably useful advice and suggestions, her unflagging support, and especially for staying the course.

AUTHOR BIO

AFTER GRADUATING FROM YALE, R.C. Goodwin spent six demanding but wonderful years in Dublin attending medical school before returning to the U.S. for an internship and psychiatric residency. Since then, he has worked in private practice, jails and prisons, nursing homes, a substance abuse facility, and a student mental health clinic at a major university—all of which he describes in his memoir, *Making God Laugh*. His fiction has appeared in *Elixir, Center, Northeast,* and *Writers Digest Online* among other publications. It has also been published in two anthologies, *Stories that Need to be Told* and *Coolest American Stories*. Goodwin's debut book *The Stephen Hawking Death Row Fan Club*, a prison-based collection of award-winning short stories and a novella, was named a Kirkus Indie Best Book of 2015. He has also written a novel, *Model Child*, a psychological thriller. He lives with his wife and a spoiled, bossy cat in Connecticut.

www.ingramcontent.com/pod-product-compliance
Lightning Source LLC
Chambersburg PA
CBHW052134070526
44585CB00017B/1816